WHAT PEOPLE ARE SAYING ABOUT
Saints for Our Time

"This comprehensive and highly readable work will be an essential addition to school and parish libraries. Arranged according to the calendar year, with appendices of fixed feast days and patron saints, it is a most welcome and useful resource for those planning and celebrating the liturgy, and a valuable guide for participants in the RCIA and confirmation programs. *Saints for Our Time* will challenge teachers, preachers, and indeed, all the faithful to discover the relevance of the saints to the world we live in today."

Most Reverend Thomas J. Curry
Auxiliary Bishop of Los Angeles

"This useful, practical, and pastoral collection fills the need in the RCIA to assist catechumens and candidates in understanding the role of saints in general and the opportunity for them in particular to signify their new identity in Christ by borrowing a baptismal or confirmation name."

Paul F. Ford, Ph.D.,
Professor of Theology and Liturgy
St. John's Seminary, Camarillo, CA

"I particularly like the contemporary message from each saint and the personal reflection that follows it. Both of these extras make the life of the saint alive and liveable. This book has real appeal for all readers, but I feel that RCIA Directors in particular will find this book a real resource in teaching the wonderful heritage the church has in its saints."

Sr. M. Joyanne Sullivan, SND
DRE, Sacred Heart Church, Ventura, CA

"Here the lives of the saints are chronicled in such a way as to make each come alive for the reader. Each story presents a challenge for our daily Christian living, and accompanying questions for reflection prompt the reader to put into action the virtues practiced by the saint.

"This book will be well used by teachers, catechists, and RCIA teams to lead learners into a better understanding of our heavenly intercessors."

Sr. Jean Alden, SND
Catechist, Principal, and member of a RCIA team in
Ventura, CA

"Ed Ransom reminds us in this handy tool that we encounter Christ in his saints as we study and celebrate their heroic and consecrated lives. He manages to capture the spirit and faith of these daily saints in a way that will inspire readers to look for their complete biographies."

CAPT James W. Anderson, CHC, USNR
Command Chaplain
Naval Construction Battalion Center
Port Hueneme, CA

"Church services at sea probably attract a greater percentage of a ship's population than is typical for the general public, and from personal experience, I know that a hush fell over PARGO when, just before the evening meal, I marked the end of the 'work' day by reading an ecumenical prayer over the General Announcing System. Ed Ransom's saint stories evoke some of those same hushed feelings. He has done a marvelous job."

James H. Patton, Jr., CAPT, USN (ret.)
Service on 7 nuclear submarines
Commanding Officer, USS Pargo (SSN 650)

SAINTS
for
OUR TIME

Ed Ransom

TWENTY-THIRD PUBLICATIONS
Mystic, CT 06355

DEDICATION

This book is dedicated to all inquirers, catechumens,
and candidates, as well as to those
who continue their faith journey on their own.
You are all in my prayers daily.

ACKNOWLEDGMENTS

Over the several years in which it was compiled, this book
has had many contributors, too numerous to mention here. I
would like to note, however, one person who played a major
role in getting me started on this work; that is my pastor,
Monsignor John C. Hughes. Without him and the access he
gave me to his personal library of books on the lives of the
saints, this book would not exist.

Twenty-Third Publications
185 Willow Street
P.O. Box 180
Mystic, CT 06355
(860) 536-2611
800-321-0411

ISBN 0-89622-921-1
Library of Congress Catalog Card Number 97-62563
Printed in the U.S.A.

TABLE OF CONTENTS

March

April

May

June

July

August

September

October

November

December

Saints for Our Time

INTRODUCTION

Every culture, nation, group, or community has always honored its heroes. These may be leaders who have provided years of exemplary service to the nation, such as statespersons or presidents, or they may be ordinary people who, in the circumstances of the times, became heroic figures.

Saints are the heroes of the Catholic Church. These are people we honor on special days and call on for their intercession with God. In an age when many modern-day heroes have been shown to have "feet of clay," saints provide bona fide role models.

Saints have been a part of the Christian Church since its beginning. Many of Christ's earliest disciples, both men and women, are saints. Some of these people had the opportunity to hear Jesus' words directly and yet were still capable of doubt or a breach of faith. Nevertheless, all of the saints strove to overcome their weaknesses and now stand as examples for us.

As we read the lives of saints, we come to realize that many of them were ordinary people like ourselves. They faced the same problems and had to make many of the same kinds of decisions that we must make on an everyday basis. Except for Mary, the mother of Jesus, saints were sinners like the rest of us, occasionally even notorious sinners (see St. Augustine and St. Camillus de Lillus for just two examples). Yet all of the saints heeded Jesus' words to "take up the cross and follow me" (Mt 10:38).

Becoming a saint

The process of becoming a saint has changed over two millennia. In the early Church, each of the Christian communities was quite small and members were well known to each other, very much like family members. Sainthood was conferred essentially by acclamation of the community and the concurrence of the local bishop (who might be the equivalent of the pastor of a medium-size parish in our day). A devotion to the saint would then develop as the community prayed to the saint for intercession with God, and a feast day would be declared to honor the saint. Some saints might be known to several communities and devotions would then be more widespread, as with those honoring the apostles.

As the Church grew in size, the process of canonization evolved. Today, a candidate for sainthood must first have a "cause" opened by the local bishop who then conducts thorough investigations into the life and writings of this person. One miracle must be identified which can be attributed to the intercession of the candidate for sainthood. If the outcome of these inquiries is positive, the candidate is then beatified by the pope, that is, declared "blessed." The person is acknowledged as a saint, but can be formally honored only within the country, region, or community from which the cause was advanced. Further rigorous investigations and a second miracle may lead to "canonization" of the saint, who is then recognized and honored by the universal Church.

The process is much more complex than can be explained in one or two brief paragraphs, of course. Books such as *The Making of Saints,* by Michael Freze, and *Making Saints,* by Kenneth Woodward (see Resource list at the back of the book) provide an in-depth history and explanation of the process of canonization as it exists today.

Honoring the saints

The liturgical calendar establishes the major feast days which are common throughout the Church, for example, Christmas. In addition, the bishops of a country or a region fix certain days to celebrate feasts for saints who are especially relevant to that country or region, such as St. Frances Xavier Cabrini, who was the first

American citizen to be canonized and is honored throughout the United States. A diocese or parish will honor their patron on a given day of the year, though that saint may not otherwise appear on the liturgical calendar; St. Vibiana, the patron of the Archdiocese of Los Angeles, falls into this category.

There is an order of precedence for the major events that are observed by the Church within the liturgical year, including those days set aside to honor saints. Solemnities are the highest celebration; these are generally holy days of obligation, that is, days on which Catholics must attend Mass. Easter, Christmas, and the feast of the Ascension are examples of solemnities.

Feast days are next in importance, when major saints such as the apostles are honored. Memorials follow in order, and these are split into obligatory and optional memorials. Mass on the day of an obligatory memorial is always in honor of the particular saint of that day, while the celebrant may choose whether to celebrate an optional memorial or not. As with any set of rules, there are exceptions. Most notably, feast days and memorials falling on a Sunday are not celebrated on that day (although a local bishop *may* designate the following day for celebration).

The saints in this collection are ordered by the calendar days on which they are honored. Not all of the saints appearing in the liturgical calendar of the Church are included in this collection; conversely, not all of the saints in this collection appear on the liturgical calendar. If the saint *does* appear on the liturgical calendar, you will find the type of feast which is celebrated in their honor next to the date of their feast; if they are not on the liturgical calendar, no designation will appear. (Appendix A lists the saints who are celebrated by the Church during the liturgical year.)

Choosing a saint for confirmation

This collection of saints began a few years ago in response to the needs of the catechumens and candidates undergoing the Rite of Christian Initiation for Adults in our parish. When asked to choose a saint's name to take at confirmation, many of them felt that they did not know enough about the saints to make an intelligent choice.

How does one go about choosing a saint's name for confirmation? You might begin by looking at the patron saints (see Appendix B). Perhaps there is a saint on this list with whom you have something in common. Or maybe there is a saint with a feast day on some momentous occasion in your life, a birthday or wedding anniversary, for example. If either of these options does not lead you to a saint, browse through the book and choose a saint whose life style and deeds appeal to you.

After each saint's biography, this book offers a brief paragraph highlighting one of the saints' characteristics or qualities which holds relevance to our lives today. This is followed by one or two questions for reflection that may help you incorporate an element of that saint's life into your own life.

The saints whose lives are summarized in this collection are only a very small percentage of the saints in the Church. If you don't find the particular saint you are looking for in here, there are many other sources of information on the lives of saints. A few of them are mentioned in the Resource List at the end of the book. Many public and parish libraries hold some of these references. If you have a Catholic university or high school near you, they may be able to offer some help in researching particular saints.

In any case, jump in. My hope is that everyone who reads this book, whether new to the Church or a member of long standing, will find the information in this book helpful and inspiring.

JANUARY

Mary, Mother of Jesus: First Century

The greatest and first among all of our saints, Mary was chosen by God to be the mother of his son. Very little is known about Mary outside of the New Testament. By tradition, she was born in Jerusalem, the daughter of Joachim and Ann. Catholics believe in Mary's immaculate conception, which means that Mary was born without original sin, the only human so honored by God.

In the Gospels of Matthew and Luke, we learn that the angel Gabriel came to Mary and announced that she was to be the mother of Jesus. We further learn about the angel's visit to Joseph; Mary's journey to visit her cousin, Elizabeth, who acknowledged her as the mother of God; and about the birth and early life of Jesus. This is most of what we know about Mary until Jesus began his ministry.

Mary is mentioned from time to time in all of the Gospels. We come to know that she was instrumental in having Jesus perform his first miracle by turning water into wine at Cana. We also know that she was there at Jesus' crucifixion, and present with the disciples in Jerusalem before Pentecost. It is believed that she was also present with the apostles after Jesus' resurrection and at the ascension.

Mary has been the intercessor for all people who call upon her for many different causes. Over the centuries, her appearance on earth has often been reported: at Lourdes, Fatima, La Salette, Guadalupe, and Medjugorje. There are many feast days in honor

5

of Mary. By tradition, her birthday is celebrated on September 8. Besides the Solemnity of Mary celebrated on this date, some of the other feast days for which, at least in part, we honor Mary are the Annunciation (March 25), the Visitation (May 31), the Assumption (August 15), the Queenship of Mary (August 22), Our Lady of Sorrows (September 15), Our Lady of the Rosary (October 7) and the Immaculate Conception (December 8). Under the title of the Immaculate Conception, Mary is the patron of the United States.

Mary's message today: Our greatest saint, Mary did one simple thing. She listened to God's will—that she be the mother of Jesus—and she accepted God's will. "Here am I, the servant of the Lord: let it be with me according to your word" (Lk 1:38).

Have you accepted God's will in your life? Pray for an understanding of what God is calling you to do.

Basil the Great, Bishop and Doctor: 329–379

Basil was one of ten children of St. Basil the Elder and St. Emmelia. He was born in Caesarea, Asia Minor (now southeastern Turkey) and educated by his father and grandmother. He took advanced studies in Constantinople and Athens where he was a fellow student of St. Gregory Nazianzen, who became his closest friend, and Julian, the future emperor and apostate.

Upon completing his education, Basil returned to Caesarea where he taught rhetoric and seemed destined for a brilliant career as a teacher. Through the influence of his eldest sister, St. Macrina the Younger, however, he decided to pursue religious life. Basil traveled to the principal monasteries of the eastern world to learn about monastic life, and upon his return, settled in a secluded spot and devoted himself to prayer and study. A group of disciples soon gathered around him, and with them he founded the first monastery in Asia Minor. Within this community Basil formulated the principles which have regulated the lives of monks in the Eastern Church down to the present day.

While Basil was establishing his monastic community, the Arian heresy (a claim that Christ was not divine) was then at its height, and orthodox Christians were being persecuted by Arian emperors. Basil was called upon to help defend the faith against the Arian heresy. In 363, he was persuaded by his friend St. Gregory to be ordained, and in 370 Basil was elected bishop of Caesarea.

The Arian emperor, Valens, put great pressure on Basil to allow Arians full communion with the Church, but Basil was firm in his refusal to allow this. The emperor, fearful of using violence against Basil, decided to exile him. But as Valens attempted to sign the order of banishment, the pen broke in his hand three times. Astonished, the emperor backed down and eventually left Caesarea, never again to interfere in ecclesial affairs.

Basil was untiring in his efforts to unite and rally his fellow Catholics, but he was often misunderstood, misrepresented, and accused of heresy and ambition. Even appeals to the pope went unanswered. "For my sins, I seem to be unsuccessful in everything," he wrote. In all of these trials, Basil never forgot his pastoral duties. He preached morning and evening to congregations so vast that he compared them to the sea, and helped the sick and the poor. Basil organized a hospital near Caesarea, described by St. Gregory as one of the wonders of the world.

Basil was one of the great orators of the Church, as well as a prolific writer. His doctrinal writing and four hundred letters have had tremendous influence on the Church. He is a Doctor of the Church, as well as the patron of both hospital administrators and eastern monks.

Basil's message today: Basil's trials and tribulations were perhaps harder to bear than physical suffering, but he continued to look after the needs of his people and fight against heresy. He prayed, "Show us the way we are to take," and found strength in God's grace. We can join Basil in this prayer.

Have you sought God's help when things did not seem to be going your way? Have you accepted the direction and guidance which God has given to you, even if it has not been easy?

Gregory Nazianzen, Bishop and Doctor: 329-390

Gregory, later known as "the theologian," was the son of St. Gregory the Elder and St. Nonna and the brother of two other saints. A contemporary and friend of St. Basil with whom he shares a feast day, Gregory studied rhetoric in Caesarea and Cappadocia, then later moved on to Athens for further study.

When about thirty, Gregory joined Basil at Pontus where the two chose to live the contemplative life as hermits. For Gregory, this respite was short-lived. His father, now over eighty and the bishop of Nazianzen (in those days, a bishop did not have to be an ordained priest), called for him to return home to help manage his diocese and estate. Reluctantly, Gregory was ordained by his father in about 362. Soon his reputation as a learned and zealous man began to grow. Gregory the Elder, in the hope of reconciling the Arians, agreed to some compromises which alienated many of the Catholics. Gregory, through tact and powerful oratory, prevented a schism from developing.

Around 372, Gregory's friend, Basil, now the metropolitan (the name for bishop in the Eastern Church) of Caesarea, named Gregory to the bishopric of Sasima, a newly created see in the middle of a territory beset by the Arian heresy. This severely strained the friendship between Gregory and Basil, as Gregory chose to remain with his father in Nazianzen.

After the death of the Arian emperor Valens in about 380, Gregory was called to Constantinople as bishop to help revitalize the Church. He arrived in the capital bald, poorly dressed, and prematurely stooped, a far cry from the dignified prelates which the sophisticated populace of Constantinople was accustomed to. This signaled the beginning of Gregory's trials with these people.

In Constantinople, Gregory stayed at the home of a friend which then became the only orthodox church in the city. Here Gregory began preaching the sermons on the Trinity which won for him the title of "theologian." He rekindled the spark of faith which had been nearly extinguished by the Arian heresy and paved the way for a return to orthodoxy.

Although his reputation spread and his congregation grew, Gregory was still beset by enemies. Eventually, fearing that the unrest would lead to bloodshed, he left the office of bishop and retired to a life of austerity. Here he devoted much time to writing, until his death in 390.

Gregory's message today: Like his friend Basil, Gregory wished for the contemplative life of a monk. But God chose him to replant the seeds of faith in a city that had succumbed to heresy. The personal attacks and abuse which Gregory suffered did not deter him from his calling until the job was done.

How strong are you when others attack you for your faith? Can you stand up to abuse and, by your example, show what it means to be a Christian?

Genevieve, Virgin: c. 422-500

Genevieve was born in the small village of Nanterre near Paris around the year 422. When she was only about seven, St. Germanus, the bishop of Auxerre, passed through Nanterre on his way to Britain and decided to spend the night. The bishop conducted a prayer service for the villagers of Nanterre, and as he was speaking, he took particular notice of Genevieve. After the prayer service, he sought out her parents and told them of Genevieve's future sanctity. The young girl then told the bishop that it was her desire to have his blessing and be consecrated to God.

When Genevieve was fifteen, she was presented, along with some other girls, to the bishop of Paris to be dedicated to God. Though Genevieve was the youngest one there, the bishop put her before the other girls, noting that heaven had already sanctified her. From that time on, Genevieve lived a very austere life, frequently eating only on Sundays and Thursdays and then only bread and beans.

After the death of her parents, Genevieve went to live with her godmother in Paris. From there she made several journeys to other places in Gaul (France) where she became known for her miracles and prophecies.

Around the middle of the fifth century, the Franks were overrunning Gaul, and Childeric, their king, occupied Paris. During the long siege of that city, the people were reduced to famine. Genevieve led a company out of the city to obtain provisions, and brought back several boats loaded with corn. Childeric respected Genevieve for her bravery and her wisdom. Through her intercession, he spared the lives of many prisoners and performed other generous acts. Genevieve also influenced a later king, Clovis, who converted to Christianity and released many prisoners.

Later in the fifth century, Attila the Hun was marching toward Paris with an intent to sack the city. As the people were preparing to abandon Paris, Genevieve assured the citizens of God's protection and encouraged them to fast and pray. As a result, the Huns, otherwise inexplicably, changed course and spared Paris.

Many miracles were attributed to St. Genevieve in the years following her death. Among the better known was one involving a deadly plague which struck Paris in 1129. In a very short time, many thousands of Parisians died from this plague, and physicians were at a loss to find a cure. Stephen, the bishop of Paris, led the people in prayers and fasting, calling on divine mercy. All this was to no avail, however, until a statue of St. Genevieve was carried in a procession from her shrine to the cathedral. The plague immediately ceased, and until the French Revolution when the relics of the saint were destroyed, it became customary to carry the statue in solemn procession to the cathedral whenever extraordinary calamities struck the city.

St. Genevieve is the patroness of women in the Army.

Genevieve's message today: Rarely does God bless someone with the wisdom and holiness with which he endowed Genevieve. Through her sacrifices, gifts, and talents, this saint earned the love and respect of the people of Paris. In turn, she led them through many difficult times, both before and after her death.

Think about how you can use your talents to benefit those with whom you come in contact. Are you willing to give of yourself to help others?

Elizabeth Ann Seton, Religious: 1774–1821

Elizabeth Ann Bayley Seton was born in New York City on August 28, 1774, just two years before the Declaration of Independence was signed. She might truly be called a daughter of the American Revolution.

Elizabeth's father, Dr. Richard Bayley, was a professor in the medical school of what is now Columbia University. Her mother, and later, her stepmother, were staunch Episcopalians who instilled in her an appreciation of prayer and the Scriptures. At nineteen, Elizabeth married a handsome, wealthy businessman named William Magee Seton, with whom she had five children.

In the first years of her marriage, Elizabeth plunged into social work and in 1797, helped to found the Society for the Relief of Poor Widows with Small Children. Just a few years later, in 1803, her husband's business failed, and William contracted tuberculosis. He and Elizabeth went to Italy hoping to effect a cure, but he died shortly after they arrived.

Elizabeth stayed on in Italy for some months after, and while there, observed Catholicism in action. She became convinced that the Catholic Church led back to the apostles and to Christ. After her return to the United States in 1805, she became a Catholic. This action angered her family and friends; in turn, they rejected her and left her without support. To provide for herself and her children, she opened a school in Boston.

In 1809, the rector of St. Mary's Seminary in Baltimore invited Elizabeth to open a school there. Shortly thereafter, Elizabeth founded a religious community along with four companions. The sisters opened a school for poor children in Emmitsburg, Maryland, which was the beginning of the Catholic parochial school system in the United States.

Archbishop Carroll of Baltimore approved the rule of

Elizabeth's community in 1812, and in 1813, Elizabeth and eighteen other women took vows in the new order, the Sisters of Charity, the first American religious society. The order spread throughout the United States and numbered some twenty communities by the time of her death.

Elizabeth Ann Seton became the first American-born saint when she was canonized by Pope Paul VI in 1975.

Elizabeth's message today: Accepting our faith sometimes leads to rejection by those we love. Remembering that God loves both us and those who have forsaken us can help to ease the pain of rejection. We must learn to pray not just for those who love us and accept us, but also for those who have turned their backs on us.

Have you prayed for those who have rejected you? Have you forgiven them?

JANUARY 5–MEMORIAL

John Neumann, Bishop: 1811–1860

John Neumann was born in what is now the Czech Republic. At an early age, he was attracted to the religious life and entered the seminary. Unable to be ordained in Bohemia due to a surplus of priests, John went to the United States where he was ordained in 1836.

The next few years were spent in missionary work, primarily among German-speaking Catholics in upstate New York. In 1840, he joined the newly established branch of the Redemptorists in Pittsburgh and became the first Redemptorist to take his vows in the United States. John continued his missionary work in Maryland, Ohio, Pennsylvania, and Virginia, and in 1847, he was named superior of the American Redemptorists.

In 1852, John Neumann was consecrated as the fourth bishop of Philadelphia. He now had an opportunity to make great inroads into what had become his passion: the education of poor German, French, Irish, and Indian Catholics.

During his eight years as bishop of Philadelphia, he reorganized the diocese, as well as opened eighty new churches and nearly one hundred schools. To staff these schools, John brought in many religious orders of priests and nuns. At the first national council of Catholic bishops, he helped to map out a plan of Catholic education for the whole United States.

Although active in his support of education and busy with the duties of leading a diocese, John Neumann was never far from his people. By the time he became bishop, he spoke twelve languages and made it a point to address each of his people in their own language. At the time of his death, John was renowned for his holiness, charity, pastoral work, and his preaching.

John Neumann was canonized in 1977 by Pope Paul VI, becoming the first American male saint and the first American bishop to be sainted.

John's message today: John Neumann's goal was to have a school in every Catholic parish. This was very nearly realized by the middle of the twentieth century. While the number of Catholic schools has fallen in the years since, the need for educating our children in their faith remains as strong as ever.

Consider how you could use your talents in the religious education program in your parish. Could you teach a grade? Be a classroom helper? Coordinate schedules?

Blessed André Bessette, Religious: 1845–1937

Born in Quebec, André was a sickly child. This kept him from attending school on a regular basis and meant that he went through life unable to read and write.

As a young man, André came to the United States and worked there for a few years. He then returned to Canada and entered the Congregation of the Holy Cross as a brother. His lack of skills relegated him to menial tasks, and he was assigned as a doorkeeper at the College of Notre Dame in Montreal for over forty years. He was also the janitor, infirmarian, barber, gardener, and lamplighter on the campus.

André developed a great devotion to St. Joseph, and eventually succeeded in having a chapel built to St. Joseph. He charmed the students of Notre Dame and their parents with his piety and his willingness to help all in need. Often, people came to him to seek his advice or his prayers. André always complied with their requests, entrusting all to St. Joseph.

After his death on January 6, 1937, the chapel which André had helped build in honor of his patron grew into the great basilica of St. Joseph's Oratory in Montreal, a place that draws pilgrims from all over the world.

André's message today: Although André was a simple man, he had the gift of holiness, a gift greater than most. To some degree, we are all given the gift of holiness. It is up to us to nurture this gift and to use it in God's service, as André did.

Have you ever asked God to make you holy? Take stock of the gifts which God has given you.

Raymond of Peñafort, Priest: 1175–1275

Raymond was born into the noble family of Peñafort, and during his one hundred years of life had the opportunity to accomplish many things. He had an excellent education and was teaching philosophy—without earning a fee—in Barcelona by the age of twenty. Some ten years later, Raymond earned a doctorate in both canon and civil law, and taught these subjects, too.

In 1222, at the age of forty-seven, Raymond entered the Dominican order, only eight months after the death of its founder, St. Dominic. As a novice, Raymond was as humble as any of the younger men despite all the accomplishments of his life to that time. He asked his superiors to impose a severe penance on him for having sometimes been complacent in his teaching, but the penance given was not exactly what Raymond had in mind. He was assigned to write a book of cases for confessors which led to the compilation of the *Summa de casibus poenitentalibus,* the first work of its kind.

Raymond became noted for his preaching and for converting heretics, Jews, and Moors, as well as for reforming fallen-away Christians who had been held as slaves by the Moors. Pope Gregory IX called Raymond to Rome in 1230 and, besides appointing him to various offices, took him as his own confessor. During this time, Raymond compiled five books of the *Decretals,* a work which served as part of the body of canon law until the publication of *Codex Juris Canonici* in 1917.

In 1235, the pope named Raymond Archbishop of Tarragona, capital of Aragon, a post which Raymond did not want. His anxiety led to serious illness and he persuaded the pope to recall the appointment. Raymond was not to enjoy his peace for long, and in 1238, he was elected master general of the Dominican order. He worked hard in this position, visiting all of the Dominicans and establishing a new constitution for the order. In this constitution, he included a provision that the master general be allowed to resign. When this constitution was accepted, he resigned at the age of sixty-five, citing age as his reason.

But Raymond was not quite ready to retire. He resumed his work of preaching and conversion, and established friaries in Spain and North Africa. Raymond died on January 6, 1275 and was canonized in 1601.

Raymond's message today: Raymond of Peñafort preferred the humble roads in life rather than avenues to power. He was an extraordinary person; in God's eyes, so is each one of us. We, like Raymond, are called upon to use our talents for the good of our community and, indeed, for the world.

What gifts of talent has God given to you? How are you using them to help those around you? Do you use your gifts with humility?

JANUARY 12–OPTIONAL MEMORIAL (CANADA)

Marguerite Bourgeoys, Religious: 1620–1700

Born in Troyes, Champagne, France, Marguerite was the sixth of twelve children. She was inclined to a religious life from her early years, but, at the age of twenty, she was turned down by both the Carmelites and the Poor Clares. The Abbé of the Augustinian convent in Troyes felt that her rejection was a sign that she should lead a new order of nuns who would not be cloistered. Marguerite's first attempt at establishing such an order failed, but another opportunity would present itself later.

In 1652, the governor of the French settlement at Ville-Marie (present-day Montreal) was visiting Troyes. He invited Marguerite to become the schoolmistress in his small colony, and she agreed to go. The first few years in Ville-Marie were spent in taking care of the few children in the colony, helping at the hospital, and preparing a chapel for the arrival of priests from France. In 1658, a school was opened with fewer than a dozen students.

From this small start, Marguerite Bourgeoys looked ahead to future growth for the school. Sailing to France, she returned to Canada with four young women as volunteer teachers. Later growth brought more volunteers and, in 1676, the women formed a community called the Congregation of Notre Dame.

In 1683, the bishop of Quebec attempted to combine the Congregation of Notre Dame with the Ursulines, who had been in Quebec since 1639. Mother Bourgeoys suggested that this would force her nuns to live a cloistered life, which would make their work impossible. The bishop acquiesced, but his successor raised similar issues before finally accepting the Congregation as the first non-cloistered foreign missionary community for women in the Church. Even so, it was not until 1698, five years after Mother Bourgeoys resigned as superior of the order, that twenty-four of the sisters were able to take simple vows.

Meanwhile, the first boarding school had been opened in Ville-Marie in 1673, and the first missionary school for Indians began there in 1676. Other schools were established outside of the colony, including a school on the island of Montreal. The little order faced the many hardships of colonial pioneering, along with a lack of understanding by their superiors. Through it all, Mother Bourgeoys was an indomitable figure who steered the order through rough times.

From the time that Mother Bourgeoys resigned as superior, her health began to fail. In late 1699, she offered God her life in place of the life of the young novice-mistress of the order who was seriously ill. The younger nun recovered and Mother Bourgeoys died on January 12, 1700.

St. Marguerite Bourgeoys is especially honored in Canada.

Marguerite's message today: Marguerite Bourgeoys felt God's call at an early age, but the direction of that calling was not clear to her until she was in her thirties. When it did become clear, she thrust herself wholeheartedly into the work which God chose for her. Only by prayer can we, too, become aware of what God's plan is for us.

When you feel unsure of your direction in life, take a few minutes to pray for God's guidance. Have the patience to wait for the right direction to become clear.

JANUARY 13–OPTIONAL MEMORIAL

Hilary, Bishop and Doctor: 315-368

Whenever the Church needs a strong voice against heresy, it seems that God sends the proper instrument to counter it. In this case, it was St. Hilary. St. Augustine called him the "illustrious Doctor of the churches"; St. Jerome said he was a "most eloquent man, and the trumpet of the Latins against the Arians."

Hilary was born in Poitiers, a member of a prominent Gallic family. Although raised as a pagan, Hilary reasoned that man is a moral and free being placed in the world to practice the great virtues. From this conclusion, he set about determining that there could be only one God, a supreme being, all powerful and eternal. At this point, Hilary was introduced to Scripture. He read the works of the prophets and then the New Testament. After this, apparently in middle age, Hilary was baptized into the Christian community.

Married and with a daughter, Hilary was elected bishop of Poitiers around the year 350. He tried to decline this office, but his humility made the people even more convinced that he was the proper choice. His scholarly writings, some of which are still in existence, began at this time.

A few years after his consecration, Hilary became involved in the Arian controversy. This heresy was widespread in the Christian world at the time due, at least in part, to the strong support from the emperor Constantius. In 355, the emperor called a synod in Milan of all the bishops in the Church. The purpose was to condemn bishop Athanasius, a strong opponent of Arianism. The emperor required all of the bishops to sign the condemnation; failure to do so meant banishment. Hilary refused to sign, and along with many others, was sent into exile in Phrygia. Here he continued his writing.

The emperor, still determined to involve himself in Church affairs, called together a council of Arians at Seleucia to offset the decrees of the Nicaean council, which had been called in 325 specifically to counter the Arian heresy. Hilary was invited out of exile to attend this council. Once there, however, he strongly defended the decrees of the Nicaean council rather than accede to the arguments of the Arians. He then withdrew to Constantinople.

Shortly after the Seleucia council, Hilary, a compelling speaker as well as a writer, made a request to the emperor that he be allowed to hold a public debate with Saturninus, the leading Arian bishop. Considering Hilary's reputation, the Arians viewed such a debate with dismay and prevailed upon the emperor to send him away from the eastern Church. Accordingly, in 360, the emperor sent Hilary back to Gaul where he was received with great joy by his people.

While Arianism began to ebb with the death of Constantius in 361, Hilary continued his strong defense of the faith until his death. He died in 368, though the date is uncertain. Hilary was named a Doctor of the Church by Pope Pius IX in 1851.

Hilary's message today: Hilary reached Christianity through reasoning and then put his formidable ability to work defending the doctrines of the Church. Most of us come to a strong acceptance of Christianity through faith and the examples provided by our families and community. No matter how it has come to us, we should remember to thank God daily for the enormous gift of faith which has been given to us.

Take time each day to thank God for all the gifts which have been given to you, most especially for the gift of faith.

Paul the Hermit: 230–342

Even though this saint lived as a solitary person in the desert for ninety years of his long life, quite a bit is known about him through the writings of St. Jerome and St. Athanasius.

A native of Egypt, Paul was orphaned in his early teens. His parents had given him not only a good education and a fair-sized estate, but a strong background in Christianity. When the harsh persecution of Christians by the emperor Decius began in the year 250, Paul hid himself in the house of a friend. Learning that his brother-in-law, who wanted Paul's estate, was ready to turn him in, Paul fled to the desert. Choosing a cave near a palm tree and a spring, Paul determined that he would serve God in the desert until such time as the persecution should end.

As time went on, Paul realized that a prayerful existence and meditation suited him, and he resolved to stay in the desert. The fruit from the palm tree, the leaves of which also gave him with clothing, provided Paul with food until he was forty-three years old. From that time until his death, a raven miraculously brought a half loaf of bread to him daily.

While his daily routine over the ninety years of his contemplative life is unknown, an incident which took place shortly before his death is illuminating. Anthony, who was the abbot of a monastery in the vicinity of Paul's cave, was himself a saintly and holy man. But Anthony, then ninety years of age, succumbed to the temptation of vanity and believed himself to be the first and longest-lived ascetic. In a dream, God directed Anthony to find one more perfect than himself. Anthony set out the next morning and, after two days and a night of searching, found Paul's cave by the bright light shining out of it.

The two saints warmly greeted each other by name, which they had learned through God's revelation. Paul inquired whether idolatry still prevailed in the world and, while they were discussing this, a raven came and dropped a loaf of bread at their feet. At this Paul said, "Our good God has sent us dinner." He then told Anthony how he had received a half loaf of bread every day for the previous seventy years and commented, "now that you have come to see me, Christ has doubled his provisions for his servants."

The next morning, Paul told Anthony that he was near death and that Anthony had been sent to bury him. He requested that Anthony return to his monastery and bring back the cloak which Athanasius had given to him. Paul then directed Anthony that he wrap him in the cloak before he was buried.

As he was returning to Paul's cave with the cloak, Anthony had a vision of Paul's soul being lifted to heaven by angels. Entering the cave, however, Anthony found Paul's body kneeling with his hands outstretched in prayer. Supposing him to be alive, Anthony joyfully knelt beside him to join in prayer, but Paul's silence soon persuaded Anthony that he was dead.

Anthony had no idea how he would dig a grave for his friend. While he was considering this, two lions came up slowly as if in mourning. Pawing at the ground, they dug a hole large enough to hold the saint's body. After burying Paul, Anthony returned to his monastery and told his followers all that had happened. He kept, and on great occasions wore, the palm leaf garment which Paul had fashioned for himself.

St. Paul the Hermit died in the year 342 while in his one hundred and thirteenth year. He is the patron saint of weavers. His feast day is celebrated in the Eastern Church on January 15 and is commemorated in the canon of the Mass in the Coptic and Armenian rites.

Paul's message today: Very few of us are called to the contemplative life of an ascetic. Nevertheless, we can all take a few minutes each day, perhaps before going to bed at night, to consider God's impact on our lives.

Consider keeping a journal and recording how God is an active part of your life each day. Come back to review it in a few months. You will marvel at the progress which you have made in your journey of faith.

Anthony the Abbot: 251–356

The death of his parents while he was still a teenager left Anthony with a large estate and a younger sister to care for. Some months later while attending Mass, Anthony heard the words of the Gospel: "Go, sell what you have, give the money to the poor, and follow me." Although the young man in Scripture did not follow Jesus' advice, Anthony knew that those words were directed at him.

Signing over the best of his lands to his neighbors, Anthony sold the rest and gave most of the money to the poor, keeping only enough for the care of his sister and himself. They began to live an austere life of prayer and sacrifice.

Again, a few months later, he heard the words of Jesus: "Do not be anxious about your life, what you shall eat." Anthony gave away his few remaining possessions, put his sister into a convent, and became a hermit. He lived a life of prayer, penance, and the strictest austerity, taking only bread and water once a day. Even this he considered too soft and so, after a few years, he moved to an old fort on top of Mount Pispir, in Egypt. Here he lived in complete seclusion, eating only what was thrown over the wall to him.

According to the writings of St. Athanasius, Anthony was constantly engaged in struggles with temptation during this time. Yet his life style attracted many followers. In 305, after twenty years on the mountain, he came down to organize his followers into what became the first Christian monastery. While loosely organized, the followers lived in solitude, except for worship, and were guided by a rule.

In 311, at the height of the persecution of Christians by Emperor Maximinus, Anthony traveled to Alexandria to visit the prisons and encourage those Christians being held there. He had expressed the desire to suffer martyrdom himself, but that was not to be. When the persecution subsided, he returned to Mount Pispir, organized another monastery, and then retired to a cave near the Red Sea.

Around 355, Anthony again returned to Alexandria, this time to fight the Arian heresy. Here he worked with his friend, St. Athanasius, for a time before returning to his cave, where he lived out the remainder of his long life.

St. Anthony is the patron of domestic and farm animals, basket makers, and butchers.

Anthony's message today: Like his friend, Paul the Hermit, Anthony chose a life of contemplation, and put himself entirely in the hands of God. It is difficult to trust that God will take care of our needs unless we have unquestioning faith in God's goodness; this we can only develop through prayer.

What is God's plan for your life? Do you accept it? How willing are you to put your trust in God?

Fabian, Pope and Martyr: d. 250

St. Fabian was a Roman and a layman who was in the assembly to elect a new pope. The story is told that a dove flew in and settled on the head of Fabian. This was taken as a sign from God by the clergy and people assembled, who then elected Fabian pope on January 10, 236.

Little is known of Fabian's pontificate. We do know that he brought back the body of St. Pontian, pope and martyr, from Sardinia for burial in Rome. He also condemned Privatus, a bishop in Africa who had authored a new heresy.

Fabian was martyred in 250 under the persecution of the emperor Decius. He was buried in the cemetery of St. Callistus where his tomb still exists. St. Cyprian, in writing of this man, said that the glory of his death corresponded with the purity and holiness of his life.

Fabian's message today: Most likely, Fabian never expected to be elected pope, but, as St. Cyprian tells us, he was equal to the task. We never know what God has in store for us, so we should live each day ready to accept God's will as it becomes known to us.

Do you pray for the wisdom to accept God's will? Do you have faith that whatever mission God gives to you, he will give you abilities equal to the task?

Sebastian, Martyr: c. 257-288

The only facts known about this saint are that he was martyred about 288 in Rome; that he was buried along the Appian Way, probably near the present basilica of St. Sebastian; and that he was venerated in Milan from the early fourth century on. He is mentioned in several martyrologies, dating from as early as 350. The rest of the knowledge about this saint is contained in legends based on long-standing tradition.

It is thought that Sebastian was born in Narbonne, Gaul around 257 and became a soldier in the Roman army around 283, a time of heavy Christian persecution under the Emperor Carinus. He encouraged two Christian men who were under sentence of death to remain firm in their faith. Sebastian was so convincing in his arguments that many converted, including the jailer and his wife. Hearing of miracles that Sebastian had performed, the prefect of Rome, Chromatius, sent for him and was himself converted along with his son. Chromatius released the prisoners, freed his own slaves, and resigned as prefect.

Diocletian became emperor soon after and, impressed by Sebastian's courage and character, named him captain of the praetorian guard without being aware that Sebastian was a Christian. The following year, Diocletian went east to Constantinople and named Maximian as joint emperor in Rome, and Sebastian retained his prestigious position in the palace guard under Maximian.

In the year 286, persecution of the Christians became fiercer under the new emperors and some of Sebastian's converts were martyred. Sebastian himself was discovered to be Christian, and impeached before the Emperor Diocletian who bitterly reproached him for his ingratitude. Sebastian was sentenced to be shot to death by archers. His body was pierced with arrows and he was left for dead.

The widow of St. Castulus soon came to get his body for burial. She found Sebastian still alive, however, and nursed him back to health. When he was fully recovered from his wounds, Sebastian refused to flee, but instead took up station one day in a place where Diocletian was to pass. When the emperor came by, Sebastian accosted him and denounced the atrocities which Diocletian was committing against the Christians. Stunned at first by the sight of a man he believed dead, the emperor could only listen. When he recovered from his surprise, the emperor ordered Sebastian seized and beaten to death.

The legend of St. Sebastian is depicted in early Christian, medieval, and Renaissance art. He is always represented as pierced with arrows or holding an arrow. St. Sebastian is the patron of archers, athletes, and soldiers.

Sebastian's message today: Sebastian, like other Christians of his time, encouraged the members of his Christian community to remain strong in their faith in the face of persecution.

While the persecution suffered by Christians today usually does not result in death, it is still very real. Can you remain strong when you are the subject of ridicule because of your faith?

JANUARY 21—MEMORIAL

Agnes, Virgin and Martyr: c. 291–304

As is the case with many of the early saints, much of what we know about Agnes is based on legend. What is generally agreed upon is that Agnes was a young girl when she died (thirteen years of age according to St. Ambrose and St. Augustine). She was a very beautiful girl and of a wealthy Roman family. Agnes was sought after by many young men in Rome, but she resolved at an early age to consecrate her virginity to God.

One of Agnes' spurned suitors denounced her to the governor as a Christian during the persecution by Emperor Diocletian. The governor, first by gentle persuasion and then by a display of instruments of torture, tried to induce Agnes to give up her faith. When that failed, he condemned her to a house of prostitution. Her saintly bearing deterred all of the men who approached her except one. Legend tells us that he was struck blind. His friends, terrified, carried him to Agnes who, by prayer, restored his sight and health.

The governor then sentenced Agnes to death. The stories vary on whether she was beheaded, burned, or stabbed, but all agree that Agnes was martyred. Her body was buried a short distance from Rome on the Nomentan Road. At this spot, in the year 354, a basilica was erected in her honor by Constantina, the daughter of Emperor Constantine.

St. Agnes (her name is derived from the Greek word for "pure") has become the great Christian symbol of virginal innocence. She is honored by mention in the Mass and is the patron of the children of Mary and of young girls.

Agnes' message today: Agnes dedicated herself to God. None of the threats or the prospect of death could turn her from this course. Like many martyrs, indeed, like Jesus himself, Agnes prayed for her persecutors.

How do you treat those who persecute you: the person at work who spreads gossip about you, the neighbor who constantly complains, or the merchant who tries to cheat you?

Vincent of Saragossa, Deacon and Martyr: d. 304

While still young, Vincent was instructed in Scripture. He was then ordained deacon by St. Valerius, bishop of Saragossa, and instructed to preach and teach the people.

In 303, during the Christian persecution, Dacian, the proconsul of Spain, arrested Valerius and Vincent and tried to induce them to sacrifice to pagan gods. Valerius, who had a speech defect, authorized Vincent to speak for both of them. Vincent told Dacian that neither would give up their faith and that they were prepared to suffer for the true God. The proconsul banished Valerius, but retained Vincent. Noted for his cruelty, Dacian was determined to break this young man's resolution.

Dacian ordered progressively harsher tortures for Vincent. He was stretched out on the rack and his flesh was torn with iron hooks, but none of this had any effect on his faith. Dacian then ordered Vincent to be placed on an iron grill over a fire. Vincent cheerfully mounted this grill and endured even the salt being rubbed into his wounds. In writing of Vincent, St. Augustine pointed out that the flames seemed to strengthen Vincent rather than torture him.

Finally, Dacian ordered Vincent to be thrown into a dungeon and left without food, with his legs placed in a stock to immobilize him. He further ordered that no one was to be allowed in to see Vincent. God, however, sent his angels to console him. His jailer noted bright light through the chinks in the dungeon walls. He saw Vincent walking and praising God, and the jailer converted to Christianity on the spot. All of this further enraged Dacian, but he finally allowed visitors to come in and dress Vincent's wounds. They prepared a bed for him and no sooner was he laid on it than God called him home.

Dacian ordered Vincent's body to be thrown out into a field

where animals and birds of prey could attack it, but a raven fended off these attackers. His body was then thrown into the sea, but washed ashore where two Christians found and buried it. St. Vincent had an early and large following all over the Christian world. In early art, he was often depicted with a raven.

St. Vincent is honored by the vinedressers of Burgundy as their patron. In some countries, he shares his feast day, January 22, with St. Vincent Pallotti. The latter, who died about 150 years ago, was the founder of the Society of Catholic Apostolate, a fellowship of *all* Catholics (not just clergy and religious) organized to spread the faith.

Vincent's message today: The strength that one gains from faith is unfathomable. Certainly in Vincent's case, this strength allowed him to withstand the worst tortures which Dacian could conceive and accept them willingly.

Through prayer, our faith grows. With this faith, God gives us the grace to confront the trials which we face in our daily lives. Do you turn to God when you are faced with uncertainties and hardships?

Francis de Sales, Bishop and Doctor: 1567–1622

Born in Savoy in the south of France, Francis studied in Paris and at the University of Padua where he received his doctorate in law at the age of twenty-four. Despite the opposition of his father and an offer of a high government position, Francis chose to become a priest and was ordained in 1593. Unknown to Francis, his cousin had proposed him as the provost of the chapter of Geneva. The pope appointed Francis to this academic post and, somewhat reluctantly, Francis took up these duties.

Francis' first love, however, was ministering to the poor and preaching, and these things he did with great enthusiasm. His preaching style was very simple, but effective. The oration style of the times called for filling sermons with quotations from Greek and Latin, but although he was an excellent scholar, Francis chose to preach in clear language and thus won a large following.

But a greater mission was in store for Francis de Sales. The people of Chablais, an area south of Lake Geneva, had fallen into Calvinism, and the few Catholics left in the area were too afraid of violence to declare themselves openly. Francis volunteered to go to Chablais and win back the people to Catholicism. Within months of his arrival, Francis was the target of two assassination attempts and other trials, but his simple message of love had its effect.

During this period, Francis began writing tracts which set forth the teachings of the Church versus the errors of Calvinism. These papers—the originals are still preserved in the archives at Annecy—were copied many times and distributed widely. When Claude de Granier, the bishop of Geneva, came to visit Francis a few years after his arrival in Chablais, he found that the Catholic faith had been firmly reestablished there.

The bishop had for some time considered Francis as a worthy successor and proposed to the pope that Francis be appointed coadjutor of the see of Geneva. Pope Clement VIII, having heard of the good works of Francis, invited him to Rome where he was to be examined before his appointment. The pope and others, including St. Robert Bellarmine and Cardinal Frederick Borromeo (cousin of St. Charles), put thirty-five complex theological questions to Francis. These he answered knowledgeably, yet with simplicity and modesty, and his appointment was confirmed.

Francis succeeded to the see of Geneva upon the death of Claude de Granier in 1602. As bishop, Francis continued to live in an austere manner. While preaching in Dijon in 1604, he met Jane

Frances de Chantal with whom, in 1610, he founded the order of the Visitation nuns. Francis also continued to write. In his *Treatise on the Love of God,* he wrote, "The measure of love is to love without measure."

Francis de Sales died in 1622, having carried on his preaching and ministrations almost up to his death. The beatification of Francis took place in St. Peter's Basilica in Rome, the first beatification to take place in that church. He was canonized three years later, and declared a Doctor of the Church in 1877. Francis was named patron of journalists by Pope Pius XI; he is also the patron of authors, other writers, and of the deaf.

Francis' message today: Despite the clear danger to himself, Francis did not hesitate to volunteer to help bring back the "lost sheep" of Chablais. Each of us probably knows some lost sheep, family members or neighbors who no longer go to church. We can encourage them to return to the faith by prayer, our example, and a quiet word or two.

Have you prayed for those people who have fallen away? Invite someone who has left the fold to attend church with you.

Conversion of Paul, Apostle: c. 5–64

Paul—named Saul at birth—was born of Jewish parents around the year 5 A.D. in Tarsus, which also made him a citizen of Rome. He studied under a renowned rabbi in Jerusalem, and became a rigid Pharisee and an obsessed persecutor of the Christians. According to Scripture, Saul was present at the stoning of Stephen, but only as a spectator. Sometime between the years 34 and 36, he was on his way to Damascus to arrest some Christians and bring them back to Jerusalem for trial. It was on this journey that he experienced the vision of God which led to his conversion.

Following his conversion, Saul spent the next three years in Arabia before returning to Damascus to preach. He went to Jerusalem sometime between the years 36 and 39 where he met the other apostles and, under the sponsorship of Barnabas, was accepted into the Christian community. With Barnabas, he began the first of his three missionary journeys around the year 45. It was during this journey that his name was changed to Paul.

On his return from this first journey, Paul was successful in convincing Peter and the other apostles that Gentile Christians need not have Jewish law imposed upon them. Armed with the approval of Peter, Paul and Barnabas set out on their second missionary journey to the Gentiles in 49. This mission was followed by a third journey between the years 53 and 58.

When he returned to Jerusalem in 58, Paul was attacked by a mob for his missions to the Gentiles and was placed under protective arrest by Roman soldiers. Paul was eventually sent to Rome for trial (which was his right as a Roman citizen) and remained under house arrest for two years. This is the last mention of Paul in the Acts of the Apostles, the main source of material about him.

According to writers a few years after his death and to tradition, Paul made yet another journey in the years following his imprisonment (63–67). During this last journey, he was again arrested and returned to Rome where, according to Eusebius, he was executed on the same day as St. Peter during the persecution of Christians by the Emperor Nero.

Paul was an important writer and apostle, who had a tremendous impact on the early Church. His influence shaped the entire Christian experience, and continues to this day. His epistles to the Romans, his pastoral letters to Timothy and Titus, and his letters to the various Christian communities which he was instrumental in converting form an important part of Church teaching.

We celebrate the conversion of St. Paul on this date, while the Solemnity of Sts. Peter and Paul, Apostles, is celebrated on June 29.

Paul's message today: None of us are likely to have as strong an influence on the Church as Paul has had through history. However, we are all capable of influencing our community and those with whom we live and work.

Ask yourself: what kind of influence am I on my family? My neighbors? My coworkers?

Timothy, Bishop and Martyr: died c. 97

Timothy was the son of a Greek father and Eunice, a Jewish mother who converted to Christianity along with her mother, Lois. These two women were responsible for Timothy's early instruction in the faith and were commended by St. Paul in his second letter to Timothy.

Timothy was living in Lystra when St. Paul visited there around the year 47. He joined Paul for the second and third of his missionary journeys and is frequently mentioned in both the Acts of the Apostles and Paul's letters. Timothy was with Paul at the founding of the Church in Corinth. He was probably with Paul when the apostle was imprisoned in Caesarea and, later, in Rome. Timothy was himself imprisoned, but was later set free.

Paul chose Timothy as his successor, and wrote two letters to Timothy outlining his wishes for the Church. In the first letter, Paul charges Timothy to use his gifts well, to select his bishops and deacons carefully, to take care of widows, to preach only sound doctrine, and to "no longer drink only water, but take a little wine for the sake of your stomach and your frequent ailments."

In the second letter, the most personal of all his writings, Paul is nearing the end of his life ("I have fought the good fight, I have finished the race, I have kept the faith" 2 Tm 4:7). He gives

Timothy further advice on how to conduct his ministry, and tells him to "be strong in the grace which is ours in Christ Jesus." Paul also speaks of his loneliness in prison, his great friendship with Timothy, and his desire for Timothy to visit him.

According to tradition, Timothy became the first bishop of Ephesus and was stoned to death there when he opposed a pagan festival.

Timothy's message today: Tradition tells us that Timothy followed Paul's advice and used his gifts well. He was indeed "strong in the grace which is ours in Christ Jesus." Jesus asks us to do the same, that is, to use our gifts well and be strong in the grace which God gives us.

How do you use the gifts which God gives you? Do you sometimes forget that Jesus is with you, giving you the grace which will help you be strong?

Titus, Bishop: First Century

Titus was a Greek who was apparently converted to Christianity by St. Paul. In Titus 1:4, Paul called Titus "my true child in our common faith." Our knowledge of him comes from Paul's letters to Titus and to the Corinthians. Titus accompanied St. Paul on his third missionary journey and acted as Paul's secretary at the council in Jerusalem.

Titus served as a mediator for Paul on several missions. Paul sent Titus to Corinth to correct errors and smooth out the dissension which had arisen there. He was received by the Corinthians with great respect, and interceded with Paul on their behalf. Titus returned to Corinth a second time at Paul's direction to collect alms for the poor.

Paul and Titus traveled to Crete, where Paul consecrated Titus and left him to serve as the first bishop. Paul's letter to Titus, similar to his first letter to Timothy, instructs Titus on how to conduct his mission and summarizes the major qualities which a bishop should have. Paul tells Titus that a bishop is God's steward and, as such, must be blameless and have a firm grasp of the Word so that he can preach with sound doctrine and refute those who dispute that doctrine.

Titus died in Crete, probably at an advanced age.

Titus' message today: In his letter to Titus, Paul mentioned many qualities which a bishop should possess. All good Christians should also possess many of these qualities: hospitality, a love of goodness, and prudence, among other things.

Are you an active member of your church community? Have you welcomed others into that community?

Angela Merici, Virgin: 1470–1540

Angela Merici was orphaned at the age of ten and, together with an older sister and a younger brother, was raised by an uncle. As a teenager, Angela became a member of the Third Order of St. Francis and lived a life of great austerity. She gave up all her possessions and lived almost entirely on bread and water.

When Angela was twenty-two, her uncle died and she returned to her home town of Desenzano, in Lombardy (Italy). Appalled at the ignorance among poorer children, she recognized that she had a greater calling than the quiet contemplative life. With other members of the Third Order, she began bringing the little girls of her neighborhood together on a regular basis for instruction in religion and in the basic skills of running a household. This proved to be so successful that Angela was asked to open a school in Brescia where she gained a reputation for her charity and saintliness.

In 1533, Angela brought together a number of the young women who had been helping in her schools and began an informal novitiate. Two years later, she founded the first teaching order of women in the church, called the Company of St. Ursula, who was the patroness of medieval universities and venerated as a leader among women. This order is today called the Ursuline order.

The sisters met together for classes and for worship. Because the idea of a teaching order of nuns was so novel, this group did not live in a community or seclude themselves as did most other orders of nuns. Though the early rule prescribed poverty, chastity, and obedience, the members continued to live at home, wore no special habit, and took no formal vows.

The Ursuline order was dedicated to re-Christianizing family life by giving future wives and mothers a solid Christian education. Even today, the work of Ursuline nuns stresses the religious education of girls, especially the poor.

Angela's message today: Angela recognized and met a need in the Church of her time—that of educating young girls in their faith as well as in running a household. Today, Catholic schools and parish religious education programs provide an opportunity for all children to be educated in the faith.

Every parish has a religious education program for its young people. How could you contribute your talents to the success of this program?

Thomas Aquinas, Priest and Doctor: 1225–1274

Thomas was the son of a count and a relative of both the Emperor of the Holy Roman Empire and the King of France. At the age of five, his parents sent him to the Benedictine monastery at Monte Cassino to be educated, in hope that he would eventually become the abbot there.

In about 1239, the Benedictines sent Thomas to the University of Naples to complete his education. He disappointed both the Benedictines and his family by joining the Dominicans at Naples in 1244. This move was so strongly opposed by his family that they had him kidnapped and held him in the family castle for over a year in an attempt to dissuade him. Thomas persisted, however, and after more studies in Paris and Cologne with St. Albert the Great, was ordained a Dominican around 1250.

Continuing his studies, Thomas became a master of theology. He then moved on to teaching and writing, first in Paris and then at Naples, Rome, Orvieto, Anagni, and Viterbo. It was during this period, from 1259 to 1268, that Thomas began his greatest opus, the *Summa Theologica*, a work which deals with the whole of Catholic theology.

Although Thomas drew a sharp distinction between faith and reason, he emphasized that the fundamental Christian doctrines, though impossible to establish by reason, are not contrary to reason and reach us by revelation. Nevertheless, he believed that such truths as the existence of God—as well as God's eternity, creative power, and providence—can be discovered by natural reason.

Thomas Aquinas is considered the preeminent spokesperson for the Catholic tradition of reason and divine revelation. His writings are required study for all theological students even to this day. He was canonized a saint in 1323 and declared a Doctor of the Church by Pope Pius V in 1567. St. Thomas Aquinas is the patron of students, schools, colleges, and universities.

Thomas' message today: Thomas Aquinas was a theologian of unparalleled insight. For hundreds of years, his writings have been the basis for almost all theological study. While not everyone would want to delve into the writings of Aquinas, all Catholics should strive to learn more about the teachings and traditions of the Church.

Spend some time learning about the Catholic faith. Check your parish library or a religious book store to see what is available there.

John Bosco, Priest: 1815–1888

John was born in Piedmont, Italy, the son of poor parents. He entered the seminary when he was sixteen and was ordained at Turin. Shortly after, John began to work with neglected children. With his mother, he opened a refuge for boys and began a school for them. By 1856, he was housing 150 boys and had placed another 500 boys in oratories.

As an educator, John Bosco was noted for using a minimum of restraint and discipline along with a great deal of love and encouragement. He kept careful watch over the development of the boys in his care. Interested not only in their spiritual growth, John established workshops for the boys in shoemaking, tailoring, and printing. To pay for all this, John preached, wrote popular books, and relied on donations.

His need for reliable assistants led him to found the Society of St. Francis de Sales (the Salesians). By the time of his death, there were some sixty-four Salesian foundations in Europe and the Americas and about 800 Salesian priests. In 1872, he founded the Daughters of Our Lady, Help of Christians, to provide the same care and education for poor and neglected girls.

St. John Bosco's interest in vocational education and publishing justify him as the patron of editors, laborers, and Catholic publishers.

John's message today: The care of young boys and girls is as necessary today as it was in John's time. Many agencies exist to help young people who are in need—for example, Catholic Charities and Boys/Girls Clubs—but these agencies cannot do the work alone.

Have you done anything to help keep children out of trouble? Could you visit a teenager who is serving in confinement for a juvenile crime and offer encouragement?

Brigid, Religious: c. 450–525

Brigid (sometimes called Bridget or Bridie) is one of many legendary Irish saints. According to tradition, her father was Dubhthach, an Irish chieftain, and her mother, Brocca, was a slave at his court. Brigid's parents were baptized by St. Patrick and Brigid herself developed a close friendship with that saint.

As a young girl, Brigid became interested in the religious life and probably professed her vows to St. Mel of Armagh while still in her early teens. About 470, she founded a double monastery at Cill-Dara and became abbess of the convent, which was the first in Ireland. The monastery developed into a great center of learning and spirituality, and around it grew the cathedral city of Kildare.

Brigid also founded a school of art at Kildare, and the illuminated manuscripts produced there became famous. One, the *Book of Kildare*, was praised as one of the finest of all Irish illuminated manuscripts before its disappearance about three centuries ago.

The *Dictionary of Saints* tells us that Brigid was one of the most remarkable women of her times, even discounting some of the fantastic legends which surround her. Stories of the miracles which she performed grew in incredibility as each of her biographers tried to surpass what had been written earlier about her. Butler's *Lives of the Saints* recounts one beautiful legend about this saint which indicates the love and compassion Brigid held for her sisters.

One evening, as the sun went down, Brigid sat with Sister Dara, a holy nun who was blind. They talked of the love of Jesus Christ and the joys of paradise. Their hearts were so full of joy that the night fled while they spoke together, and neither knew that so many hours had passed.

Then the sun came up from behind the Wicklow mountains, and the pure white light made the earth bright and gay. Brigid sighed when she saw how lovely were earth and sky, as she knew that Dara's eyes were closed to all this beauty. So Brigid bowed her head and prayed, extended her hand, and signed the dark orbs of the gentle sister. Then the darkness passed away from Dara's eyes, and she saw the golden ball in the east and all the trees and flowers glittering with dew in the morning light.

Dara looked a little while, then turning to the abbess, said, "Close my eyes again, dear Mother, for when the world is so visible to the eyes, God is seen less clearly to the soul." So Brigid prayed once more, and Dara's eyes grew dark again.

Called the "Mary of the Gael," Brigid is buried at Downpatrick with St. Columba and St. Patrick. She has become almost as popular in Ireland as St. Patrick, and is honored as well in parts of Scotland, Wales, and Australia. St. Brigid is a patron of scholars and dairy workers, and along with St. Patrick, is a patron of Ireland.

Brigid's message today: The legend of Sister Dara teaches us about Brigid's compassion, but also offers a lesson in the distractions of the world. Although it is not possible for most of us to focus only on the spiritual life, it is important to spend some time each day recognizing God's presence in our lives.

Do you try to spend a little time in prayer each day? A good way to begin is to ask God's help as you begin each day and thank God for blessings received as you end each day.

Blaise, Bishop and Martyr:
c. early Fourth Century

Blaise (sometimes spelled Blase) was martyred around 316 by order of Governor Agricolaus in Sebastea, Armenia, during Licinius' persecution of Christians. This is the only certain knowledge which we have about this saint.

According to legend, Blaise was born in Armenia to wealthy Christian parents and was made a bishop in his youth. He was known as a good bishop who encouraged the spiritual and physical health of his people. When the persecution of Christians began in Armenia, Blaise was forced to flee. He went to live as a hermit in the back country, where he cured wild animals that were sick or wounded.

One day, while seeking animals for the amphitheater, a group of hunters came across Blaise kneeling in prayer, surrounded by patiently waiting wolves, lions, and bears. Recognizing him as a Christian, the hunters hauled Blaise off to prison. On the way there, a mother came to him with her young son who was choking to death on a fish bone caught in his throat. Blaise cured the boy; thus, he later became the patron and protector of throats. Many Catholics in this country still have their throats blessed on St. Blaise's feast day.

Blaise's message today: All of God's creatures, great and small, are entitled to our care and compassion. There are many people, young and old, who may not be able to look after their own needs. It is up to us to help them in whatever way we can.

Are you aware of the needs in your own community? What can you do to alleviate the suffering of others?

Agatha, Virgin and Martyr: died 251

Agatha is another of the early saints about whom most of our knowledge is based on legend. She was born in Sicily, either in Catania or Palermo, both of which claim her as a patron, and was martyred in Catania, most likely during the persecution of Christians by the Roman emperor Decius around the middle of the third century.

Agatha dedicated herself to God and to a life of chastity. When she refused the advances of a Roman consul, he denounced her as a Christian, and subjected her to torture and indignities in an effort to change her mind. But Agatha's continued dedication to God and her calm acceptance of torture infuriated her captors. They cut off her breasts and rolled her over red-hot coals until she died.

Early Christian art depicted Agatha holding a tray with her breasts on it. In the Middle Ages, the breasts were mistakenly seen as two loaves of bread. This led to the custom of blessing bread on St. Agatha's feast day and bringing the bread to the altar on a tray.

Sometime after her death, an eruption of Mt. Etna was stilled after the people prayed to St. Agatha for intercession. As a result, people have continued to ask St. Agatha to protect them from fire. She is also a patron of nurses, and she could well be an appropriate patron for women undergoing a mastectomy.

Agatha's message today: Not many of us have to endure torture today, but all of us do bear distressing pain, whether physical, mental, or emotional, from time to time. Although this practice has been out of favor for awhile, we might offer up our suffering to God in reparation for our sins.

Do you accept the sufferings that come into your life with grace, or do you tend to let everyone know that you are suffering?

Paul Miki and Companions, Martyrs: died 1597

During the 1550s, St. Francis Xavier evangelized much of Japan and made hundreds of thousands of converts to Christianity. Some forty years later, Paul Miki, a Jesuit scholastic studying for the priesthood, and twenty-five others died for their faith at Nagasaki. The group included Jesuit and Franciscan priests, brothers, laymen, a doctor, teachers, a soldier, old people, and young altar servers. Their nationalities included Spaniards, a Mexican, and an Indian, as well as native Japanese. Of this group of twenty-six, Paul Miki became the best known. As he was dying on the cross, Paul, who was native Japanese, preached to the crowds and prayed for his executioners.

The Shogun who had these martyrs killed wished to wipe out Christianity in Japan, calling it a religion brought by foreigners who intended to conquer the country. A great show was made of the killing. The victims were maimed then led through several towns to a hill, known today as Holy Mountain, for their execution. This action was meant to terrorize the people into giving up the Christian faith.

When missionaries returned to Japan almost three hundred years later, they initially found no sign of Christianity. After they were established, they found thousands of Christians living around Nagasaki who had secretly preserved their faith, a tribute to the steadfastness of Paul and the others, as well as to St. Francis Xavier. Paul and his companions were beatified within a few years after their deaths, and canonized in 1862.

Paul's message today: Like many other martyrs, Paul forgave and prayed for his slayers. It is never easy to forgive those who have hurt us in some way, but if Paul could forgive those who killed him, can't we forgive those who have caused us to suffer in some lesser way?

Do you have some family member or close acquaintance who has hurt you? Think about how you can shed this burden by forgiving that person.

Dorothy, Virgin and Martyr: died c. 303

There is a beautiful story told about St. Dorothy, who was persecuted during the reign of the emperor Diocletian. The governor of Caesarea, Fabricius, imposed cruel punishments on Dorothy because of her refusal to worship idols or to marry. Dorothy spoke of the garden to which God would take her and the sweet fruits of the garden. The crowning blow for Fabricius occurred when two women, sent to induce Dorothy to give up her faith, were themselves converted. This led to a sentence of execution.

As Dorothy was being led to her execution, a young lawyer in the crowd, Theophilus, jeered at Dorothy and yelled at her to send him fruits when she reached the garden where she was going. Dorothy promised that she would. Just before her execution, Dorothy knelt and prayed. Suddenly an angel appeared with a basket containing three apples and three roses which Dorothy sent to Theophilus, telling him that she would wait for him in the garden. After tasting the fruit, Theophilus became a Christian and, later on, was himself martyred.

Based on the story recounted above, St. Dorothy is depicted in medieval art with flowers and fruit. She is the patroness of florists and gardeners.

Dorothy's message today: Dorothy is a witness to the importance of forgiveness, something all of us can imitate today. She forgave the one who callously taunted her, inviting him to share in the glories of paradise.

Are there people in your life who taunt you for your choice to follow Jesus more closely? Do you pray for them? Forgive them?

Jerome Emiliani, Religious: 1486–1537

Jerome was born in Venice and became a soldier for that city-state. As commander of the League of Cambrai forces at Castelnuevo, Jerome was captured and imprisoned when that outpost town fell in battle. He spent the time in prison thinking about his life and learning how to pray. Jerome escaped from prison, and returned to Venice where he began studies for the priesthood. He was ordained in 1518.

The years which followed saw much plague and famine in Europe. While aiding the victims of this pestilence, Jerome became especially affected by the condition of orphans and decided to devote himself to helping them. He founded several orphanages and a hospital. Around 1532, Jerome and two other priests founded a congregation which became known as the Clerks Regular of Somascha (named after the town in which their first house was established). The order was dedicated to the care of orphans, and to educating children and priests.

Jerome died in 1537 of an infectious disease which he caught while ministering to its victims. St. Jerome is the patron of abandoned children and orphans.

Jerome's message today: Jerome was a good and caring person, even a heroic one. All of us know someone who has been abandoned by friends or family, or who is spiritually orphaned. We, like Jerome, can reach out to these abandoned ones.

Is there someone in your life who needs God's healing touch right now? As a follower of Christ, are you willing to offer it?

Apollonia, Virgin and Martyr: died 249

St. Dionysius wrote an account of the heavy persecution of Christians by the pagan populace in the city of Alexandria in the last year of the reign of the Emperor Philip. An enraged mob killed several older Christians who would not blaspheme God or worship the false gods. Many other Christians fled the city, leaving all of their possessions behind rather than renounce their faith. St. Dionysius noted that he knew of none who yielded to the pressure.

Among the older Christians martyred at this time was Apollonia, a deaconess. The pagans first beat her severely, knocking all of the teeth out of her head. Then, dragging her out of the city, they lit a great fire and threatened to throw her into it unless she blasphemed God. Apollonia asked for a moment's delay which, interpreted by the pagans as a sign that she was considering it, was granted. When she was freed, Apollonia threw herself onto the flames. While we, as Christians, believe it a sin to hasten one's own death, St. Augustine was of the opinion that Apollonia was guided by the Holy Spirit in her action.

St. Apollonia, the patron saint of dentists, is invoked against toothache and all dental diseases. In ancient art, she is often depicted holding a tooth in a pair of pincers or with a golden tooth hung from a necklace.

Apollonia's message today: Standing up for one's faith is only easy if that faith is strong. Faith will remain strong only if we ask God to give us the strength we need to face the many obstacles and temptations which cross our paths.

When times of trial occur in your life, do you turn first to God for help?

Scholastica, Virgin: 480–547

Scholastica was the twin sister of St. Benedict, and was a member of a wealthy family from the central area of present-day Italy. Like her brother, Scholastica was drawn early on to a religious life. After Benedict founded a monastery at Monte Cassino, south of Rome, she joined a convent in Plombariola, a town which was located a few miles away from Monte Cassino. Scholastica became the abbess of a convent and is considered to be the first Benedictine nun.

Scholastica and her brother visited each other once each year. Because Scholastica was not permitted in the monastery, they met at a nearby farmhouse. In these meetings, the twins discussed spiritual matters. During one meeting, Scholastica sensed that her death was near at hand. She asked her brother to remain overnight so that they might continue their discussion. Benedict refused because he did not want to remain outside of the monastery overnight as this would break his own rule.

According to the writings of St. Gregory, Scholastica then prayed to God that her brother remain. Hardly had she finished her prayer when a major storm came up which prevented Benedict from venturing outside the farmhouse. Benedict cried, "God forgive you, sister. What have you done?" Scholastica answered him, "I asked a favor of you and you refused. I asked it of God and he granted it." The twins parted the next morning after a long discussion.

Three days later, Benedict saw a vision of his sister's soul in the form of a dove, ascending to heaven. He announced the death of his sister to his fellow monks and sent them to bring her body to the monastery. Benedict then interred her in the tomb which he had prepared for himself.

St. Scholastica is often called upon to intercede with God when children suffer convulsions.

Scholastica's message today: The story of Scholastica's last meeting with her brother provides an excellent example of how God listens to all of our prayers and grants even our smallest requests. Yet often, we do not put our trust in God but try to get along without God's help.

Faith can move mountains, but only if it is strong. Do you pray with faith that God will answer your prayer? Do you really believe it?

FEBRUARY 14—MEMORIAL

Cyril, Monk: 825–869 and Methodius, Bishop: 826–884

Cyril and Methodius were brothers born at Thessalonika, Greece, of a senatorial family. Cyril was sent to study at the imperial university in Constantinople at an early age. In time, he was ordained and assumed the chair of his teacher, Photius. Methodius, meanwhile, was governor of one of the Slavic colonies in Greece before becoming a monk.

Both brothers wanted to live out their lives in a monastery. In

861, however, Emperor Michael III sent them to convert the Khazars in the Dneiper-Volga regions of Russia. The brothers learned the Khazar language and made many converts before returning to their monastery several months later. In 863, Photius, now the patriarch of Constantinople, sent the two brothers to Moravia (now part of the Czech Republic) to convert the Moravian people, since German missionaries had achieved little success in their evangelization efforts there.

The brothers put their knowledge of the Slavonic language to good use. They invented an alphabet, based largely on Greek capital letters, which marked the beginnings of Slavonic writing. (The Cyrillic alphabet attributed to Cyril was probably the work of his followers.) With the new alphabet, the brothers began translating liturgical books into Slavonic and began using the Slavonic tongue in their church services. Because of this, and the fact that they were from Constantinople where heresy was abundant, they incurred the wrath of the German clergy and bishops.

Summoned to Rome in 869 to defend their position, the brothers were received warmly by Pope Adrian II, who, convinced of their orthodoxy, approved the use of the Slavonic language in their liturgies and announced that they were to be consecrated bishops. But shortly after, Cyril died on February 14, 869; it is not known whether he ever was consecrated a bishop. Methodius was consecrated, however, and returned to Moravia as bishop. Later he was named archbishop of Velehrad, Czechoslovakia.

Methodius' problems with the Germans continued. In 870, King Louis and the German bishops deposed Methodius at a synod and threw him into prison. He was released two years later by order of the pope, now John VIII, but Pope John deemed it advisable to forbid the use of the Slavonic language in the liturgy. Methodius was again summoned to Rome in 878 when his orthodoxy was questioned. He was able to convince Pope John of his conformity and the need for the use of the vernacular in the liturgy.

Methodius finished the translations of the Scriptures which his brother had begun. He and Cyril are called the "Apostles of the Slavs," and to this day the liturgical language of the Russians, Serbs, Ukrainians, and Bulgars is that designed by Cyril and Methodius.

Sts. Cyril and Methodius are the patrons of Moravia and are specially venerated by Catholic Czechs, Slovaks, Croatians, Orthodox Serbians, and Bulgarians. Their memorial was extended to the universal Church by Pope Leo XIII.

Cyril and Methodius' message today: Over a thousand years ago, Cyril and Methodius translated Scripture into the language of their people and used the vernacular in worship. Ministering to their people in this manner brought condemnation from others, but Cyril and Methodius persevered despite obstacles.

Do you defend those principles that you know are right when others condemn them? Do you spend time studying the background so that you can apply persuasive arguments to your defense or do you just base your stand on a "feeling?"

Valentine, Martyr: died 269

There is some confusion about the life of Valentine. There may have been two Valentines, one a priest and physician in Rome, the second the bishop of Interamna, a town about sixty miles from Rome. Many scholars believe that these were one and the same person.

Valentine, the priest, cared for Christians who were being persecuted under Claudius II. Arrested for this, he was sent by the emperor to the prefect of Rome who tried to persuade Valentine to renounce his faith. The prefect failed in his efforts, and he ordered

Valentine to be beheaded. The execution took place on February 14, 269. He was buried on the Flaminian Way in Rome where a church was erected in his honor and a gate, the Porta Valentini (now known as the Porta del Popolo) was named for him.

Valentine, the bishop, was also beheaded and buried on the Flaminian Way though he is said to have been executed in Interamna where a great devotion to the saint built up immediately. Tradition has it that he also was killed on February 14, however the year of his death is put at 273. It is entirely possible that Valentine, the bishop, was brought to Rome where he was put to death, thus, it is likely that Valentine, the priest, and Valentine, the bishop, are the same person.

The custom for young men and women to choose each other as Valentines on this day is based on the popular medieval belief, recorded in literature as early as Chaucer, that birds began to pair on this day. Early references to the custom were contained in a letter written in 1477 by Elizabeth Drews to a prospective bridegroom concerning her marriageable daughter, Margery, and Margery's letter which refers to him as "my right well beloved Valentine."

Valentine's message today: Since we know that God is love, it seems appropriate that we should associate one of God's saints with love. We should remember, however, that God does not want us just to love those who are near to us. Jesus told us that we must love our enemies as well.

Do you pray for your enemies? Do you make an effort to understand their position? Have you tried to make peace with them?

Peter Damian, Bishop and Doctor: 1001–1072

Peter was orphaned when he was very young. He was raised for a time in the household of a brother who put him to work at the heaviest chores as soon as Peter was able to handle them. Another brother, Damian, who was a priest in Ravenna (Italy), felt pity for the boy and took charge of raising and educating him. Perhaps in gratitude, Peter took his brother's name as his surname.

Peter was educated first at Faenza and then at Parma. He was an excellent student and went on to become a noted professor. Yet this was not the life which Peter wanted to lead. Even while teaching, he practiced austerities; it is said he fed the poor from his table on a regular basis. In 1035, Peter entered a Benedictine hermitage at Fonte Avellana and resolved to spend the remainder of his life as a humble monk, praying, studying Scripture, and living a life of great austerity.

Around the year 1043, Peter became abbot of Fonte Avellana. Not only did he govern with great wisdom and piety, but Peter founded five other monasteries and appointed the priors who led their communities under Peter's general direction.

Peter Damian's wisdom commended him to several popes and his skills were employed by many of them in the service of the Church. In 1057, Pope Stephen II prevailed upon Peter to leave his hermitage and appointed him cardinal-bishop of Ostia. In this see, he began a program of ecclesiastical reform. While severe with the clergy, Peter treated penitents with kindness and mildness. Peter wanted to return to simple monastic life, however, and he constantly sought permission from Stephen's successors to resign his office.

Pope Alexander II was finally persuaded to allow Peter to resign on the condition that he be available if his help were needed. Peter considered this papal consent to not only relieve him from the responsibility of governing his see, but also from the governance of his religious settlements. He thus returned to the life of a simple monk.

In his retirement, Peter set an example of piety, humility and penitence. He also used this period to write extensively, continuing to push for ecclesiastical reform. He often called upon monks to strictly observe their vows and denounced simony, which is the practice of paying for ecclesiastical favors. Peter also wrote on the sacraments of penance and Eucharist, as well as other theological and religious topics. Many of his letters exist today.

Peter died in a monastery near Faenza on February 22, 1072. For many years, devotions to St. Peter Damian were celebrated in the areas where he lived and worked. In 1828, Pope Leo XII extended the saint's feast to the entire Church and declared the saint a Doctor of the Church.

Peter's message today: Peter, though a brilliant man, sought a simple life of prayer and penance. Yet when God called on him to undertake a different mission, Peter said yes. We too are sometimes called upon to step out of our "comfort zones" and to respond to a call for a particular purpose in God's plan.

What are you doing to prepare yourself to respond to God's call? If your pastor asked you to lead a parish ministry, for example, what would you answer?

Chair of St. Peter, Apostle: died c. 64

Peter, as Scripture tells us, was a son of John and the brother of Andrew. He was a native of Bethsaida, a small village near Lake Tiberias. With his father and brother, Peter, at that time called Simon, worked as a fisherman on Lake Gennesaret.

Through the Gospels and the Acts of the Apostles, we know much more about Peter than we do about many of the early saints. We know, for example, that Peter was present at the marriage feast at Cana when Jesus worked his first miracle. Peter and the other apostles would join Jesus whenever he was teaching in their vicinity. Jesus came to Peter's home in Capernaum and cured his mother-in-law, and Peter's boat was always available to Christ. Peter, together with James and John, was privileged to witness the Transfiguration. Later, as we know, it was Peter who denied Christ three times in the courtyard of Pontius Pilate.

When Peter acknowledged Jesus as "the Messiah, the Son of the living God," Jesus replied, "And I tell you, you are Peter, and on this rock I will build my church" and "I will give you the keys of the kingdom of heaven. Whatever you bind on earth will be bound in heaven; whatever you loose on earth will be loosed in heaven" (Mt 16:16–19). Thus, Peter was chosen to be the first pope.

Following the ascension of Jesus into heaven, Peter assumed his role as head of the Church on earth. He was the first apostle to preach to the Gentiles, and was the first of the apostles to perform miracles.

Imprisoned by Herod Agrippa in about the year 43, Peter escaped, guided by an angel. At the assembly in Jerusalem, he proclaimed that Christ wanted the Good News preached to all. This is the last mention of Peter in the New Testament, but very early tradition says that Peter then went to Rome where he became Rome's first bishop. He was crucified in Rome around the year 64 during the reign of Nero and was buried on Vatican Hill. Excavations under St. Peter's Basilica in recent years have uncovered what is believed to be his tomb. Bones found in the tomb are still under intensive study.

This feast is called the Chair of St. Peter, and commemorates the action of Christ when he handed over the leadership of the Church to St. Peter and his successors. We celebrate the Solemnity of Sts. Peter and Paul on June 29.

Peter's message today: Peter provides a good example of Jesus' love for us. Peter denied Jesus three times, yet Jesus still loved Peter and did not withhold the position he had promised. Likewise, Jesus loves us and forgives us our sins when we ask his forgiveness.

Have you asked for Jesus' forgiveness? If you will be received into the Church at the Easter Vigil, have you begun to prepare for the sacrament of reconciliation?

FEBRUARY 23–OPTIONAL MEMORIAL

Polycarp, Bishop and Martyr: c. 69-155

A follower of St. John the Evangelist, Polycarp was one of the second generation of Church leaders known as Apostolic Fathers. As the bishop of Smyrna (modern-day Izmir, Turkey), Polycarp was the acknowledged leader of the Eastern Church. He traveled to Rome to meet with Pope Anicetus and discuss certain issues. Among these was the timing of Easter, which the Eastern and Western Churches differed on. Neither was able to persuade the other on this point, so they concluded that each should follow their own custom. Despite this disagreement, the pope, to signify his respect, asked Polycarp to celebrate the Eucharist in his own papal church.

During the persecution of Christians by the Emperor Marcus Aurelius, Herod, the chief of police, sent soldiers to the place where Polycarp was staying. The bishop greeted them, ordered supper for them, and requested some time for prayer before he went with them. He prayed for his own people and for the whole Church with such intense devotion that some of his captors regretted the mission which they were carrying out.

While Polycarp was being brought to his judgment, he was met on the road by Herod and Herod's father, Nicetas, who took Polycarp into their chariot and attempted to persuade him to show compliance by acknowledging Caesar as divine or by offering incense to Caesar in order to save his life. When Polycarp refused, he was brought before the proconsul who, also failing to sway Polycarp, ordered him burned at the stake.

When the fire was lit, the flames swirled around Polycarp's body, but did not touch him. Seeing this, the proconsul ordered him pierced with a lance. As the soldiers speared him, a dove flew from him and blood spewed forth to quench the fire.

One of Polycarp's writings, his letter to the Philippians, is still in existence and was commended by St. Irenaeus, one of his followers, and St. Jerome among others. The narrative of his martyrdom is taken from eyewitness accounts written by his followers. St. Polycarp, though not named as a patron, has been invoked to save those threatened by flames.

Polycarp's message today: The determination and strength that Polycarp displayed when the soldiers came to arrest him can only be attributed to a solid faith. Polycarp knew that God was with him and he knew that his prayers would bring strength to the whole Church.

All of us are on a journey of faith. In your prayers, ask that you may develop a strong faith, which will carry you through the toughest times.

Gabriel Possenti, Religious: 1838–1862

Born the eleventh of thirteen children, Gabriel was christened Francis, a name appropriate to the place of his birth, Assisi. His father was an official of the papal states, and the family was quite well off. As a young boy, Francis developed an interest in bird hunting, a sport quite popular in Italy at the time. In his teens, Francis lived the life of a typical young man. He became interested in the theater, and was discriminating in his personal appearance and dress.

Francis' family moved to Spoleto when his father was assigned there, and Francis began attending the Jesuit school in that city. It was during this period that Francis first felt the stirrings of a vocation. Falling sick, he promised to devote his life to God if he recovered. During this illness, someone brought him a relic of the Jesuit martyr, St. Andrew Bobola. Francis, believing himself cured due to the intercession of this saint, interpreted this as a sign that he should become a Jesuit. He applied to the Society of Jesus and was accepted, but, not yet seventeen, he delayed entry.

A favorite sister of Francis died during an outbreak of cholera and this spurred him to think again about his vocation. Believing that he was being called to a more penitential life than what was offered by the Jesuits, Francis chose the Passionists and entered their novitiate in 1856, at the age of eighteen. It was here that he was given the name Brother Gabriel of Our Lady of Sorrows.

The remainder of Gabriel's short life was marked by his strong desire to perfect himself through obedience and humiliation. He constantly sought more severe forms of bodily mortification, which in most cases was denied by his superiors. Having asked permission many times to wear a chain with sharp points next to his body, an exasperated spiritual director finally said, "Wear it by all means, but you must wear it outside your habit and in public, too, so that all may see what a man of great mortification you are."

Gabriel looked forward to his ordination and the wonderful things he could accomplish for God, but this was not to be. He developed tuberculosis and died on February 27, 1862, a few days before his twenty-fourth birthday. Humble to the end, he did not want anyone to think him extraordinary. Just a few days before his death, he destroyed his personal notes, in which he had described the many blessings God had showered on him.

St. Gabriel of Our Lady of Sorrows is the patron saint of clerics. While his feast day is not on the liturgical calendar in the United States, he is honored by his order and by others on this date.

Gabriel's message today: Like Gabriel, we all go through periods in our lives in which we are not sure what God's plan is for us. Although Gabriel felt a calling to a religious life from early in his teens, he had second thoughts before finally committing to this life. We too have second thoughts about what course we are to take in our lives. Prayer can provide the answer when the time is right.

Think about a time when you may have had second thoughts about a decision. Did you turn to God in prayer and ask for guidance?

MARCH

David, Bishop: c. 520–c. 589

David was born around the year 520. He was educated in a monastery in Cardigan where his fellow students told of seeing a "dove with a golden beak playing at his lips and teaching him to sing the praise of God." After ordination as a priest, David retired to an island to study under the Welsh saint Paulinus for several years.

When he emerged from his studies, David became very active. He is said to have founded twelve monasteries, the last of which, Mynyw (later called Menevia and now St. David's) in the far southwest corner of Wales, became his home for most of the remainder of his life. The discipline of his community was extremely severe. Hard manual labor and bare subsistence were the norm. The monks drank only water (which earned for St. David the surname, "the Waterman"). Silence was the rule unless absolutely necessary to speak, and prayer was constant, even when laboring.

Sometime during the mid-500s, a synod was called in Cardigan to suppress the Pelagian heresy, which was reemerging in Britain at that time. (This heresy denied the concept of original sin.) David was invited to attend, but declined until St. Deiniol and St. Dubricius arrived at the monastery and persuaded him to go. At the synod, David's eloquence and grace so overwhelmed the attendees that he was unanimously elected bishop of Cambria, replacing St. Dubricius who resigned in his favor. David accepted only on the condition that the episcopal seat be relocated to Mynyw. As bishop, David later convened another council which ratified the decrees of the earlier assembly and drew up the regulations which became the governing documents for the Church in Wales.

Little else is known of St. David, but he is said to have died in his monastery in Mynyw sometime around the year 589. Another Welsh saint, St. Kentigern, saw his soul being carried to heaven by angels.

St. David is depicted in art standing on a mound with a snow-white dove on his shoulder. Legend holds that when David was speaking at the first synod in Cardigan, a dove came to rest on his shoulder. At the same time, the land on which he was standing rose up so that, towering above the assembly, all present could clearly hear his words. St. David is the patron of Wales, and is honored in that country on this date.

David's message today: While little is known for certain about St. David's life, we can assume that he lived a life devoted wholly to God and accepted God's will. It isn't always easy to accept God's will in our lives, but with prayer we can accomplish anything.

Set aside some part of your day for prayer and reflection if you do not do this regularly. Ask God for help in speaking with conviction about your faith.

MARCH 3—OPTIONAL MEMORIAL

Blessed Katherine Drexel, Virgin: 1858–1955

Katherine was the daughter of Francis A. Drexel, a wealthy Philadelphia banker. When she was just five weeks old, Katherine's mother died, and she was raised by a loving stepmother, Emma Bouvier Drexel.

Katherine traveled extensively with her parents and two sisters, and received the best education available. But she was also given a firm foundation in faith. Her mother—Katherine refused to allow anyone to call Emma a stepmother—had an oratory (prayer room) built into the family home. All of the family members used this retreat for prayer and meditation. Three days per week, Emma, supported by her husband, opened her doors to the poor of Philadelphia and gave them food, clothing, and money for rent. It is said that the family spent about twenty thousand dollars per year in this charity. Her family also contributed generously to the missions which served the American Indians and blacks, and Katherine found herself working in this ministry even as a young girl.

Katherine chose to devote her life to the care of Indians and black people. Shortly after her father's death in 1883 (Emma had died two years earlier), Katherine became aware of the gross injustice with which Indian affairs were being handled. Over the next several years, she and her sisters gave $1.5 million to the construction of missions and schools, including money for equipment and teachers' salaries. An efficient, practical businesswoman, Katherine oversaw the disbursement of most of this money and the design of simple, but serviceable buildings for the Indian schools.

In her early twenties, Katherine had considered a religious vocation. She was doing much good in her charitable works, however, and the fullness of her life left little time for thoughtfully pursuing that vocation. A bishop who acted as her spiritual advisor was initially unconvinced that Katherine had a calling to the religious life. After a time, he recommended that Katherine found her own order to minister to Indians and blacks. At first, Katherine felt unworthy to do this, but at the bishop's urging, agreed to the mission.

In 1889, Katherine entered the convent of the Sisters of Mercy in Pittsburgh to prepare herself for her mission. In 1891, she founded a new order, the Sisters of the Blessed Sacrament for Indians and Colored People. Katherine did much for the Indians and blacks over her long life. Schools for Indians covered most of the West from the Canadian border to Mexico. In 1915, she founded Xavier University in New Orleans for the black people of that city. It has been estimated that in her lifetime, Katherine spent approximately $12 million in her ministry to the Indians and blacks.

> **Katherine's message today:** While Jesus said that it is easier for a camel to go through the eye of a needle than for a rich man to enter the kingdom of heaven, he never said that it was impossible. The Drexel family provides an excellent example of the proper use of wealth. Although most of us will never be in this position, we can follow the example of Katherine and use our resources to help those who are less fortunate than us.

> *Do you volunteer regularly at your parish or help in one of your local charities? Do you provide financial support to your parish and to charity?*

Casimir of Poland: 1458–1484

Casimir was one of thirteen children of King Casimir IV of Poland and Elizabeth of Austria, daughter of Emperor Albert II. Even as a young child, Casimir was drawn toward a life of holiness and practiced harsh penances such as wearing a hair shirt under his clothes. This did not affect his demeanor, however, which was always pleasant and cheerful.

Casimir showed his strong love of God and of the Blessed Mother by caring for the poor. He gave away all of his own possessions for the benefit of the needy, and used his influence with his father when necessary on their behalf.

When the boy was only fifteen, nobles from Hungary came to

his father and asked him to place Casimir on the throne of that country, replacing Matthias Corvinus. Though reluctant to do so, Casimir, in obedience to his father, led an army to the borders of Hungary. There, confronted by the large army assembled by Matthias, many of the Polish troops deserted. With this and a strong conviction that the war would be unjust, Casimir returned with his army to Poland. While his father was unhappy with this decision, Casimir would never take up arms again. As a result of this action, the Poles gave Casimir the title of "the Peacemaker."

Casimir devoted most of his life to study and prayer, as well as to caring for the poor. He served as the viceroy of Poland from 1479 to 1483 while his father was out of the country.

His austere practices did not help a lung disease, probably tuberculosis, from which he suffered and Casimir died at the age of twenty-six in 1484. He was canonized by Pope Adrian VI in 1522 and named the patron saint of Poland and Lithuania.

Casimir's message today: "Blessed are the peacemakers." Casimir, recognizing the casualties that would result from an unjust war, withdrew from the battlefield. His action shows that sometimes it is better to back down, although this course may be the harder one to follow.

Is there a cause that you would fight for? Is it a just cause or one motivated by ego?

MARCH 7–OPTIONAL MEMORIAL

Perpetua and Felicity, Martyrs: died c. 203

Perpetua was a young woman of noble birth and the mother of an infant son. She was arrested in Carthage during the persecution of Christians by Emperor Severus, along with several other catechumens who included Felicity, a slave. Perpetua kept a record of the trials and sufferings which the group endured while imprisoned and of the visions which she experienced. This journal, which went up to the day before their deaths, was completed by an eyewitness. (A more complete transcription of Perpetua's diary can be found in Butler's *Lives of the Saints*.)

Perpetua wrote of the discussions which she held with her father, an old man at the time and a pagan. Perpetua was his favorite child and he tried very hard to convince her to give up her faith. "Father," she said to him, "Do you see this vessel, a waterpot? Can it be called by any other name than what it is?" "No," he replied. "So also I cannot call myself by any other name than what I am—a Christian."

The Christians were brought before Hilarian, the procurator of the province, who, failing to shake their faith, sentenced them to be killed in the amphitheater by wild animals. While awaiting their deaths, these Christians converted many more by their strong faith. Among them was their jailer, Pudens.

Felicity, pregnant at the time of her arrest, was fearful that she would not be allowed to suffer martyrdom due to her condition. Joined by the others, she prayed that she might be delivered before the games began. Her prayers were answered when Felicity gave birth to a daughter who, after her death, was adopted by a fellow Christian. Pudens also arranged for Perpetua, who was greatly concerned for her son, to have the baby remain in prison with her.

When the day came for their deaths, the group was led to the amphitheater where some members expressed the hope that they would be set upon by several kinds of animals to gain a more glorious crown. But none of the animals would attack Perpetua and Felicity. They were then ordered beheaded by gladiators. Perpetua directed the sword of the nervous gladiator to her throat after he missed with his first stroke.

Perpetua and Felicity's message today: Nothing could shake the faith of these young women, along with the other martyrs, not even the fear of a painful death. While our faith is normally not tested in the manner of the martyrs, we should still be prepared to meet death at any time since we never completely know God's plan for us.

If God were to call you home today, would you be ready? What would it take to prepare yourself?

John of God, Religious: 1495–1550

John, born in Portugal, was a soldier in the wars between Spain and France as well as in the war against the Turks in Hungary. Later he was a shepherd in Seville and also served as an overseer of slaves in Morocco.

During the early years of his life, John had given up the Christian faith. But when he was about forty years of age, John decided to atone for his previously immoral life by going to Africa to rescue Christian slaves and to seek martyrdom. Instead, he got as far as Gibraltar where he peddled religious books and holy pictures. In 1538, he went to Grenada and opened a religious goods store.

Soon after, he heard a sermon by St. John of Avila which filled him with remorse. He engaged in a public beating of himself, begging forgiveness for his sins and wildly repenting his former ways. For this, he was thrown into an insane asylum. Helped by John of Avila, who suggested that he apply his energies to helping others rather than to practicing the harsh penances which he had imposed on himself, John of God found new purpose in his life. Upon his release from the asylum in 1539, he devoted himself to helping the sick and the poor.

John opened a house to care for these ill-fated people, at first begging for alms to supply the basic needs of his house. Soon his wisdom, zeal, dedication, and holiness in serving the unfortunates so impressed the people of Grenada that the wealthy clamored to support his efforts. The work of John and his supporters was the beginning of the Order of the Brothers Hospitalers, also known as the Brothers of St. John of God, an order which has spread throughout the world.

St. John of God is the patron saint of booksellers, heart ailments, hospitals, nurses, printers, and the sick.

John's message today: God never gives up on anyone, but loves all of us equally as his children. Like many of our own children, it took John a little longer to determine what it was that God was asking him to do with his life. Nevertheless, once he had chosen the right course, John launched into it with fervor.

Have your children or others close to you sometimes disappointed you with the life choices they have made? They still need and want your love, as well as your prayers. Find a way to show them some compassion.

MARCH 9–OPTIONAL MEMORIAL

Frances of Rome, Religious: 1384–1440

The daughter of wealthy parents who lived in Rome, Frances was wed in an arranged marriage to Lorenzo Ponziano when she was thirteen. Always desirous of a life in service to God, Frances began ministering to the poor of Rome soon after her marriage. She was joined in this by Vannozza Ponziano, wife of her brother-in-law, Paluzzo.

While living a life of great holiness, Frances neglected none of her obligations to her family even when, upon the death of her mother-in-law, she was required to assume the duties of head of the household for the Ponziano family. When her first son, John Baptist (Battista), was born in 1400, Frances, though well able to afford help, allowed no one but herself to look after him. The same was true for her other two children, Evangelist and Agnes.

When a plague struck Rome in the early 1400s, Frances and Vannozza worked to relieve the suffering of the people. To support their efforts, Frances, with the consent of her father-in-law, sold her jewels, emptied the family storerooms, and with Vannozza, went door-to-door begging for food to feed the hungry.

Around this time, a great schism had divided the Catholic Church. When Ladislaus of Naples, an ally of the anti-pope, captured Rome, Lorenzo was wounded and Paluzzo was taken prisoner. Ladislaus' governor also demanded little Battista as a hostage. While Frances was praying in the church, Battista was released under circumstances which were described as miraculous.

In a later raid, Lorenzo escaped but Battista was captured. (He later escaped and joined his father.) Ladislaus' soldiers sacked and burned the Palazzo Ponziano and many farms and villages under the family's control, slaughtering animals and killing many of the peasants. Frances and Vannozza (whose husband was still a prisoner), together with Evangelist and Agnes, lived in a corner of the burned-out palazzo while still offering whatever help they could to their poorer neighbors.

Another pestilence struck Rome around 1413 during which Evangelist died. Twelve months after his death, while Frances was praying, her dead son appeared to her with an archangel. He told her of his happiness in heaven, but warned her that his sister, Agnes, would soon die. As a consolation, the archangel who came with Evangelist would stay with Frances to be her guide. About a year later, Agnes died at the age of sixteen. The archangel, who appeared to Frances as a child about eight years old, remained with her and was seen only by her.

Frances' fame had spread all over Rome, and her advice and counsel were sought from all quarters. She formed a society of women, living in the world and bound by no vows, who pledged themselves to God and to the service of the poor. These women were known initially as the Oblates of Mary. After seven years, the society thought it appropriate to come together in a house and a building known as the Tor de' Specchi was acquired for them. They then became known as the Oblates of Tor de' Specchi.

Three years later, Lorenzo died and Frances announced her intentions to join her sisters at Tor de' Specchi. The superior immediately resigned her position and, together with the other sisters, insisted that Frances take her place. Frances reluctantly accepted. She was now able to live even closer to God and her visions became more frequent. She was sometimes known to spend whole nights in prayer.

Frances died in the spring of 1440. When word of her death spread, throngs of people came to the Palazzo Ponziani to mourn. To this day, countless pilgrims come to her tomb in the Church of Santa Maria Nuova and to Tor de' Specchi and the Casa degli Esercizi Pii (the successor to the old Palazzo Ponziani) on March 9, the anniversary of her death. St. Frances is the patron of motorists.

Frances' message today: Frances' undying love and concern for her family and for the needs of the sick and the poor stand out as a model for all of us today. While all of us have our families first and foremost in our hearts, we sometimes forget about those who are not as fortunate as ourselves.

Have you considered the needs of the poor in your community? In the world? Do you ever visit a sick person who is not a family member or close friend?

Patrick, Bishop: 385-461

So much of what is commonly accepted about Patrick is clouded in legend and myth. The facts about Patrick's life are drawn primarily from his *Confessio,* a short treatise written against his detractors. Even these few facts are sketchy.

Patrick was the son of a Roman-British official and was probably born somewhere on the island of Britain (though some sources say he may have been born in Gaul). At about the age of sixteen, Patrick was captured by raiders and carried off in slavery to Ireland, then a pagan land. He was put to work as a shepherd for six years until he escaped.

During his captivity, Patrick experienced a conversion, and he turned from being a thoughtless youth to one with a deep faith in God. Upon returning to his family and his homeland, Patrick began his studies in the monastery at Lerins (an island off Cannes in France) and was probably ordained around the year 417.

Patrick felt called to preach the Good News to the Irish people who had held him captive. He was consecrated a bishop by St. Germanus about 432, and sent back to Ireland to succeed St. Paulinus who had died in the previous year. Patrick traveled to all corners of Ireland, meeting fierce opposition from Druids and hostile chieftains. He usually overcame his opposition by miraculous means and eventually converted most of the island to Christianity. During his nearly three decades in Ireland, Patrick baptized hundreds of thousands of people, raised intellectual standards, founded several monasteries, ordained many priests, divided Ireland into dioceses, held church councils, and brought the Irish into closer relations with the rest of the Western Church.

One legend about St. Patrick explains the association of this saint with the shamrock. Upon arriving in Ireland, Patrick traveled to Ulster where he sought to gain favor with the High King

Laoghaire. Although the king himself apparently never became a Christian, many of his people and members of his family were converted. In instructing the king's two daughters, Patrick used the three-leaved shamrock to exemplify the Holy Trinity.

The Irish have been strong defenders of the faith since accepting Christianity through St. Patrick. Soon after Patrick's time, Irish missionaries began to spread out over northern Europe, bringing the whole of that region into Christianity. To this day, Irish missionaries continue to spread the Good News throughout the world. St. Patrick is the patron saint of Ireland.

> **Patrick's message today:** It is not easy to "forgive and forget" one's enemies. When we have a problem forgiving others, it is well to recall the words which Jesus taught us in the Lord's Prayer: "Forgive us our trespasses as we forgive those who trespass against us." Patrick well heeded these words when he returned to Ireland to serve the people who had previously enslaved him.
>
> *How easily do you forgive your enemies? Would you give of yourself, as Patrick did, to help an enemy?*

MARCH 17

Joseph of Arimathea: First Century

One of the early saints of the Church, Joseph of Arimathea is mentioned in all four Gospels. According to Luke 23:50, Joseph was a "virtuous and righteous man" who was "himself awaiting the kingdom of God" (Mk 15:43). He was a member of the Sanhedrin and was secretly a disciple of Jesus. Like many Christians of that time, he kept his discipleship to himself "for fear of the Jews" (Jn 19:38).

When Jesus was brought before the Sanhedrin to be condemned to death, Joseph opposed their decision. After Jesus died on the cross, however, Joseph went to Pilate and asked for his body. Pilate consented, so Joseph wrapped Jesus' body in clean linen and laid it in a new tomb which had been hewn out of rock.

Legend tells us that Joseph went with Philip the apostle to Gaul to spread the Good News. Philip later sent twelve missionaries, under the direction of Joseph, to the British Isles. Though he did not accept Christianity, the king gave the missionaries an island, later to become Glastonbury, on which they constructed a church in honor of Our Lady. Joseph is also said to have inherited the chalice used by Jesus at the Last Supper, the Holy Grail, which has been the subject of many fictional quests. In the Middle Ages, when these legends reached the peak of their popularity, British clerics used them to support their claim that Britain was the first country of the western world to accept the teachings of Christ.

St. Joseph of Arimathea is the patron of funeral directors. Though he has no memorial on the liturgical calendar, he is honored on this date.

Joseph's message today: After Jesus' death on the cross, Joseph chose to reveal himself as a follower of Christ, a move which must have caused his expulsion from the Sanhedrin. We too are sometimes asked to make sacrifices in the name of Jesus.

Do you offer those sacrifices which Jesus asks of you willingly or do you try to find a way to avoid them?

Cyril of Jerusalem, Bishop and Doctor: c. 315–386

Cyril is thought to have been the son of Christian parents and, if not born in Jerusalem, he certainly was raised there. He received an excellent education from his parents which helped to prepare him for his coming trials.

Ordained by St. Maximus, the bishop of Jerusalem, one of Cyril's first duties was to instruct catechumens as they prepared for the reception of the sacraments at the Easter Vigil (what we call the period of purification and enlightenment), and during the Easter season after the sacraments had been received (mystagogy). Much of what we know about the way catechumens were prepared for baptism in the early Church has been gleaned from the writings of Cyril, and his work has been instrumental in developing the Rite of Christian Initiation for Adults as it is used today.

Cyril succeeded St. Maximus as bishop of Jerusalem. The Arian heresy, which was rampant throughout most of the Christian world in the mid-fourth century, hit hardest in Palestine. It should be noted that during this time, the young and growing Church was still in the process of defining itself. Beliefs that we take for granted today were not so sharply determined in the fourth century. The Council of Nicaea was called in 325 specifically to counter the Arian heresy, but, as with many Church councils, it was many years before the full effects were felt.

Cyril's troubles began when Acacius, the Arian bishop of Caesarea, claimed jurisdiction over Jerusalem as the metropolitan of Caesarea, and tried to advance the Arian heresy in Cyril's episcopate. When Cyril disputed both the claim and the heresy, open warfare broke out. Acacius called a synod of Arian bishops and accused Cyril of being rebellious against authority. The Arian bishops condemned Cyril, and he was driven out of Jerusalem.

When Cyril finally returned to Jerusalem about the year 387, he found chaos at reign. Schisms and heresy abounded and party factions were literally at war with each other. Cyril requested help from the Council of Antioch, and Gregory of Nyssa was sent to assist him. This saint found the troubles of Jerusalem to be more than he could handle and soon left the city. Gregory did report back to the council, however, that while major problems existed in Jerusalem, Cyril's faith was orthodox.

In 381, Cyril and Gregory both attended the Council of Constantinople where an amended Nicene Creed was adopted. At this council, many of his contemporaries praised Cyril as a champion of orthodoxy against Arianism. In 1882, Pope Leo XIII declared him a Doctor of the Church.

Cyril's message today: Cyril took a strong stand for what he believed in. At the cost of placing ourselves in the middle of controversy, we too must sometimes stand up for what we believe.

Do you tend to "go along with the crowd" or do you defend those things you strongly believe in?

Joseph, Husband of Mary: First Century

Most of our reliable information on Joseph is contained in the first two chapters of the Gospels of Matthew and Luke. Here we find out that Joseph was of royal descent from David, that his family was from Bethlehem in Judea, and that Joseph, who was a builder, had moved from Bethlehem to Nazareth in Galilee.

Joseph was engaged to Mary. Upon learning that she was pregnant, he resolved to divorce her. Described in Matthew as a righteous man, Joseph did not want to expose Mary to public disgrace; therefore, he intended to dismiss her quietly. An angel appeared to Joseph in a dream to tell him, "do not be afraid to take Mary as your wife for the child conceived in her is from the Holy Spirit" (Mt 1:20).

Shortly after the birth of Jesus, Herod ordered the death of all children in Bethlehem under the age of two. An angel again appeared to Joseph to tell him to take Mary and Jesus and flee to Egypt. After Herod's death, an angel came to Joseph for the third time, instructing him to return to Israel with his family. While this is all we know definitively about Joseph, we can surmise more from the few brief references to this saint found in Scripture.

Luke may have interviewed Mary as he was writing his Gospel. He notes that Mary, upon finding the twelve-year-old Jesus in the temple after three days of searching, says to the boy, "your father and I have been searching for you in great anxiety" (Lk 2:48). Luke then tells us that Jesus went down to Nazareth with his parents and was obedient to them. This reference suggests that Mary and Joseph, like any other parents, loved and cared for their child.

Charged with supporting his family and raising the boy Jesus, Joseph worked as a carpenter. We know that he taught his trade to Jesus, as was the custom of the times. We can also assume that Jesus, like most boys, picked up the mannerisms and speech of Joseph. Finally, we can surmise that this holiest of families was like most any other family, with the same joys, sorrows, love, and concern for each other.

Devotions to St. Joseph began to grow in the Middle Ages, but only became widespread in the fifteenth century when his feast day was added to the Church calendar in 1479. St. Teresa and St. Francis de Sales particularly popularized devotion to the foster father of our Lord. Pope Pius IX declared St. Joseph patron of the universal Church in 1870 and later popes pronounced St. Joseph the patron of workers and of social justice, with Pope Pius XII establishing May 1 as the feast of St. Joseph the Worker.

Joseph's message today: In a time when families are breaking up, often with fathers abandoning their wives and children, Joseph provides a model for fathers who love their families.

When the weight of the world seems to have settled on your shoulders, try saying a prayer to St. Joseph. Ask him to help you carry your burden.

MARCH 23–OPTIONAL MEMORIAL

Turibius de Mongrovejo, Bishop: 1538–1606

As a young man, Turibius was educated in law and soon recognized as a brilliant scholar. He became a professor of law at the University of Salamanca where he attracted the notice of the king, Philip II. After some time, the king appointed Turibius chief judge of the Inquisition, an unusual appointment for a layman. He fulfilled his duties in a most humane manner, with wisdom and discretion.

Some years later, the archbishopric of Lima, Peru became vacant. Peru had been troubled by outrageous abuses against the Indians on the part of Spanish conquerors. The clergy, if not actually contributing to the abuses, condoned them by ignoring the plight of the natives. Missionary work was at a virtual standstill.

An archbishop who could change all of this was required, and Turibius, who had impressed all with his judiciary skills and the strength of his character, was selected. Stunned by this decision, Turibius argued that canon law prohibited laymen from performing ecclesiastical duties. Undeterred, the hierarchy ordained him, consecrated him a bishop, and put Turibius on the next ship for Peru.

Soon after his arrival in 1581, Turibius undertook a journey though his diocese. His first order of business was to straighten out the clergy, which he did with firmness. The powerful among the laypeople were a little more intractable, but he succeeded in removing some of the most extreme abuses.

The archbishop established many churches, hospitals, and the first seminary in the New World. In order to converse directly with the Indians, he studied the native dialects and his efforts succeeded in converting many of them. He confirmed Rose of Lima and Martin de Porres, who themselves later became saints. The charities of Turibius were numerous. The bishop recognized that many of the poor Spaniards would not accept charity publicly or from anyone they knew. In these cases, he provided assistance without the beneficiaries knowing where the help came from.

Turibius was traveling in the north of the country when he fell ill, but he continued his travels until he knew that the end was near. Turibius made a will leaving all of his property for the benefit of the poor, then died on March 23, 1606. Together with St. Rose of Lima, he is considered one of the first two saints of the New World.

Turbius' message today: In his lifetime, Turbius became known as a wise, humane, and just administrator, first during the Spanish Inquisition, then during his tenure in Peru. He met strong opposition from many who preferred the excesses of abuse and corruption. But this did not deter Turbius from seeking justice for the oppressed.

Many of the stands which we, as Catholics, take are not fashionable in our culture now. Nevertheless, we are obliged by our faith to take the moral high road, whether politically correct or not.

APRIL

Isidore of Seville, Bishop and Doctor: 560–636

This saint's family is thought to be of Roman origin, but his father was from Cartagena, Spain, and Isidore was born in Seville. As a boy, Isidore was entrusted his older brother, Leander, for his education. He received a very strict but firm grounding, later becoming known as the most learned man of his time and a strong supporter of good education. (Incidentally, Leander and another brother, Fulgentius, also became bishops and saints; a sister, Florentia, founder and abbess of several convents, became a saint as well.)

Isidore worked as an assistant to Leander, who had become the bishop of Seville. Upon Leander's death in about 599, Isidore succeeded him in this post. As bishop, Isidore accomplished much. He completed the conversion of the Goths from Arianism to Catholicism and adapted a missal and breviary for them, both tasks having been started by his brother. Isidore was responsible for establishing seminaries or church schools in every diocese of Spain. These schools did not teach merely the liberal arts and the classical languages, but had medicine, law, the sciences, and Aristotlean philosophy as part of their curriculum.

Isidore presided over two Church councils during his episcopate, the second Council of Seville in 619 and the fourth Council of Toledo in 633. He hosted the Council of Seville, but the other bishops chose him to preside over the Council of Toledo in recognition of his superior distinction as the greatest teacher in Spain.

Isidore was a prolific writer, with many books to his credit on topics ranging from astronomy to theology. One book, written about the Goths, provides the only source of information available on a particular period in the history of that people. Another, called the *Etymologies* or *Origins,* was a virtual encyclopedia of all the knowledge of his age.

Isidore lived an austere life throughout his years, taking very little for himself and giving away what he did have. When he was near death, Isidore invited other bishops to visit him. At his request, they clothed him in sackcloth and ashes, the clothing of penitents, and he prayed for forgiveness of his sins. After receiving the last rites, Isidore distributed all his remaining worldly goods to the poor, forgave those indebted to him, then returned to his house where he died.

Isidore's message today: Isidore had a strong drive to spread education throughout Spain at a time when generally, only the aristocracy and priests were educated. He managed to do all of this while living an austere life and tending to the needs of the poor.

How well do you put to work the gifts which God has given you? Are you helping those who have less than you, whether materially or spiritually?

APRIL 7–MEMORIAL

John Baptist de la Salle, Priest: 1651–1719

The eldest of ten children born into a wealthy family, John Baptist showed early signs of a desire for the priesthood. He was named a canon of the cathedral at Rheims when only sixteen and, as such, was assured of a steady and comfortable income for life. In 1670, he began studies for the priesthood which led to ordination in 1678.

In 1679, a chance meeting with a layman, Adrian Nyel, changed the course of John Baptist's life. Nyel came to Rheims to open a school for poor boys, and with John Baptist's encouragement, opened two such schools. De la Salle took a great interest in the men who taught in these schools. He rented a house for them, provided them with meals, and tried to infuse in them high standards of education.

Later, John Baptist moved into the teachers' quarters to be in closer solidarity with them. He soon realized, however, that the income which he had from the canonry and his ample private fortune separated him from the schoolmasters who had no assured earnings, so John Baptist gave up the canonry and his fortune as well. He sold all of his property and distributed the money to the poor, then began living a very austere life.

Four more schools were soon opened, and John Baptist faced the problem of training all of the teachers needed to staff the schools. Calling together the men who had worked longest with him, John Baptist laid the groundwork for the order which he was to establish. The brothers were to take annual vows of obedience until such time as they were certain of their vocation. Since he wanted to eliminate any class distinctions between his teachers and their students, he imposed a rule that no brother could ever become a priest and no priest could become a Christian Brother. The order would be called the Brothers of the Christian Schools (now, more familiarly, the Christian Brothers).

The growth of the order, though not always smooth, was quite rapid. Other schools opened around the country and along with them, new houses for the Christian Brothers. John Baptist undertook to organize his order and his teaching method, while overseeing the training of his teachers, as well. He wrote a book, the *Conduct of Schools,* which largely revolutionized elementary school teaching and is still the basis for teaching in these schools today. He also laid out what was then a radical idea in education: to teach in the vernacular—French, in this case—rather than in Latin as had been the norm.

John Baptist's successes were not without a price. He was bitterly opposed by secular schoolmasters who saw his methods as encroaching on their turf. Others attacked him for providing a broad education to the poor who, they felt, should only receive instruction in the trades. He was the object of several lawsuits by both of these groups.

By about 1700, the Christian Brothers had schools all over France and their work had spread over the Alps to Italy. John Baptist resigned his position as superior in 1717 and lived like the humblest of his brothers. In the period before his death on Good Friday in 1719, he wrote several books and spent his time teaching novices in the order.

Today the Christian Brothers are the largest teaching order in the Church and have a worldwide presence on all levels of education, from elementary schools to universities. St. John Baptist de la Salle was canonized in 1900. In 1950, Pope Pius XII named him the patron saint of schoolteachers.

John's message today: Catholic schools today often face the same opposition from the public sector that John Baptist de la Salle saw in his day. There are attempts to deprive private schools of the rights and privileges to which they are legally entitled. Fortunately, many people, like John Baptist, are willing to stand up for Christian education.

Do the students in Catholic schools in your area receive the rights to which they are entitled? If not, would you be willing to fight to see that they do?

Stanislaus, Bishop and Martyr: 1030–1079

Stanislaus was the only child of a noble family from a town near Cracow, Poland. Childless for many years of marriage, his parents' prayers were answered with his birth. In thanksgiving, they dedicated his life to God.

Stanislaus was educated in Gnesen and in Paris and was ordained by Bishop Lambert Zula of Cracow who later appointed him his archdeacon. The young priest soon became known for his preaching and he was able to bring about a reformation in the morals of the people of Cracow including many clergy.

Bishop Lambert wished to resign his episcopacy in favor of Stanislaus, but the priest would not hear of it. Nevertheless, upon the death of Lambert, he was overwhelmingly chosen bishop by the people. Their choice was ratified by the pope and Stanislaus reluctantly became the bishop of Cracow in 1072. The bishop proved a worthy shepherd, tireless in the care of his flock and tending especially to the poor of his see.

Boleslaus II, the ruler of Poland at the time, was noted for his uncontrolled lust and brutality. Stanislaus was the only person who would speak out against this tyrant's cruelty. For a time, Boleslaus appeared to be repentant, but this soon wore off and he fell back into his old ways. The final straw occurred when Boleslaus had the beautiful wife of a nobleman abducted and carried off to his palace. The Polish nobles went to the archbishop of Gnesen, then the capital of Poland, and his court to have them denounce this act; but the fear of offending Boleslaus caused them to remain silent.

Stanislaus was not so restrained. He went to Boleslaus and condemned him for this abduction. He warned the king that he would be excommunicated if he persisted in his sinful ways. The king reacted angrily, and he set about slandering the bishop.

Finding that his reprimand had no effect on Boleslaus, Stanislaus followed through with the excommunication. At first, the king ignored this sentence, but upon his entering the cathedral, the services were suspended at Stanislaus' order. This completely enraged the king. With a small band of troops, Boleslaus followed Stanislaus to a small chapel outside of Cracow where they found the bishop celebrating Mass. The king ordered his troops to go in and kill the bishop. When they could not carry out this command, Boleslaus himself went into the chapel and killed Stanislaus.

St. Stanislaus is the patron of Cracow.

Stanislaus' message today: This saint finds himself in the good company of saints like John the Baptist, Thomas Becket, and Thomas More. Like them, he opposed the tyranny of a despot and, like them, he paid with his life. We often hear a great hue and cry about the separation of church and state and, usually this is a good thing. There are times, however, when the church must take a stand for what is right in the same way that Stanislaus did.

Do you support your bishops when they take a position in opposition to the government on some moral issues?

APRIL 21

Conrad of Parzham, Religious: 1818–1894

Born in Parzham, Bavaria on December 22 and baptized John Birndorfer, this saint was the youngest of nine children of a peasant family. The boy was noted for his diligence and hard work, though his knowledge was based more on common sense than education. Later in his life he was to say, "The Cross is my book."

From his youngest days, John held a strong devotion to the Blessed Mother. He went to Mass every day, and prayed the rosary daily, as well. This piety was inherited from his family who, typical of the families in the region, were simple, pious people.

In 1849, after his parents had died, he became a Capuchin lay brother and took the name Conrad. After taking his vows, Conrad was sent to Altötting, home of a famous shrine to Our Lady. He served as a porter in this shrine for forty-one years.

In this capacity, Conrad answered the door whenever any visitors came, no matter what the hour. He was also charged with feeding the many poor who came to the monastery. The menu was the same as the one for the monks: bread and soup, and maybe a little beer. Occasionally, a beggar would complain about the blandness and monotony of the diet and throw the soup away. Conrad, with quiet humor, would suggest that maybe they could change from bread and soup to soup and bread.

Besides his devotion to Mary, Conrad was noted for his charity, as well as his ability to prophesy and to read people's hearts. While the shrine to Our Lady was the major attraction at Altötting, many pilgrims came to see Conrad himself.

Conrad died at Altötting on April 21, 1894. Although his life may seem less remarkable than some other saints, Conrad's piety and virtue were of such notoriety that he was canonized in 1934, only forty years after his death. While he is not on the liturgical calendar in the United States, the Franciscan Capuchins honor St. Conrad on this date.

Conrad's message today: Conrad did not have the benefit of an education, and therefore, spent most of his life doing menial labor. Yet he did this cheerfully and without complaint. Conrad was content to fulfill God's humble purpose for him. We do not always accept our lot in life, but sometimes wish that we were smarter, wealthier, or more powerful.

Do you work to develop, to their fullest extent, the talents which God has given you? Pray that God grant you the strength to accept the fullness of his gifts.

George, Martyr: died c. 303

A ll that we know for certain about this saint is that he was martyred in the early fourth century. During this period, a great persecution of Christians was taking place under the emperors Diocletian and Maximian.

George, a Christian knight from Cappadocia, saw that some Christians were being terrified into giving up their faith. He went into the public square and announced loudly that the Christian God is the only true god. Arrested by the provost, Datianus, George was tortured unmercifully, but, in the night, Jesus came to him and restored him to good health. Next a magician was sent to give him a potion containing a deadly poison. George drank this with no ill effects and the magician, converted by this act, also died a martyr. Further attempts to crush the saint between two spiked wheels and to boil him to death in a vat of molten lead had no effect.

Datianus then tried promises and cajolery to sway George. Pretending to agree to sacrifice to the false gods, George prayed and a fire rained down from heaven which destroyed their temple and idols. Even though his wife had also converted after witnessing these events, Datianus then ordered the saint beheaded. After this was carried out, a fire from heaven consumed the provost.

No story about St. George would be complete without the tale of the dragon slaying. While this account was not added to his lore until the twelfth century, it was widespread throughout Europe during the Middle Ages. There is, however, no factual basis for it.

According to legend, George was riding in the province of

Libya when he came upon a city called Sylene, near which was a marshy swamp. In this swamp lived a dragon which the people could not kill because its breath was so terrible that none could approach it. To keep the dragon at bay, the people supplied it with two sheep every day, but when sheep became scarce, a human victim had to be substituted.

On the day that George arrived, the victim, chosen by lot, was the king's daughter. Dressed as a bride, she was going forward to meet her fate. Coming on the scene, George pierced the dragon with his lance. Then he fastened a belt around the dragon's neck and the princess led the captive dragon into the city. The people were about to flee, but George told them to have no fear. If they would just believe in Jesus Christ and be baptized, he would slay the dragon. The king and all of his subjects readily agreed and some fifteen thousand men (not counting women and children) were baptized.

George then killed the dragon and four ox carts were needed to carry the carcass to a safe distance. The king offered the knight great treasures, but George told him to give these to the poor. Upon leaving, George left four orders for the king: that he maintain churches, that he honor priests, that he himself attend religious services, and that he show compassion for the poor.

Probably as a result of this myth, St. George became the patron of England and of the Order of the Garter. St. George is also the patron saint of Portugal, Germany, Aragon, Genoa, and Venice.

George's message today: We have all met people like the provost, Datianus, who, even when presented with overwhelming evidence, refuse to believe. We may even have someone like this in our families. Our quiet and regular prayer may do wonders for these people.

Are you praying for those people in your life who do not believe in Jesus?

Mark, Evangelist: died c. 74

Mark's gospel is very likely the first one written (sometime between 60 and 70 while in Rome) and is the shortest of the four. He often goes into much more detail in describing Jesus' ministry than do the other evangelists.

Mark apparently was writing for Gentiles who were unfamiliar with Jewish customs. Mark is not mentioned in any of the gospels, though he may have been referring to himself when he wrote of the young man who attempted to follow Jesus after his arrest in the Garden of Gethsemane (Mk 14:51–52). Modern biblical scholars believe that Mark's gospel provided Matthew and Luke with a common source for their gospels.

In the Acts of the Apostles and the letters of Peter and Paul, Mark is mentioned several times. He was the son of Mary at whose house in Jerusalem Peter and the other apostles stayed. He was a cousin of Barnabas. He accompanied Paul and Barnabas on Paul's first missionary journey, and he was with Paul in Rome during Paul's first imprisonment. Mark was evidently a disciple of Peter who refers to him as "Mark, my son." An early, though uncertain, tradition about Mark is that he was the first bishop of Alexandria.

St. Mark is the patron of Venice. This city claims that his body was brought from Alexandria to Venice, where it now lies in St. Mark's Cathedral. He is also the patron of notaries.

Mark's message today: Imagine telling the story of Jesus' life to people who have never heard it before. Some of today's evangelists are the teachers of religious education, who tell Jesus' story to children.

Have you considered offering to teach or help in some way the religious education program in your parish? Your help would be most appreciated.

Peter Chanel, Priest and Martyr: 1803–1841

Peter was the fifth child of Francis and Mary Ann Chanel, peasants living in Cluet, France. Mary Ann recognized that her son could perform great service to God and she dedicated him to Mary. His education was turned over to the priest in their parish who saw him through his elementary schooling. Peter then chose to enter the seminary, where he was esteemed by both students and faculty.

After his ordination in 1827, Peter was assigned to a rundown and lax country parish which, by simply caring for the sick, he completely revitalized in three years. Peter's ambition had always been to become a missionary, however, and when the Society of Mary (Marist) order was founded, he joined in 1831.

Peter's first assignment was to teach at the Marist seminary, which he did for five years. In 1836, the Marists were given the New Hebrides Islands in the Pacific for their evangelical work, and Peter was assigned as the superior of seven Marists sent to the Islands as missionaries. Upon their arrival in Oceania the group split up, and Peter Chanel and a lay brother went to the island of Futuna.

The two missionaries were well received by the pagan islanders on Futuna, and the king, who had recently abolished cannibalism, was among their welcomers. Chanel and the lay brother had some initial success in their conversion efforts, but real progress came only after they learned the islanders' language.

As the number of conversions began to grow, the king realized that the adoption of Christianity by his people posed a threat to some of his prerogatives. When his own son expressed a desire to be baptized, the king sent his warriors to club Peter Chanel to death and cut his body to pieces. Thus, on April 28, 1841, Peter Chanel became the first Marist to be martyred and the first martyr in Oceania.

A measure of the success of Peter Chanel's mission work is in the fact that within months of his death, the whole island of Futuna was converted to Christianity. St. Peter Chanel, the patron of Oceania, was canonized in 1954.

Peter's message today: Given the success that he was having and the initial welcome from the king, Peter probably did not expect to suffer martyrdom. That is true of most people today in a civilized world. And yet martyrdom still occurs in our times, even in some so-called civilized countries.

Do you remember the missionaries and the important work which they accomplish in your prayers each day?

APRIL 29–MEMORIAL

Catherine of Siena, Virgin and Doctor: 1347–1380

Catherine was the youngest of twenty-five children. At the age of six, she began to have the mystical experiences which she would have throughout her life. Catherine resisted the urging of her parents to marry, and entered the Third Order Dominicans when she was sixteen.

Her calling was to minister to the ill in hospitals and Catherine devoted herself to caring for those with particularly distressing illnesses such as leprosy. Increasingly, she experienced visions of Christ, Mary, and the saints. Her supernatural gifts and her outspoken support of the pope attracted ardent supporters, as well as enemies. The latter caused her to be brought before a chapter general of the Dominicans in 1374 at Florence where, upon investigation, the accusations against her were dismissed.

Returning to Siena, Catherine dedicated herself to caring for those stricken by a plague that was devastating the city, as well as to ministering to condemned prisoners. She was widely acclaimed for her holiness and for her abilities as a peacemaker. In 1376, Catherine was instrumental in returning the papacy to Rome from Avignon, France, where it had been moved some seventy years earlier. She also helped reconcile the differences between the city-state of Florence and the Holy See, a situation which had caused great turbulence throughout all of Italy.

On Pope Gregory XI's death in 1378, the great schism of the Catholic Church began when Urban VI's election as pope was disputed by a group of dissident cardinals. This group elected an antipope and set up a papal court in Avignon. Catherine worked unceasingly to secure support for Urban though she never hesitated to criticize him for some of his actions. The pope brought her to Rome as his advisor, where she continued her efforts on his behalf until her death in 1380.

St. Catherine of Siena is the patroness of Italy, of fire prevention, and of nursing. She was declared a Doctor of the Church by Pope Paul VI in 1970.

Catherine's message today: In our own times, we can see an example of what St. Catherine of Siena must have been like in Mother Teresa of Calcutta. Both were saintly women, and neither was afraid to care for those sick with the most virulent diseases, or to get involved in the affairs of the church and of the world.

Is there an area of parish or community life where your influence and action could make a positive difference?

Peregrine Laziosi, Priest: 1260–1345

Peregrine started out his life in a somewhat less than saintly manner. Born into a well-to-do family in Forli, Italy, he received his religious training from his mother. His political training, however, came from his father who was a member of the Ghibellines, a political faction aligned with the German emperor against the pope.

When Peregrine was about eighteen, the pope sent St. Philip Benizi, the Prior General of the Servite Order, to Forli to mediate the dispute. While the saint was speaking to the crowd, Peregrine approached him and struck him on the face. The saint immediately turned the other cheek. This so impressed Peregrine that he begged the saint's forgiveness and, from that moment, reformed his life.

Peregrine began spending hours each day on his knees in the chapel of Our Lady in the cathedral. After a time, Mary appeared to him and directed him to join the Servite Order. Peregrine at once obeyed, setting out for Siena where he was welcomed into order by St. Philip Benizi himself.

Peregrine labored for several years as a lay brother before being ordained. After becoming a priest, he was sent back to Forli to found a new monastery for his order. Peregrine developed a reputation for the wise and provident advice which he gave to those who visited his monastery. He was tireless in his ministering to the poor. It is said that he never sat down for thirty years. Several miracles by Peregrine were reported in these years. During famine, he multiplied food for the poor and, on at least one occasion, he raised a person from the dead.

During a plague which began in 1323, Peregrine was stricken with a painful cancer in his right leg, which left him almost completely incapacitated. It was recommended that Peregrine's leg be amputated in order to stop the disease from spreading. As he prayed in front of a crucifix in his room the night before the operation was to take place, Peregrine beheld a vision of Christ descending from the cross, reaching toward him with an outstretched hand. The next morning, the doctors could find no trace of the cancer. As a result of this miraculous cure, St. Peregrine became known as the patron of cancer victims.

Peregrine lived another twenty years following his cure, and continued ministering to the sick and the poor and preaching. He died on May 1, 1345, his eighty-fifth birthday.

Peregrine's message today: It sometimes takes a revelation to change our way of thinking. In Peregrine's case, the simple act of St. Philip Benizi turning the other cheek was enough to transform his life. We, too, can be transformed by others if we are open to the love of Christ.

Remembering Christ's command, could you turn the other cheek? Are you able to love your enemy?

MAY 2–MEMORIAL

Athanasius, Bishop and Doctor: 295–373

A thanasius was born into a Christian family and was given an excellent education. At the age of about twenty-one, he was ordained a deacon and became the secretary to Bishop Alexander of Alexandria. In this position, he attended the council of Nicaea.

This council was called to denounce Arianism, the heresy which denied the divinity of Jesus, and it is from the decrees of this council that the Nicene Creed came about. While Athanasius did not play an especially active role in the council, it at least presaged the later work of his life.

Elected bishop of Alexandria following Alexander's death in 327, Athanasius set out to visit his far-flung diocese, which included Ethiopia. It was probably during this journey that Athanasius came to know St. Anthony the Abbot, a friend who came to his aid in the fight against Arianism and about whom Athanasius wrote in later years.

The Council of Nicaea provided only a temporary setback to the Arians, who were joined in Egypt by the Meletians, another dissident group. Athanasius provided a strong voice against the heresy and made many enemies by the position he took. In one case, his adversaries accused Athanasius of murdering a Meletian bishop. The "dead" bishop was actually in hiding; Athanasius, aware of this, ignored the summons to answer this charge.

The Arians then persuaded the emperor Constantine to call a council, which was held in Tyre in 335. Realizing that a guilty verdict had been reached prior to the council meeting, Athanasius left the council and presented himself to the emperor. Constantine at first sided with Athanasius, but then agreed with the condemnation of Athanasius and sent him into exile in northern Gaul.

Upon the emperor's death in 337, Athanasius was returned to his see. But Eusebius, who was the Arian bishop of Nicodemia, persuaded Pope Julius to hold a synod in Rome for the purpose of reopening the charges against Athanasius. During this time, an Arian bishop was installed in Alexandria. Although he was wholly vindicated by the synod, Athanasius was unable to return to Alexandria and remained in exile in Rome.

Athanasius' third exile came after Roman soldiers broke into his church one night while a vigil celebration was going on. Several people were killed or wounded in this raid, and Athanasius had to flee to a monastery in the desert. He remained hidden there for many years, during which time he completed most of his major writings.

Under the emperor Valens, Athanasius was finally able to return to his see in Alexandria. He remained there for the last seven years of his life and continued his writing. A greatly beloved shepherd of his people, Athanasius was also the strongest bulwark of the faith during the Arian heresy. He was praised by John Cardinal Newman as the principal instrument by which the faith has been "secured to the world."

Athanasius' message today: Athanasius kept the faith when it would have been easy to give in to the heavy pressures which he was under. There are a lot of false gods in our times: more money, a bigger house, a fancier car. Our culture would have us put these things into our life at the cost of our faith.

Are you strong in your faith, enough to resist the cultural influences which may put you in conflict with it?

MAY 3–FEAST

James, Apostle: died c. 62

This Saint James is called "the Less" or "the Younger" to distinguish him from the other apostle named James. He has also been called "James the Just" in recognition of the respect in which he was held by the Christians of his time.

A number of things can be inferred from the references to James in the gospels, together with tradition and what has been passed on in the writing of others. (Many Church historians believe that there was a third James who was prominent in the Church in first-century Jerusalem, and some of what follows might be attributed to this other James) James was the son of Alphaeus.

St. Paul tells us that Jesus made a special appearance to James prior to the Ascension. The other apostles were still suspicious of Paul when, three years after his conversion, he visited Jerusalem. But James, along with Peter, gave Paul a cordial welcome.

James was recognized by Peter as one whose preeminence was acknowledged by the Christians of Jerusalem. Indeed we know that James (or, perhaps, the third James) was the bishop of Jerusalem. At the Council of Jerusalem, the bishop appears to have taken a major role. It was at this first Church council that the decision was made that Gentiles who accepted Christian teaching need not follow all of the Jewish laws. James suggested that "we should not trouble those Gentiles who are turning to God" (Acts 15:19). After consulting with Peter, it was James who announced the conclusions to the assembly.

Early writers tell us that James was stoned to death by the scribes and Pharisees who were afraid that, because of his influence with the people, he would bring all of Jerusalem to Christ. As he was being stoned, James knelt down and prayed for his tormentors. One of the priests tried to stop the stoning, shouting to the others that James was praying on their behalf. But another priest then took a heavy stick and struck James on the head, killing him. The year of his death is commonly accepted to be 62 A.D.

St. James is the patron of druggists, hatmakers, and fullers (people who make cloth "full" by pleating or gathering). He shares a memorial with another apostle, St. Philip, on this date.

James' message today: Like many other martyrs and like Jesus, James prayed for his persecutors. It is not easy loving those with whom we are in strong disagreement, but that is what Jesus asks us to do.

Have you forgiven your enemies or is your animosity still allowing them to rule your life? Ask Jesus to help you to learn to forgive those who have hurt you.

Philip, Apostle: First Century

Philip was from Bethsaida in Galilee, and is thought to have been a disciple of St. John the Baptist when Jesus called him. He is listed as an apostle in the gospels of Matthew, Mark, and Luke, but these make no further mention of Philip.

In John's gospel (1:43), we are told that Jesus "found Philip" and instructed him to "Follow me." Several other times, John mentions Philip. Philip, for example, was responsible for bringing his friend, Nathanael (believed to be the apostle Bartholomew), to Jesus. Philip was present at the marriage feast at Cana and at the feeding of the five thousand. It was here that Jesus tested Philip when he saw the large crowd who had come to hear him. "Where are we to buy bread for these people to eat?" (Jn 6:5), he asked Philip. Philip, not recognizing that Jesus was about to perform a sign for all of them, replied, "Six months' wages would not buy enough bread for each of them to get a little."

Again, Philip is the apostle at the Last Supper who asks Jesus to show them the Father, a tribute to his, as well as the other apostles' earnestness. Jesus responded to Philip, "Whoever has seen me has seen the Father," (Jn 14:9), a message for all of us. The Acts of the Apostles notes that Philip was with the other ten apostles in the upper room awaiting the Holy Spirit, but makes no other mention of him. (Philip the Apostle shouldn't be confused with Philip the Deacon, who is spoken of later in Acts.)

Early Church tradition was recorded by Eusebius the historian, as well as by other writers. This tradition states that Philip preached the gospel at Phrygia and later died at Hierapolis. He is said to have had three daughters, one of whom recounted to Papias, a later bishop of Hierapolis, the story of a miracle performed by the saint, in this case, raising a man from the dead.

Depending on the account—and here some confusion between

the two Philips may have entered—Philip either died a natural death or was crucified at Hierapolis. It has been stated that the remains of St. Philip were eventually brought to Rome and have been preserved in the basilica of the Apostles since the time of Pope Pelagius (c. 561).

Philip's message today: Just as he tested Philip about feeding the crowd, Jesus sometimes tests our faith with adversity. While these trials can seem overwhelming, we should remember that God is with us even when we cannot feel his presence.

Do you trust that God is there with you when you experience hard times in your life? Renew your trust that God is always with us.

Matthias, Apostle: died c. 64

Our only certain knowledge of Matthias comes from the Acts of the Apostles. After the Ascension, Peter stated that they should pick a successor to Judas Iscariot to fulfill the Scripture. The apostles selected Joseph Barsabbas and Matthias as candidates and prayed for guidance before drawing lots. Matthias was selected.

Tradition handed down by the great historians of the early Church, Clement of Alexandria, Eusebius, and St. Jerome, tell us that Matthias first preached in Judea then moved on to Cappadocia and to the shores of the Caspian Sea where he planted the faith. He is said to have suffered great persecutions and was martyred in Colchis.

Matthias' message today: Although he was a disciple of Jesus throughout most of his ministry, Matthias had no idea that he might be selected as one of the twelve after Jesus ascended into heaven. We too have no idea what God may have in store for us, so we must live our lives anticipating that we may be called at any time.

Are you ready to answer God's call? Have you been living the kind of life which Jesus has asked you to live so that you may join him in heaven?

MAY 15–OPTIONAL MEMORIAL

Isidore: 1070–1130

Unlike his namesake honored on April 4, this Isidore was not well educated; nevertheless, he had a lasting influence on the people of Spain. Born of poor parents in Madrid, Isidore began working in the fields of a wealthy Madrid landowner, John de Vargas, when he was very young. He spent his whole life in those fields.

Isidore's parents instilled a great love of prayer and a revulsion of sin in him. He rose early each morning to go to Mass and, while laboring all day in the fields, communed with God and the saints. But his attendance at daily Mass angered some of his fellow workers, as it caused Isidore to arrive at work later than they did. John de Vargas hid himself one day to confirm this, and sure enough, Isidore did arrive after his coworkers. De Vargas was about to take him to task for his lateness when he saw a team of snow white oxen plowing the field parallel to Isidore's team. With unknown figures driving this team, de Vargas realized that supernatural help was compensating for the work that Isidore missed.

Isidore married a girl as simple as himself and they had one child, a boy who died young. His wife, Maria Torriba, is also a saint, honored under the name Santa Maria de la Cabeza.

Though poor himself, Isidore and Maria always shared what they had with those who had less. Isidore often invited the poor into his house for a meal and ended up with only the leftover scraps for himself. On one occasion, Isidore was late for a confraternity dinner. When he arrived, he had with him a train of beggars. His hosts noted that they had saved only his portion and that there was not enough for the large group who had come with him. Isidore replied that there would be plenty for himself and Christ's poor. When the food was served, there was ample for everyone with food left over.

Many other miracles have been attributed to Isidore. About eighty years after his death, Isidore appeared in a vision to the King of Castile who was then fighting the Moors. Isidore showed him a hidden path which allowed his soldiers to surprise and defeat the enemy. Another time, the intercession of Isidore brought King Philip III of Spain back from the brink of death to good health. His shrine in Madrid has been the site of many other miracles.

St. Isidore is one of the "five saints of Spain" (together with St. Ignatius, St. Francis Xavier, St. Teresa of Avila, and St. Philip Neri). He is the patron of farmers and of Madrid. He is also a patron of laborers and of the national Rural Life Conference in the United States.

Isidore's message today: Saints have been profound and learned scholars and saints have been very simple people. It matters not to God what station you have in life as long as you use the talents which he has given to you in his service—in most cases, this means service to your neighbor.

Do you give unselfishly of what you have to the poor, the sick, and the other members of your community?

Brendan, Abbot: c. 484–577

Brendan is a very popular Irish saint about whom little is known outside of legend. He was probably born near Tralee in Kerry, Ireland. When he was six, he was sent to a monastic school in Tuam for his education. He was ordained in 512 by Bishop St. Erc.

Brendan founded many monasteries in Ireland. The most famous of these, Clonfort, was a center of missionary activity for many centuries. Some three thousand monks lived, worked, studied, and prayed there under his direction.

Brendan made many missionary journeys by small sailing boat (a *curragh*) around Ireland and to England, Scotland, and Wales, but his most famous journey, lasting from five to seven years, was to a place he called the Land of Promise. His epic manuscript on this adventure, *Navigatio Sancti Brendani Abbatis,* was translated into many languages and was a bestseller in Europe in the Middle Ages.

In this saga, Brendan described what may have been a voyage to North America. While many people doubted this over the centuries, some modern scholars believe that Brendan actually was the first European to visit North America. In the 1970s, Tim Severin, an expert on exploration, followed the directions in *Navigatio* and sailed a hide-covered *curragh* from Ireland to Newfoundland. His observations, documented in his book, *The Brendan Voyage,* demonstrated the accuracy of Brendan's directions and the descriptions of the places he wrote about.

St. Brendan is a patron of sailors. His feast day is celebrated in Ireland on this date.

Brendan's message today: Brendan is one of those saints who, while fully dedicated to God, were also devoted to advancing the state of human knowledge. We often think that living a life for God means shunning the ways of the world. Brendan proved otherwise by his love of exploration and ability to communicate with others through the tales of his adventures.

Where do you most often find God in your everyday life? Where do you most see God's presence in the world?

Bernardine of Siena, Priest: 1380–1444

B ernadine degli Albizzeschi was the son of the governor of Massa Marittima, Italy. Orphaned at the age of seven, Bernardine was raised by an aunt. He chose to join the confraternity of Our Lady at seventeen and, by the age of twenty, was running a hospital in his hometown of Siena for victims of the plague. After several months of this work, however, he was overcome by a lingering fever.

After his recovery, Bernardine spent another year caring for the aunt who had raised him. At her death, he began to fast and pray that God's will would be made known to him. At the age of twenty-two, he entered the Franciscan order. Ordained in 1404, Bernardine spent the next several years in solitary at the monastery.

A dynamic person, Bernardine began to preach in Milan in 1417 against the evils of paganism which was widespread at that time. He soon became known for his eloquence and attracted crowds of as many as 30,000 as he followed St. Francis' advice to preach about "vice and virtue, punishment and glory." Bernardine traveled on foot throughout Italy, and might preach for several hours in one town before walking on to speak in another town.

Bernardine was attacked by enemies who found his preaching dangerous to their way of life. On three occasions, they sought to have the pope censure him, but his holiness and intelligence, as well as his piety, cleared him of any charges. Bernadine was elected vicar general of a branch of the Franciscan order in 1430. Under his leadership, the order was reformed and regenerated, growing from about three hundred members to over four thousand by his death.

In Europe at the time, the use of pagan symbols was widespread. To counteract this, Bernardine devised a symbol for Christ which is still in use today. He took the first three letters of Jesus' name in Greek—IHS—and superimposed them in Gothic letters on a blazing sun.

There is a story about Bernardine, who, while preaching against the evils of gambling in Bologna, lit a huge bonfire to destroy all instruments of vice: playing cards, dice, and other things. Seeing this, a manufacturer of playing cards complained that Bernardine was taking away his livelihood. The saint told him to start making medals which bore the symbol IHS, instead of cards. The man did so, and made more money that ever before.

St. Bernardine died on May 20, 1444 while on a mission trip.

Bernardine's message today: Sometimes it takes a while for God's call to take shape in our lives. While Bernardine learned fairly early in his life that he wanted to serve God, it was some years before he recognized his call to preach, as well as to lead his Franciscan order in reform.

Have you found your calling in life? If not, what are you doing in the meantime?

Bede, the Venerable, Priest and Doctor: 673–735

At the age of three, Bede was entrusted to the care of the Abbot at the St. Paul monastery in Jarrow, England. The happy combination of an inquiring intellect and willing, able teachers made Bede one of the most learned men of his time.

Bede was ordained at the age of thirty and spent virtually his entire life in the monastery studying, teaching, and writing. While he was knowledgeable in mathematics, the sciences, and philosophy, he devoted most of his time to the study of Scripture and English history. His writings are regarded as major influences on English literature. One book in particular, *Ecclesiastical History,* is the primary source of the history of Christianity in England up to that time (729).

Bede was honored as a saint even in his own lifetime. In recognition of his saintliness and his scholarship, he was called "the Venerable." His advice and counsel were sought after by noblemen and even the pope. Except for a brief period when he taught at the school of the bishop of York, however, he remained in the monastery. His final work, finished the day before he died, was an English translation of the Gospel of John "to break the word to the poor and unlearned." Unfortunately, this work has been lost.

Bede is known as the father of English history. He was also the first to date events *anno Domini* (A.D.), meaning "in the year of our Lord." At the Council of Aachen in 853, the title "the Venerable" was formally added to his name. In 1899, the Venerable Bede was named a Doctor of the Church, in recognition of his wisdom and learning. He is the only English saint so honored.

Bede's message today: Bede advanced the state of knowledge not just in ecclesiastical matters, but also in math, science, and history. Like Bede, those of us who teach—and non-teachers, as well—should advance our own knowledge, not just in our own specialized fields, but across the spectrum of art, humanities, science, and Scripture.

How do you try to continue your education? Do you enjoy learning about new things, or are you generally content with what you already know?

Philip Neri, Priest and Doctor: 1515–1595

Philip Neri was born in Florence, Italy, the son of a minor government official. As a young man, Philip was sent off to pursue a career as a businessman, but he gave this up almost immediately for the religious life. After three years of studying philosophy and theology in Rome, Philip discarded, for the time being, the idea of being ordained. Instead, he began preaching in the streets and markets of Rome as a layman.

Philip had a large circle of friends from all walks of life. His sermons were marked by cheerfulness and good humor, which was in sharp contrast to the type of preaching people usually heard at that time. Philip also became an influential leader in the Counter-Reformation.

With his confessor, Fr. Persiano Rossa, Philip founded the Confraternity of the Most Holy Trinity in 1548. This was a group of laymen who banded together to minister to needy pilgrims. At the urging of Fr. Rossa, Philip was ordained in 1551. He was successful in encouraging many priests to conduct conferences for the pilgrims, who sought spiritual guidance and solace. This group of laymen, in time, became known as Oratorians because of their custom of inviting groups to their oratory for meditation and consultation.

Philip Neri became known as "the apostle of Rome." He was sought after by popes and bishops, rich and poor, rulers and common people. The whole college of cardinals came to him for counsel and spiritual guidance. Visitors to Rome from other parts of the world sought appointments with him.

Philip believed that there was no conflict between spirituality and having a good laugh. "I will have no sad spirits in my house," he said. "Cheerful people are more easily led to perfection." He belied the idea that sanctity requires putting on a long face. Indeed, while this saint has not been declared a patron saint, he might very well join St. Vitus as a patron of comedians.

Philip Neri died in Rome on May 26, 1595 and was canonized in 1622 by Pope Gregory XV. He was later declared a Doctor of the Church.

Philip's message today: It is said that Philip Neri prayed, "Let me get through the day, and I shall not fear tomorrow." With that prayer, and a sense of humor, Philip was ready to face the trials that we all encounter in our day-to-day lives.

Do you sometimes take yourself too seriously? Remember that God has a sense of humor and wants us to be joyful.

MAY 27–OPTIONAL MEMORIAL

Augustine of Canterbury, Bishop: died c. 605

St. Gregory the Great, pope during Augustine's adult life, had a vision of re-evangelizing Anglo-Saxon England. To accomplish this, he selected about thirty monks from his monastery in

Rome, including their prior, Augustine. This group set out for England in the year 596.

When the group reached the English Channel, they received warnings that the Anglo-Saxons were a wild and fierce people, and that the monks would be in great danger if they crossed over the Channel into England. The monks asked Augustine to seek reassurance from the pope, so Augustine returned to Rome. There Gregory encouraged him and his monks to continue with their mission, promising them that he was certain that the English were ready for conversion.

Arriving in the territory of Kent, the missionaries sent word to the English king that they had come to spread the good news. King Ethelbert (later St. Ethelbert), whose wife was a Christian though he himself was not, came to meet them. Ethelbert had no objection to the monks preaching, and allowed them to convert any of his people who would believe in Christ. King Ethelbert himself was baptized in the following year. Having learned well from his teachers, the king would not force any of his people to become Christian, the service of Christ being voluntary. Upon his conversion, however, many of his followers were also baptized. Soon after, Augustine was consecrated the bishop of the English.

Augustine's success in his mission overjoyed the pope who sent another band of missionaries to assist him. Gregory outlined for Augustine the steps which he should take to establish the Church in England. Local customs were to be maintained as far as possible, substituting the feast days of saints for heathen festivals. Pagan temples were to be purified and consecrated as Christian churches for, as Gregory wrote, "he who would climb to a lofty height must go by steps, not leaps."

Augustine kept busy spreading the faith. In Canterbury, he rebuilt an ancient church as the center of his see, which stood on the site of the present-day cathedral. Outside the walls of Canterbury, he established an abbey which he dedicated to Sts. Peter and Paul. After his death, this abbey became known as the

Abbey of St. Augustine. He also established sees in London and Rochester.

Augustine died on May 26 in about the year 605, seven years after his arrival in England. He is honored in England and Wales on that date. In this country, his memorial is celebrated one day later, on the 27th of May.

Augustine's message today: Like many of us, Augustine had doubts before he set off on his mission. With God's reassurance through the pope, he proceeded on to great successes.

From who have you received reassurance when unsure about a particular undertaking? Have you brought the issue to someone you love and trust, perhaps to your pastor?

MAY 28

Bernard of Montjoux, Priest: 996–1081

Probably born in Italy, almost nothing is known about this saint's early life. After his ordination, the picture becomes more clear. As vicar general of the diocese of Aosta in the Italian Alps, Bernard spent forty-two years traveling up and down that rugged country, even into neighboring jurisdictions, bringing Christianity to isolated areas where heathen superstition still lingered. He founded schools, restored clerical discipline, and insisted that churches should be well built.

Bernard's diocese included two of the major mountain passes over the Alps. His solicitude went out to all in need, but he was particularly concerned about travelers, many of them French and German pilgrims en route to Rome. Some of these travelers lost their way in the snow and froze to death or were set upon and robbed by highwaymen.

With the help of the bishop and others, Bernard built hospices at the summits of the two passes which were later renamed the Great and Little St. Bernard. These hospices were to take care of all travelers indiscriminately and were placed under the care of clerics and laymen. Eventually the keepers of these havens became Augustinians and a monastery was built to house them. The Augustinians continue to man these shelters to this day.

St. Bernard, after whom the breed of dog is named, was declared the patron of Alpinists, skiers, and mountain climbers by Pope Pius XI in 1923. He is honored by those groups on this date.

Bernard's message today: Bernard was concerned with the spiritual well-being of the people in his diocese, but he also cared for the physical well-being of travelers who came over the Alps into his region. We too are called to live a life balanced between spiritual and temporal care for those in our community who need our help.

Are the streets in your city safe? Have you taken the lead in correcting problems facing your city?

Joan of Arc, Virgin: 1412–1431

J oan was only thirteen when she experienced the first of her visions which she described as a voice accompanied by a blaze of light. She later identified the voices as those of St. Michael, St. Catherine, St. Margaret, and others. They revealed to Joan that her mission in life was to save France by assisting the Dauphin, the rightful heir to the throne of France.

When she tried to embark on her mission, she was scoffed at by the French commander and initially ignored by the Dauphin, who preferred a life of luxury to pursuing his father's throne. Eventually, however, Joan convinced the civil and Church authorities that she was not a heretic and did have a mission to save France. Clothed in a suit of white armor, Joan led an expedition to relieve the besieged city of Orléans. After this success, she gained a great victory over the British and, shortly after, captured Troyes.

The Dauphin was crowned King Charles VII in 1429 as a result of her victories, and Joan stood at his side during the coronation. But she failed in an attempt to capture Paris and, in 1430 during a new campaign, was captured and sold to the British who occupied much of France at this time. Charged by the British with heresy and witchcraft, her visions were declared to be of diabolical origin. She was tricked into signing a recantation, but a few days later, she again dressed as a boy, a practice which she had agreed to abandon.

Joan was charged as a lapsed heretic and condemned to be burned at the stake. This occurred on May 30, 1431 in Rouen, France. Joan was cleared of the charges against her by a court appointed by Pope Callistus II in 1456 and she was canonized in 1920. Together with St. Denis, she is a patron of France. Her memorial is celebrated in that country on this date.

Joan's message today: Joan was cast into an unfamiliar and unexpected role by God and sent on a mission with specific goals. We are often asked to perform unusual, if less dramatic, tasks than Joan's. Usually, the only ill consequence to us might be embarrassment or inconvenience.

Have you ever been asked to run an errand for a sick neighbor, or visit a lonely person? Have you done it with good grace or do you privately grumble?

JUNE

Justin, Martyr: c. 100–165

Justin, a layman, was the first great apologist of Christianity; a number of his lengthy writings remain with us today. Born of Greco-Roman parents, Justin received the best education available in his day. He studied rhetoric, history, and poetry, and was especially interested in philosophy. But none of the philosophers whom he studied seemed to have exactly what he was looking for.

One day, as Justin was walking along the seashore pondering one of Plato's maxims, he found himself being followed by a venerable-looking old man. This stranger aroused Justin's interest by telling him of a philosophy more virtuous and satisfying than any he had studied to that time. It was one, the man told him, revealed by God to the Israelite prophets of ancient times which had reached its culmination in Jesus Christ. Inspired by the man's words, Justin began a study of Scripture and undertook to learn more about Christianity. Justin was baptized when he was about thirty.

Up to this time, Christianity's beliefs and practices were largely unknown to those outside of the faith. Justin, however, felt that many more people would accept Christianity if it were presented to them properly. He began teaching and writing about the Christian faith and also about what took place at their secret meetings (the celebration of the Eucharist).

Traveling to various lands, Justin debated with pagan philosophers, heretics, and Jews. Eventually, he came to Rome where he argued in public with a Cynic named Crescens. Having bested

Crescens in the debate, Justin earned his hatred. Crescens denounced Justin as a Christian and Justin, together with six other Christians, was brought before the Roman prefect Rusticus for trial. After admitting his Christianity and refusing to sacrifice to the Roman gods, Justin and the others were condemned to torture and death.

St. Justin is a patron of philosophers.

Justin's message today: Justin searched for a time before finding God. Once he had found God, he kept the faith even to death. Although martyrdom may not be the fate of any of us, we should be prepared to defend our faith at any given moment.

All of us face temptations daily which would lead us away from God. Ask God to help you to grow in faith that you will be able to stand up to temptation.

JUNE 2

Erasmus (or Elmo), Bishop and Martyr: died c. 303

Few saints have as great a following as St. Elmo. Yet at the same time, almost all that is known about him is based on legend. We know that Elmo (his name, over time, was shortened from Erasmus) was the bishop of Formiae and his relics were preserved in the cathedral of that city until it was destroyed by the Saracens in 842. At that point, his relics were moved to Gaëta where they rest today and where this saint is considered to be the principal patron.

The legends of this saint may have him confused with another bishop. According to these traditions, Erasmus was a Syrian bishop who fled to Mount Lebanon during the persecution of the emperor Diocletian. Discovered, he was brought to the emperor who ordered him to be beaten and then rolled in pitch and set afire. When the flames did not harm him, he was thrown into prison to be starved to death.

An angel of the Lord released him from his prison and carried him to the Roman province of Illyricum (present day Italy, along the coast of the Adriatic Sea). In this province, Erasmus converted many souls. This led to further torture and reimprisonment. The angel again released Erasmus and brought him to Formiae where he died of his wounds.

St. Elmo became the patron saint of Neapolitan sailors and eventually, seaman everywhere (although Portuguese sailors honor Blessed Peter Gonzalez as their patron). The static electric charge (blue lights) often seen at the mastheads of ships following storms are still called St. Elmo's Fire. This fire, sometimes seen before a storm as well, was believed to be a sign that the saint was protecting the ship and its crew from the tempest.

Elmo's message today: While Elmo's connection to the sea is tenuous at best, sailors everywhere have looked to Elmo for hundreds of years to protect them from raging seas. In a storm, sailors have said the prayer, "O God, thy sea is so great and my ship is so small, have mercy on me."

What saint are you named after? Who is the patron of your profession or of your interests? Offer a prayer to these saints.

JUNE 3–MEMORIAL

Charles Lwanga and Companions, Martyrs: died 1886

Charles Lwanga was the assistant to the master of pages in the court of King Mwanga of Uganda. Joseph Mkasa, a

Catholic, was his superior. Mkasa chastised the king for his murder of a Protestant missionary, as well as for the king's homosexuality and his corruption of the young pages. This served to intensify the king's hatred of Catholics and Joseph Mkasa was ordered slain by the king.

Charles, having been under instruction in the Catholic faith, asked for and received baptism on the day that Mkasa was killed. For his own unwillingness to submit to immoral acts and his defense of the other pages, Lwanga and fourteen other pages who were Christian were sent to a prison. En route, three of the pages, including Lwanga, were burned to death along with two soldiers.

During this persecution, some one hundred people were killed, including one young catechist speared by King Mwanga himself. Other martyrs included tribal chiefs and judges.

St. Charles Lwanga, together with twenty-one other martyrs, was canonized in 1964 by Pope Paul VI. He has been named the patron of African youth.

Charles' message today: What strong faith this young man had! Knowing that it would probably lead to his own martyrdom, he persevered in his request for baptism. Then he stood up to the king, defending himself and others against what he knew to be wrong.

Think of some ways that you can help a young person affirm their faith. Pray for the teenagers in your parish who will be confirmed this year.

Boniface, Bishop and Martyr: 680–754

Born in Devonshire, England and baptized Winfrid, this saint decided at the age of five that he wanted to be a monk. His parents sent him to a monastery school at the age of seven and, at fourteen, to the Nursling abbey in Winchester where he studied under Abbot Winbert. Upon completion of his studies, Winfrid was named director of the school. A very popular teacher, he attracted many students and wrote the first Latin grammar compiled in England.

Winfrid was ordained at the age of thirty and seemed destined for great things in his native country. He felt that he was called by God to evangelize in a foreign land, however, so in 716 he set forth with two companions for Germany. At this time, Christianity had made few inroads into Germany, and the vast majority of the people still worshiped pagan gods.

Winfrid was not successful in this mission, and soon returned to the Nursling abbey. Hoping to keep him in England, the monks elected Winfrid abbot upon the death of Winbert, but Winfrid was not deflected from his goal. Convinced that a papal commission was essential to his success in Germany, Winfrid set out for Rome. There Pope Gregory II gave him a commission to preach the word of God to the heathen. It was at this time that he changed his name from Winfrid to Boniface.

Boniface traveled straight to Germany in 718 where he successfully engaged in missionary work for three years under St. Willibrord. That saint, now an old man, wanted to designate Boniface as his successor, but Boniface declined, claiming his commission was to preach throughout Germany and not just minister to one area. Boniface's work in other areas of Germany was so successful and his report to the pope was so satisfactory that the pope summoned him to Rome in 722 and consecrated him a regional bishop for all of Germany.

Having stayed in touch with the English monasteries, Boniface was able to bring many monks and nuns from England to Germany to teach his converts about Christianity. Through him, Germany became a Christian country.

Almost as important as Boniface's influence on Germany was his revitalization of the Church in France. Several years of neglect under Charles Martel, the Frankish king, had resulted in many ecclesiastical abuses. With the death of Charles Martel in 741, his sons Carloman and Pepin were persuaded to call a synod to deal with these abuses. Over several years, Boniface presided over four assemblies which instilled fresh vigor into the Church in Gaul.

In 747, Boniface was once more summoned to Rome, this time by Pope Zachary. He made Boniface archbishop of Mainz, designated him primate of Germany, and named him apostolic delegate for Germany and Gaul.

Boniface was growing old and stepped down from his office in 753 to return to his first love, missionary work. This time, he went to Friesland in present-day Netherlands, where he was again successful in his evangelization. Boniface was preparing to confirm new converts in 754 when a hostile band descended upon him and his companions, killing them all.

St. Boniface is the patron of Germany.

Boniface's message today: Boniface set his sights on converting the German people, an undertaking which he was able to accomplish successfully over his lifetime. Along the way, Boniface also found time to reinvigorate the Church in France. He shows us that with God's help, we can accomplish many things.

Do you turn to God when you are overwhelmed by the extent of the tasks facing you? Do you believe that God will provide you with the strength you need to accomplish those tasks?

Norbert, Bishop: 1080–1134

Norbert was born into a wealthy family of distinguished origins, and his early life was less than saintly. Though never a bad person, he was content to take life's pleasures as they came.

As a young man, Norbert was riding his horse across the countryside one day when a violent thunderstorm occurred. A bolt of lightning startled his horse, and it threw Norbert to the ground where he lay unconscious for nearly an hour. When he regained consciousness, his words echoed Saul's on the road to Damascus: "Lord, what wilt thou have me to do?" To this, an inner voice replied, "Turn from evil and do good: seek after peace and pursue it."

Norbert retired to his birthplace, Xanten, where he adopted a life of prayer, fasting, and meditation. He studied for the priesthood and was ordained in 1115. He appeared at his ordination in lambskin clothing with a crude rope for a belt, a sign of his determination to give up worldly pleasures.

Norbert began to lead an evangelical and apostolic life, but his preaching aroused many enemies. He was condemned as a hypocrite and an innovator, and was charged with preaching without a license. In response, Norbert sold all of his estates and gave his possessions to the poor. Then, accompanied by two attendants who refused to leave him, he set out, barefoot, to visit the pope and to seek forgiveness for his misdeeds. The pope, in response, gave Norbert the right to preach anywhere he chose.

In 1120, Norbert received a grant of land at Prémontré from the bishop of Laon. On this land, with thirteen followers, Norbert founded his order which became known as the Prémonstatensians. The order grew rapidly to include eight abbeys and two convents and was recognized by the pope in 1125.

When Count Theobold of Champagne expressed a desire to join the order, Norbert, recognizing a lack of priestly vocation, advised the count to carry out the duties of his station and to marry. But Norbert also gave him a scapular to wear under his outer clothing and prescribed devotions for his use. This was the first instance of a tertiary to a religious order. (A tertiary is a layperson who is affliliated with a religious order, but continues to live in the secular world.)

In 1126, Count Theobold went to Germany and took Norbert with him. Their visit to Emperor Lothair coincided with that of a delegation from Magdeburg, who had come to ask the emperor to name a bishop for their vacant see. Lothair chose Norbert. As the delegation led him back to Magdeburg, he entered the city barefoot and was so poorly clad that he was turned away from his residence by a porter, who told him to go and join the other beggars. "But he is our bishop!" shouted the crowd. "Never mind, dear brother," said Norbert to the startled servant. "You judge me more truly than those who brought me here!"

Even while bishop, Norbert lived the austere life which he had set up for his order. He was strong in defense of the rights of the Church, and has been called the "Apostle of the Eucharist" for the strong stand he took in his preaching against the heresy which denied the presence of Christ in the Eucharist. His reforms, though ultimately successful, provoked heavy opposition, and on two or three occasions, he was the object of assassination attempts.

In Germany, St. Norbert played the same role as St. Bernard had in France. He persuaded the emperor to lead an army into Rome to re-seat Pope Innocent II, and in recognition of his services, Emperor Lothair named him as his chancellor. St. Norbert could not assume these duties as he was in ill health, and he died shortly after his return from Rome at the age of fifty-three.

Norbert's message today: "Turn from evil and do good": a simple directive, but one which led Norbert to do much in the relatively short span between his ordination and his death. Norbert's example shows us that we can take on

God's work at any time and God will help us to stay at it as long as we are needed.

What would God like you to do at this point in your life? Pray about it. You might be surprised to learn that God has great things yet in store for you.

Ephrem of Syria, Deacon and Doctor: 306–373

Ephrem (also spelled Ephraem) was born in Nisibis in present day Turkey. When he converted to Christianity as a teenager, his pagan parents threw him out of their house. Ephrem was taken in by the bishop of Nisibis, St. Jacob (or James) when he was eighteen.

The following year, the bishop had Ephrem accompany him to the Council of Nicaea where Ephrem became one of the most outspoken opponents of the Arian heresy. Upon their return, the bishop ordained Ephrem as a deacon, one of the last permanent deacons in the Church until after Vatican II. Ephrem then served this bishop, and his three successors, for several years.

In 350, the Persians overran Turkey, and they stood outside the gates of Nisibis ready to take over that city. Ephrem led his people in prayer for the safety of Nisibis, and their prayers were answered when, for no apparent reason, the Persians turned away. This was not to last, however, as the Persians were awarded Nisibis in a peace settlement around the year 363. Fearing for their safety, Ephrem and the other Christians fled the city.

Ephrem retired to a cave on a bluff overlooking Edessa in Syria. Subsisting on a little barley bread and a few vegetables, it was here that Ephrem did much of his writing. Although generally living an ascetic life, Ephrem became well known in Edessa, which he called the "city of blessing." He frequently visited the city to preach, particularly against the heresy which was widespread at the time.

Ephrem can be credited with introducing music to Christian liturgy. He found that attaching Church doctrine to popular music and performing that music during the Mass was an extremely effective way to teach.

Well known in his time as a great teacher, orator, poet, and commentator, Ephrem was also considered a staunch defender of the faith. His writings included commentary on most of the Old Testament and much of the New Testament. Readings from his commentaries often followed the reading of sacred Scripture in the eastern Church. The most famous biblical commentator, St. Jerome, mentioned St. Ephrem in his listing of the great Christian writers.

St. Ephrem was named a Doctor of the Church, the only Syrian so honored, in 1920. Along with St. Cecilia, St. Ephrem can be considered a patron of sacred music.

Ephrem's message today: God has given some of us many talents, while others may receive just a few. Like the stewards in the parable of the talents (Lk 19:12–26), we must use the gifts which we are given to accomplish God's purpose for us.

Are you using your talents in God's work or do you sit on the sidelines while others carry your share of the load?

JUNE 11–MEMORIAL

Barnabas, Apostle: First Century

B arnabas was one of three persons formally recognized as apostles who were not among the original twelve. In the Acts of the Apostles, Luke writes that Barnabas sold his estate and lay the money from this sale at the feet of the apostles as an example of his Christian calling. In recounting this incident, Luke interprets Barnabas' name to mean "son of encouragement." It is in Acts we first see the reference to Barnabas as an apostle.

We know from other references in Acts that Barnabas had a strong influence on the other apostles, and was active in the early councils and missionary activity of the Church. When St. Paul came to Jerusalem following his conversion, the apostles and the faithful were suspicious of his change of heart. It was Barnabas who took him in and vouched for him.

Barnabas and Paul traveled together on Paul's first missionary journey which carried them to Salamis in Cyprus and other Mediterranean ports. A disagreement between Paul and Barnabas later ended their association and Paul left on his second missionary journey without Barnabas. This is the last mention of Barnabas in the Acts of the Apostles. One brief further mention of Barnabas occurs in Paul's first letter to the Corinthians.

Tradition tells us that Barnabas died around the year 60, having been stoned to death at Salamis. Other traditions say that he preached in Alexandria and Rome and that he was the first bishop of Milan.

Barnabas' message today: Barnabas sold all of his possessions and laid the money at the feet of the apostles. We are not asked to take such drastic steps in support of our community, but we are asked to support the church community in whatever way we can.

Do you support your church by contributing regularly—not just financially, but also with your time and talent?

Anthony of Padua, Priest and Doctor: 1195–1231

Born Ferdinand de Bulhoes in Lisbon, Portugal, Anthony was the son of a knight in King Alphonso's court. He began his studies at the cathedral in Lisbon and joined the Augustinians when he was fifteen. Ordained in about 1219, he transferred to the Franciscans in 1221, at which time he took the name Anthony.

Anthony was sent to Morocco to preach to the Moors, but was soon forced to return because of illness. He was stationed at a small hermitage in Italy, where he spent his time studying Scripture, praying, and doing menial tasks. Once, at an ordination when no one was prepared to speak, Anthony hesitantly accepted the task. His fellow Franciscans, expecting little from him, were astounded by his sermon, and Anthony began a new ministry as a preacher.

Anthony was assigned to preach throughout Italy. Noted for his eloquence, fire, and persuasiveness, he attracted large crowds wherever he spoke, and was particularly successful at converting heretics. Recognized as a great scholar, Anthony became the first Franciscan friar to teach theology to other Franciscan friars.

Appointed minister provincial of the Franciscan order, Anthony was released from these duties in 1226 in order to resume his preaching. He settled in Padua in that year and his bold and brilliant preaching completely reformed the city. He worked to abolish debtors' prisons, helped the poor, and worked ceaselessly and untiringly with heretics. All of this took its toll on Anthony's health and he died on June 13 at the age of thirty-six.

Anthony was canonized in the year following his death and was declared a Doctor of the Church by Pope Pius XII in 1946. He is the patron of the poor and oppressed. Alms given to seek his intercession are often referred to as "St. Anthony's Bread."

Anthony is also widely invoked for the return of lost articles.

This belief comes from a story which told of a Franciscan novice who ran away, taking with him a book of Psalms which Anthony had been using. Anthony prayed for the return of the book and the novice, struck by an alarming vision, brought the psalter back to Anthony.

Anthony's message today: Anthony has been a favorite saint for hundreds of years because of the belief that he intercedes with God on behalf of those who have lost articles. We can count on the saints to help us, knowing that they, too, experienced many of the difficulties we encounter in our own lives.

Is there a special need that you have at this time which may be helped by the intercession of a saint?

Aloysius Gonzaga, Religious: 1568–1591

Aloysius was the oldest son and heir of the Marquis Ferrante of Castiglione who was in the service of Philip II of Spain. His father wished to see Aloysius become a military officer, but Aloysius had another idea in mind.

At about the age of seven, Aloysius had a spiritual awakening and began his day with regular prayers, including the Office of Mary and the Psalms. At nine, he was sent to Florence to be educated. By the time he was eleven, Aloysius was teaching the catechism to poor children and fasting three days a week, as well as practicing other austerities.

After reading a book about the Jesuits' experiences in the missions of India, Aloysius decided to enter the Society of Jesus. His father strongly objected to his decision and enlisted the aid of eminent churchmen and noblemen to persuade Aloysius to pursue a more "normal" career. After a four-year struggle, his father relented and Aloysius joined the Jesuits in 1585.

During his studies at the Jesuit seminary in Milan, Aloysius undertook different spiritual practices. Under his spiritual advisor, St. Robert Bellarmine, he was obliged to eat more than he previously had, to take exercise with his fellow seminarians, and to pray only at the appointed times. Because of his frail health, Aloysius was called to Rome and took his vows there in 1587.

Several years later, a plague struck Rome. The Jesuits, in response, opened a hospital to care for the victims. Together with the other Jesuits, Aloysius performed personal services for the patients, nursing them, washing them, and making their beds. Aloysius, already in frail health, caught the affliction himself. He became so weak that he could scarcely get up from his bed, yet he continued his daily devotions. Within three months, after receiving the last rites from St. Robert Bellarmine, Aloysius Gonzaga died at the age of 23 on June 21, 1591.

Aloysius Gonzaga was canonized in 1726. He was declared protector of young students by Pope Benedict XIII, and patron of Catholic youth by Pope Pius XI.

Aloysius' message today: Aloysius chose the path he wanted to follow very early in his life and he let nothing deter him from it. In today's world, there is much to distract us from the goals we have set for ourselves. We should try to emulate Aloysius and persevere until we reach our own goals.

Do you let yourself become distracted from your goals? Say a prayer to St. Aloysius asking his help in staying on track.

Thomas More, Martyr: 1477–1535

Thomas was the son of Sir John and Agnes More. Sir John was a lawyer who later was named a judge on the king's bench. Thomas received the best education available in London. To broaden his background, he was sent at age thirteen to be a page in the household of John Morton, archbishop of Canterbury, who was then also the chancellor of England. Thomas learned much in this atmosphere which intertwined Church and state affairs.

While completing his studies, Thomas explored a religious vocation, living for four years in a Carthusian monastery in London. There he studied Scripture and the works of the Church Fathers, as well as the law. In 1505, however, Thomas married Jane Colt with whom he had four children: Margaret, Elizabeth, Cecilia, and John. More was deemed extraordinary in his day because he espoused the education of women. In this regard, he taught his wife and all of his children to read, then instructed them in Latin and many of the arts and sciences.

Thomas More rose rapidly and dramatically to hold many high offices of state. He served variously as undersheriff of London, diplomat, speaker of the House of Commons, knight, chancellor of the Duchy of Lancaster and, finally, from 1529 to 1532, Lord Chancellor of the Realm. He was the first layman in two centuries to serve in the latter capacity.

No one was more respected in England than Sir Thomas More, a man of highest personal integrity. He was described thus by a contemporary, Robert Whittinton:

> More is a man of angel's wit and singular learning; I know not his fellow. For where is the man of that gentleness, lowliness, and affability? And as time requireth, a man of marvelous mirth and pastimes; and sometimes of a sad gravity; a man for all seasons.

During the time that Thomas was Lord Chancellor, King Henry VIII's troubles with the Church began. When his wife, Catherine of Aragon could produce no male heir for his throne, Henry VIII petitioned the pope to declare the marriage null. Thomas disagreed with Henry's stand, but took no part in the controversy at first.

Henry's actions increasingly made Thomas' position as chancellor untenable, however. Henry declared himself "protector and supreme head of the Church of England," and began directing the clergy in Church matters. Thomas openly opposed these actions, angering the king, who accepted his resignation as chancellor in May 1532.

Thomas More was in retirement (and virtually penniless) for about two years by the time King Henry VIII had the Act of Succession passed by Parliament. This Act, among other things, required all the king's subjects to take an oath recognizing the validity of Henry's divorce and remarriage and repudiating the authority of "any foreign authority, prince, or potentate." To oppose this Act was considered to be high treason. On April 13, 1534, the oath was presented to Sir Thomas More and to Bishop John Fisher. Both refused to accept it.

After a second refusal, More and Fisher were imprisoned in the Tower of London. Henry tried desperately to persuade Thomas to accept his Act because he recognized that Thomas' approval would sway all of England to agree. But Thomas More would not compromise his moral values even to save his own life.

Thomas More was tried for high treason (though much of the testimony against him was false) and beheaded at the Tower of London on June 6, 1535. He was canonized exactly 400 years later on June 6, 1935 by Pope Pius XII.

St. Thomas More is the patron of lawyers. In many places a "Red Mass" is celebrated for lawyers to mark Thomas More's feast day.

Thomas' message today: Thomas More's conscience compelled him to oppose Henry VIII's increasingly belligerent stand against the pope. This cost him his position, his wealth, and, ultimately, his life. While we probably won't be obliged to make the sacrifices that Thomas did, we sometimes are asked to bend our principles for another.

Would you be capable of standing up for something that you believe in strongly? Add a prayer to your daily routine asking God to give you the strength to defend those beliefs you know to be right.

John Fisher, Bishop and Martyr: 1469–1535

John was born in Beverly, York, England, the son of Robert and Mary Ann Fisher. His father died when he was very young, but his mother saw to it that John was well educated.

From early on, John was recognized as a gifted student. He entered the University of Cambridge where he received his Master of Arts degree, and he was ordained a priest in 1491. Chosen as proctor of the university, John continued his studies earning the degree of Doctor of Divinity in 1501. In the same year, he was named vice-chancellor of the university.

Fisher's reputation was widespread in England, particularly in intellectual circles. Lady Margaret, the Countess of Richmond and mother of King Henry VII, soon called him into service as her counselor. Already generous in her good works, Lady Margaret became more so under the influence of John Fisher. She gave alms to the needy, provided dowries for poor brides, distributed food, and provided shelter. In addition, John's influence caused her to establish two colleges at Cambridge

Also admired by the king, John was nominated by Henry VII to be the bishop of Rochester in 1504, and assumed this position at the age of thirty-five. In the same year, he was elected chancellor of the University at Cambridge. As bishop, John Fisher visited every parish in his diocese and spent much of his time attending to the sick and overseeing the care of the poor under his charge. At the same time, as chancellor of the university, John Fisher was gaining world renown for his contributions to the intellectual world as well as his confutation of the heretical stands of Martin Luther.

Upon the death of Henry VII, Fisher became counselor to Catherine of Aragon, wife of Henry VIII. Later, when Henry tried to divorce Catherine, the bishop strongly defended the validity and indissolubility of the marriage. And as Henry VIII took further steps toward separating the Church in England from Rome, John Fisher spoke out in defense of the Church and the supremacy of the pope.

Bishop John Fisher and Sir Thomas More were both called upon to take the oath of loyalty to the king, and recognize his sovereignty over the Church of England. When both refused, they were imprisoned at the Tower of London. During their imprisonment, members of the king's council tried hard to persuade both to take the oath, but both refused.

On May 21, 1535, Pope Paul III named the John Fisher a cardinal. In anger, Henry VIII had Fisher tried for high treason. Like Thomas More, he was convicted on false testimony and was beheaded on June 22, 1535.

John Fisher was canonized by Pope Pius XII in 1935.

John's message today: John Fisher refused to go against his principles. It can be easy to compromise one's belief for worldly gain, particularly when one's life is at stake. We can look to people like John Fisher as models when we are called upon to yield on what we believe in.

Have you compromised your principles for a gain in power, influence, or wealth? Do you have the strength to stand up for your beliefs?

Birth of John the Baptist: First Century

John was the son of Zachary, a priest of the Temple in Jerusalem, and Elizabeth, a cousin of Mary. He was born after the angel Gabriel had told Zachary that his wife would bear a son even though she was an old woman (at that time, old might have meant someone in their late thirties).

Following the Annunciation, Mary came to assist her cousin during her pregnancy, an event known as the Visitation. Luke (1:57–80) then gives a marvelous account of John's birth and of his naming, and tells us that "The child grew and became strong in spirit, and he was in the wilderness until the day he appeared publicly to Israel."

About the year 27, when he was around thirty years old, John began preaching on the banks of the Jordan against the evils of the time. He called for repentance and baptism, warning that "the kingdom of heaven has come near" (Mt 3:2). His preaching attracted large crowds and, when Jesus came to him, John recognized him as the Messiah. John tried to discourage Jesus from being baptized, saying, "I need to be baptized by you, and do you come to me?" Scripture continues: "But Jesus answered him, 'Let it be so now; for it is proper for us in this way to fulfill all righteousness.'"

When Jesus began his public ministry in Galilee, John continued to preach along the Jordan. Herod Antipas, the tetrarch of Perea and Galilee, became fearful of John's great power among the people. After John condemned Herod's adulterous and incestuous marriage to Herodias, wife of Herod's half-brother, Herod had John arrested and imprisoned.

Knowing John to be a righteous and holy man, Herod initially planned no further action than his imprisonment. This was to change, however. During a celebration for Herod's birthday, Herodias' daughter, Salome, danced for the guests. So impressed was Herod and the others present that he offered anything she would ask for, "even half of my kingdom" Salome consulted her mother who told her to ask for John's head on a platter. While Herod regretted his offer, he could not back down in front of his guests and ordered John beheaded. The head was presented to Salome who then gave it to her mother.

John's preaching inspired many of Christ's followers, among them the apostles Andrew and John, who first came to know Jesus through John's teaching. He is presented as the last of the Old Testament prophets and the precursor of the Messiah.

We celebrate the birth of St. John the Baptist on this date. His martyrdom is remembered in memorial on August 29.

John's message today: Scripture tells us that John was "The voice of one crying out in the wilderness: 'Prepare the way of the Lord, make his paths straight'" (Matthew 3:3). John was the voice of which Isaiah prophesied a few thousand years ago. This message is as valid today as it was in both Isaiah's and John's time.

Have you prepared the way of the Lord in your life? Will you be ready when he comes?

JUNE 28—MEMORIAL

Irenaeus, Bishop: c. 130–202

This saint, whose name means "peace lover," is considered the first great theologian in the Church. It is believed that Irenaeus was born in Asia Minor, and became a priest in early adulthood. He was a disciple of Polycarp who, in turn, was a disciple of John, the apostle and evangelist.

In an effort to evangelize the Gauls in what is now France,

Polycarp sent Irenaeus to work under Pothinus, the bishop of Lyons in Gaul. Around this time, a cult had developed in Asia Minor under Montanus, who claimed the gift of prophecy and spread erroneous interpretations of sacred Scripture. In 177, Pothinus, who had also come from Asia Minor, sent Irenaeus to Rome with a letter to the pope pleading for leniency with their Christian brothers who had fallen under the spell of Montanus and his followers.

Before Irenaeus left for Rome, a persecution of Christians had begun in Gaul. During his absence, Pothinus and others were martyred, and when Irenaeus returned to Lyons, it was as bishop.

Irenaeus was greatly known for evangelization in the areas around his see. But it is for his defense of Christianity against Gnosticism that he is most remembered today. The Gnostics believed, among other things, that Jesus was never human, but only had that appearance. They also believed that procreation was sinful.

The Gnostic heresy contained many different false tenets which had been formulated under the leaders of the various Gnostic sects. Irenaeus, a learned man, set out to master all of these tenets so that he could understand and refute them. He proceeded to lay each tenet out in writing and follow it to its logical conclusion. He then contrasted the tenets with the teachings of the apostles. The writings of Irenaeus were widely circulated and are credited with eliminating the threat of Gnosticism to Christianity. The early Latin translations of his works are still extant.

Bishop Irenaeus had one more peacemaking mission in his life. The Quartodecimans, a sect of the Eastern Church, refused to celebrate Easter at the time when the Western Church celebrated this great feast. They had been excommunicated for this by Pope Victor III. Irenaeus interceded on their behalf, pointing out that they were following an old Eastern tradition. Further, that difference had not prevented Pope Anicetus and St. Polycarp from remaining in communion with the Quartodecimans. Iraneus's mission was successful and a permanent peace was established.

Irenaeus' message today: If we are to defend our faith well, we need to know what sets it apart from other religions. For Catholics today, the documents of the Second Vatican Council provide a strong basis for understanding the principles of our Church in the twentieth century.

Can you present a persuasive argument for your point of view or do you let others mold your opinions?

JULY

Junípero Serra, Priest: 1713–1784

No person has had more influence on the settlement of California than Junípero Serra. He was born Miguel José Serra to parents of humble means, living in Petra on the Mediterranean island of Majorca. His early education took place on the island at the Franciscan convent of San Bernardino. The church there had several small chapels on either side of the main altar dedicated to saints. Young Miguel developed a strong love for these saints while attending Mass, and their names—including San Diego, San Juan Capistrano, Nuestra Señora de Los Angeles, San Francisco—later became the names of the cities and missions which he established along the Camino Real in California.

Miguel was ordained in 1737, and took the name Junípero at that time. In the same year, he was named a professor of philosophy at the university in Palma, Spain. He continued with his studies and in 1742, earned a doctorate in theology. A year later, he was elected to the Dun Scotus chair of theology at the university. He also became renowned as a preacher on the island and was chosen to preach on the highest holy days.

Since he was a boy, Junípero Serra had dreamed of becoming a missionary in the New World. When the opportunity came, he joined about thirty other Franciscan missionaries who sailed to Mexico, arriving on December 2, 1749. For most of the next twenty years, Junípero served as a missionary in the harsh environment of the Sierra Madres of northeastern Mexico and as a professor at the College of San Fernando in Mexico City.

Prior to 1768, the Jesuits had established many missions in Mexico and in Baja, California. But a dispute with King Carlos III of Spain in that year led to the order being forcibly ejected from their missions, and the priests sent back to Spain. To ensure that Spain would maintain a strong position in the New World, the king ordered the Franciscans to take over the Jesuit missions in Baja, California and to establish new missions north along the coast in the Spanish-claimed territory, which extended north to present-day British Columbia. Junípero Serra was selected to lead the Franciscan missionaries in this new assignment.

Serra believed that the colonization of California was secondary to the conversion of the Indians, and his lifework reflected this. His biographers wrote of his love for his "dear children," the more than 6,700 Indians whom he baptized and the more than 5,000 whom he confirmed. During the period in which Padre Serra worked among the Indians, he raised their health and living standards and introduced training in agriculture, letters, crafts, and music.

A man of vision, Junípero Serra's concept was to build a "ladder" of missions one day's journey apart between San Diego and San Francisco. Between 1769 and 1782, Padre Serra actually established nine missions along this route, most of which are still active today.

The process of sainthood for Junípero Serra was begun in 1934 and has continued with his beatification in 1988.

Junípero's message today: Junípero Serra undertook a bold journey in coming to the New World. Our physical travels may not be as far-reaching as Serra's, but we are all on a spiritual journey whose course can often be as dramatic. We, too, can hold steadfast to our goal of reaching God's kingdom.

How do you stay on course when your spiritual journey takes a difficult turn?

Thomas, Apostle: First Century

Thomas is probably best known for expressing his disbelief in Jesus' resurrection (hence the term "doubting Thomas"). But Thomas is also the first to expressly acknowledge the divinity of Jesus when, upon seeing the resurrected Christ, he uttered one of the most beautiful and shortest of prayers: "My Lord and my God."

While not a lot is known about this apostle, his love for Jesus was apparent in the instances where he is mentioned in Scripture. When Jesus was about to return to Judea upon the death of Lazarus, his disciples tried to talk him out of it, pointing out that the Jews had tried to stone him to death there (Jn 11:7–8). But Jesus insisted on going to Judea and it was Thomas who said to his fellow disciples, "Let us also go, that we may die with him" (Jn 11:16).

At the Last Supper, when Jesus said, "You know the way to the place where I am going" it was Thomas who replied, "Lord, we do not know where you are going. How can we know the way?" In response, Jesus effectively summarized our Christian faith, "I am the way, and the truth, and the life. No one comes to the Father except through me" (Jn 14:4–6).

Thomas also joined Peter and some of the other apostles fishing in the Sea of Tiberias after the resurrection (Jn 21:1–14). After a night in which they caught nothing, Jesus was standing on the shore as they approached. When told that they had not caught anything, Jesus directed them to lower their net. When they did, they had so many fish in the net that they were unable to pull the net in.

Eusebius, the Church historian, says that Thomas preached the gospel in Parthia. Ancient tradition tells us that Thomas later preached in India where he was martyred and buried near Madras.

St. Thomas was declared the Apostle of India by Pope Paul VI in 1972. He is also the patron of architects, builders, surveyors, the blind, Pakistan, and the East Indies.

Thomas' message today: Like all of us, Thomas was human and he had doubts. Thomas overcame his doubts through his great love of Jesus. We can do the same. Jesus told us how much he loved us when he responded to Thomas' short prayer, "Blessed are those who have not seen and yet have come to believe" (Jn 20:29).

When something occurs in your life to raise doubts, do you turn to God or do you turn away? Try saying Thomas' prayer, "My Lord and my God."

JULY 4–OPTIONAL MEMORIAL

Elizabeth of Portugal: 1271–1336

The daughter of Peter III, King of Aragon, Elizabeth was named for her great-aunt, St. Elizabeth of Hungary. She was destined for a throne from birth, but her early upbringing taught her humility and a strong sense of charity. At the age of twelve, Elizabeth was married to Denis, King of Portugal. Denis was a good ruler, but a less-than-ideal husband. While he allowed Elizabeth complete freedom to carry out her charitable work and her devotion, he did not feel obliged to emulate her.

Elizabeth rose early each morning to pray, and had other regular devotions in the afternoon and evening. Like her namesake, Elizabeth felt called upon to take care of those less fortunate than herself. She built hospitals and founded orphanages, and also ordered that pilgrims and poor strangers be provided with lodging and other necessities. In all of this, Elizabeth never neglected her official duties or the care of her family.

When Denis became seriously ill in 1324, Elizabeth devoted all of her attention to caring for him. During his long illness, Denis repented of the wanton life which he had led and died in 1325 in a state of grace.

After the death of her husband, Elizabeth wished to retire to a convent for the Poor Clares which she had built. She was dissuaded from this, however, and instead undertook a simple life in a house near the convent as a member of the third order of St. Francis.

Elizabeth earned the title of "peacemaker" because she frequently intervened between quarreling members of her family. In the royal milieu of the time, family quarrels often turned into wars. On two occasions, Elizabeth had come between the forces of her husband and of her son. Two other times, she either averted war or intervened in disputes between rulers of Spanish kingdoms.

In 1336, Elizabeth went to reconcile a quarrel between her son, Alphonsus IV, now the king of Portugal, and her grandson, Alfonso XI, king of Castile. Upon reaching Estremoz on the border of Castile where her son and his forces were deployed, Elizabeth fell ill and died on July 4, 1336.

Elizabeth's message today: In our times, maintaining peace in one's family does not usually involve averting a war. But peace among family members is no less important—or no less difficult to achieve—than it was in Elizabeth's time.

Where do you stand in your family? Are you a peacemaker? The contentious one? What can you do to bring peace where there is dissension?

Maria Goretti, Virgin and Martyr: 1890–1902

Born the third of seven children to a poor farmer near Ancona, Italy, Maria was described by her mother as "happy, good, openhearted, without whim, but with a sense and seriousness far beyond her years, and never disobedient." The family's circumstances meant that even the children had to work as farmhands for other people. Because of this, Maria and the other children received no schooling.

When Maria was nine, her father died. Maria's mother, sisters, and brother continued to work the fields while Maria cooked, sewed, and kept house for the family. At the age of eleven, Maria received her first communion, but the strongest test of her faith was yet to come.

The Gorettis were forced to take another family in to room with them. The son, an eighteen year old named Alessandro, soon began making indecent proposals to Maria. While she turned him down time and again, she never told anyone about this since Alessandro had threatened her and her mother if she told.

One day when Maria was home mending clothes and the others were working in the fields, Alessandro came home and tried to force himself on Maria. When she again resisted, the enraged youth stabbed her several times with a knife. Maria was rushed to a hospital where doctors tried in vain to save her. Before she died on June 6, 1902, she forgave Alessandro and said that she wished to see him in heaven.

Alessandro was tried for Maria's murder and sent to prison. At first, Alessandro showed no remorse for his crime. But after eight years, Maria appeared to him in a dream and his life changed completely. When his sentence was complete, Alessandro went to Maria's mother to beg forgiveness, which he received. He then became a Capuchin lay brother.

St. Maria Goretti was canonized by Pope Pius XII on July 25, 1950. Present at the canonization were her mother, her siblings, and Alessandro, her attacker. She is the patron of youth and of teenage girls.

Maria's message today: "Forgive us our trespasses as we forgive those who trespass against us." We may say these words daily, but do we pay attention to what we are saying? Maria, mortally wounded, could both forgive and pray for her attacker.

If Maria could forgive (and pray for) her killer, can you forgive someone who has done much less harm to you?

Benedict, Abbot: c. 480–547

Benedict established monasticism as we know it in the Western Church today, and most orders of monks follow at least a modified version of the rule set by him.

Benedict was born into a good family, and was raised in the ancient town of Nursia. As was the custom of his time, Benedict was sent off to Rome as a young boy for his education. After several years, however, he recognized that this was not God's choice for him, and he retreated to a mountainous region near Subiaco in Italy. There a monk named Romanus led him to an almost inaccessible cave high on the mountain where Benedict remained for three years, subsisting on a loaf of bread which Romanus brought to him each day.

Although Romanus kept Benedict's whereabouts secret, some shepherds who stumbled on his cave were so in awe of Benedict's holiness that word of him soon spread throughout the area. A nearby community of monks whose abbot had just died asked Benedict to become their abbot. Though he warned them that they might consider his life too severe, they insisted, and Benedict at last agreed. But as he had predicted, the members soon became dissatisfied with Benedict's rule and they tried to poison him.

Following this incident, Benedict returned to Subiaco, and began the great work which God had planned for him. He organized his followers into twelve communities of twelve members, each under its own prior appointed by Benedict. He made manual labor a central part of the discipline practiced by these monks. Before long, Subiaco became a center of learning and spirituality.

Around the year 525, Benedict left Subiaco and settled at Monte Cassino. Here he established the rule that today governs many of our religious communities. The rule, with its seventy-three sections, was based on common sense, along with prescribed prayer, study, labor, and moderate asceticism.

Benedict's counsel was sought by popes and kings. He never neglected the poor and the destitute of the surrounding countryside while leading his community. Benedict performed many miracles during his lifetime, which included curing the ill and, on more than one occasion, raising the dead.

St. Benedict was named patron protector of Europe by Pope Paul VI in 1964.

Benedict's message today: The monastic life led by Benedict and his followers is a life of total dedication to God and entails much hardship. All of us need to give some part of our lives back to God; in this regard, each of us should assume some hardship or sacrifice.

What sacrifices have you made for your community? Are you active in any ministry? If unable to participate, do you pray for those who are active?

Blessed Kateri Tekakwitha, Virgin: 1656–1680

Kateri was born in upstate New York, the daughter of a Mohawk warrior. Her mother died of smallpox when she was four years old, and Kateri was adopted by her two aunts and an uncle. Kateri had also contracted smallpox, and the disease left her with a lingering illness and a disfigured face.

During this time, the French Jesuits had undertaken an evangelization mission to the Indians. Kateri's uncle, a powerful Mohawk chief, warned her against the Jesuit "black robes," whom he blamed for the sickness and disease which had fallen on the tribe. The girl's experience with the Jesuits was quite different, however. She found them to be kind and gentle, and through their message, she felt called to Christianity. Converted as a teenager, Kateri was baptized at the age of twenty and dedicated her virginity to Jesus. She developed a great devotion to the Eucharist and to the crucified Christ.

Her conversion incurred great hostility among her tribesmen, but Kateri remained steadfast in her faith. She refused marriage which was considered the duty of Mohawk women in order to have a man who would provide food for the family.

Kateri's confessor, Father Jacques de Lamberville, soon began to fear for her life, and in 1678 he sent her to a new Christian colony of Indians in Canada. Here Kateri lived a life of prayer, penance, and care for the sick and the aged. Each morning, even in the bitterest winter, she rose long before dawn and stood at the chapel door until it opened at four. She remained there until after the last Mass when she went into the fields with the other women of the community. When their work was done, Kateri returned to the chapel for her daily Rosary and evening devotions. On Sundays and feast days, Kateri often spent the whole day in prayer at the chapel.

Still suffering the effects of her childhood illness, Kateri died during Holy Week in 1680. Her last words were, "Jesus, Mary, I love you." The story is told that at the moment of her death, the scars on her face disappeared.

Kateri Tekakwitha is known as the "Lily of the Mohawks." Blessed Kateri Tekakwitha is the first native American to be beatified in the Catholic Church.

Kateri's message today: Imagine the strong faith that this young woman developed in her short lifetime. When the vast majority of her tribe and the members of her family were against her, she stood resolute in her determination to dedicate her life to Jesus.

Is your faith strong enough to stand up to your acquaintances—perhaps even your family—when they try to discourage you?

Camillus de Lellis, Priest: 1550–1614

Born into a aristocratic family at Bocchianico in the Abruzzi province of what is now Italy, Camillus grew swiftly to be a big man—six feet six inches tall and similarly proportioned. When Camillus was seventeen, he went off with his father to fight with the Venetians against the Turks.

During this sojourn, Camillus became infected with a disease in his leg and was admitted to the San Giacomo Hospital for the Incurables in Rome. Here Camillus developed a gambling habit. More than once, he lost everything he owned, including the shirt off his back. Camillus became a mercenary when he was finally discharged from the hospital, but a peace treaty between the Venetians and Turks took away this livelihood. Meanwhile, the disease in his leg brought him back to San Giacomo. When his health improved, the hospital administrators employed Camillus, giving him menial jobs for small pay. But gambling generally took most of his money from him. Finally having enough of his bad habits, the administrators fired Camillus and threw him out on the street.

In a fit of remorse, Camillus vowed to join the Franciscans, hoping that he might kick his gambling habit. Perhaps with this vow in mind, he accepted work as a laborer in the construction of new buildings at a Capuchin monastery. He entered the novitiate of the Capuchins, but the problem with his leg returned and he could not continue. Returning to San Giacomo, Camillus devoted himself to the care of the sick. This time, the administrators noted his sincerity and Camillus was eventually made superintendent of the hospital.

At that time, care conditions at the hospital were deplorable, and most of the hospital workers were somewhat unscrupulous: prisoners, the very poor, or those who felt that they could somehow take advantage of the sick. Theft was common, and those near death were sometimes thrown into the burial pits with the dead so that their belongings could be stolen.

Camillus tried hard to change this disreputable situation. He wanted to form a community who would care for the sick from a motive of charity rather than from avarice, but his efforts were met with jealousy and suspicion. With the support of his confessor, St. Philip Neri, Camillus realized that he could only be successful in this ministry if he were a priest. Upon ordination, Camillus left San Giacomo and began to lay the foundation for his congregation.

During his lifetime, the congregation of Camillus de Lellis, known as the Ministers of the Sick (today called the Order of Hospitallers), opened several houses and hospitals for the care of the sick and wounded. His congregation also went along with troops who were fighting in Hungary and Croatia, thus establishing the first field hospitals.

God granted Camillus the power of prophecy and the gift of miracles. He also was known to have received personal revelation from God on many occasions. St. Camillus de Lellis was canonized in 1746 and declared the patron of hospitals, nurses, and of the sick. The health care professions honor this saint and celebrate his gifts to their field on this date.

Camillus' message today: This saint recognized the slippery slope down which he was descending and, with the grace of God, turned himself around. God's grace is available to everyone whether they need abundant help, as Camillus did, or just enough to keep them on the right path in their journey of faith.

Do you regularly ask for God's grace or do you sometimes think that you can do it all on your own?

JULY 15–MEMORIAL

Bonaventure, Bishop and Doctor: 1221–1274

This saint was born at Bagnorea in Tuscany, the son of John Fidanza and Mary Ritella. He was christened John at his baptism. Stricken with a dangerous illness as a baby, at his mother's plea, little John was prayed for by St. Francis of Assisi. As he recovered, the saint, seeing a great future for the baby, exclaimed, "O buona ventura"—O good fortune! Thus did he receive the name by which he was known throughout his life.

Bonaventure entered the Franciscan order at the age of twenty-two and was sent to Paris to complete his studies. It was in Paris that his reputation for genius manifested itself, and here that he became a close friend of Thomas Aquinas.

In 1257, Bonaventure (and Thomas Aquinas) received the degree of doctor. In the same year, Bonaventure, not yet thirty-six, was elected minister general of the Franciscan order. During this time, he laid out a set of constitutions on the rules for the order which have been a foundational part of the Franciscan community up to the present day.

Bonaventure governed the Franciscans for seventeen years. In 1273, he was named bishop of Albano, and directed by Pope Gregory X to come immediately to Rome. Upon his arrival there, the pope ordered Bonaventure to prepare an agenda and develop position papers for a council which was to be held in Lyons. The primary purpose of this council was to effect a reconciliation between the Eastern Church and Rome, and all of the best theologians would be present there. (It was while en route to Rome for this purpose that St. Thomas Aquinas died.)

Cardinal Bonaventure was the major figure at this great council, and through his efforts a reunion (later abrogated by Constantinople) was agreed upon. Bonaventure was the preacher at a celebration Mass in which the Scripture was sung in both Latin and Greek. About two weeks later, he died.

There is a story told of Bonaventure which demonstrates this saint's humility and charity. One day, Bonaventure was visiting a monastery of his order. One of the friars wished to talk with him, but out of shyness and humility, hesitated to approach his superior. When Bonaventure had departed, the friar realized that he was missing his chance to speak with him, and pursued Bonaventure down the road. When he finally caught up with him, Bonaventure spent a long time in conversation with the man. As the friar had returned home, comforted and rejoicing, Bonaventure's traveling companions showed signs of impatience. Seeing this, Bonaventure mildly rebuked them. By virtue of his office, he told them, he was both prelate and servant to his brothers. That friar, he said, "is both my brother and my master."

St. Bonaventure was canonized in 1482 and declared a Doctor of the Church in 1588. Owing to the angelic virtues credited to him in his lifetime, he is known as the "Seraphic Doctor."

Bonaventure's message today: Most of us tend to take ourselves too seriously from time to time. We sometimes see ourselves as better—smarter, richer, more successful—than others, and look down on them. Bonaventure recognized that whatever gifts he had received came from God, they did not make him a better person than his "brother and master."

Do you sometimes feel that you are superior to another? Have you used your riches and power to accomplish good in the world or merely to indulge yourself and your family?

JULY 22–MEMORIAL

Mary Magdalene: First Century

With the exception of Mary, the mother of Jesus, few women are more honored in Scripture than Mary Magdalene.

An unfounded but persistent legend identifies her as the unnamed, sinful woman who anointed the feet of Jesus (Lk 7:37–38), but this story has largely been discounted by modern Church scholars. The next chapter of Luke's Gospel mentions Mary Magdalene as the one from whom Jesus cast out "seven devils," an indication, at the worst, of extreme demonic possession, or, more likely, severe illness.

Mary probably received her name from Magdala, a place on the western shore of the Sea of Galilee near Tiberias. It seems likely that Jesus first met her during his Galilean ministry. Many legends surround Mary, but no evidence exists to confirm any of them. According to a French tradition, for example, Mary Magdalene is identified as the Mary who is the sister of Martha and Lazarus. In this story, she accompanied Martha and Lazarus to Marseilles where the three evangelized the people of Provence. While no factual evidence supports this legend, a great devotion to St. Mary

Magdalene exists today in southern France and parts of northern Italy along the Mediterranean.

Mary was one of many who helped support Jesus and his apostles during Jesus' ministry (Lk 8:3). But perhaps Mary Magdalene is best remembered for her closeness to Jesus during his passion, death, and resurrection. Mary Magdalene stood at the foot of the cross with Jesus' mother and St. John. Out of all of the disciples of Jesus who might have been selected, Mary Magdalene was the first to become aware of the resurrection when she came to Jesus' tomb on Easter morning to anoint his body.

Mary's message today: It isn't really important whether Mary Magdalene was a great sinner, possessed by demons, or very sick. What is important is that she became one of Jesus' good friends and a disciple. That is also what is important for us today: the relationship which we have with Jesus right now.

What kind of relationship do you have with Jesus? Do you consider him a friend and companion for your life's journey?

JULY 23—OPTIONAL MEMORIAL

Bridget, Religious: 1303–1373

Bridget (called "Birgitta" in Sweden) was born the fifth child of Birgir Persson, the governor of Upland, and Ingeborg, daughter of another provincial governor. From this high position, she seemed destined to play some role in the temporal affairs of Sweden.

The first of the many visions she was to have throughout her life came to Bridget at the age of seven, when she saw herself being crowned by Our Lady. At ten, she pictured Christ on the cross telling her that he was made to suffer by those who spurned his love for them. When she was thirteen years old, Bridget married Ulf Gudmarsson, himself only eighteen. Ulf, described as rich, noble, and wise, and Bridget had eight children, one of whom is St. Catherine of Sweden. Early on, the couple became heavily involved in charitable work and brought their children up to maintain a sense of humility and obligation.

In 1335, Bridget was named the principal lady-in-waiting to Blanche of Namur, wife of King Magnus II of Sweden. At one point, Bridget took a leave of absence from the royal court to go with her husband on a pilgrimage to Spain. During this trip, Ulf became seriously ill and was not expected to survive. Bridget's prayers were answered by a vision of St. Denis who assured her that Ulf would recover. Upon regaining his health, Ulf and Bridget pledged to devote the rest of their lives to God. But before they could fully implement this resolution, Ulf died in the monastery at Alvastra in 1344.

After Ulf's death, Bridget lived at the monastery for four years. She began to dress in the manner of a humble penitent and to practice severe austerities. As the result of another vision, Bridget returned to the court of King Magnus. During this period, the king liberally endowed a convent at Vadstena which became the motherhouse of the Order of the Most Holy Savior, the religious order founded by Bridget.

Bridget's correspondence with popes began as a result of a vision. She wrote a candid letter to Pope Clement VI urging him to bring peace between Edward III of England and Philip IV of France and spelling out the consequences of a failure to achieve peace. When the pope's lukewarm effort fell short, the results which Bridget foretold occurred. Along with St. Catherine of Siena, Bridget also played a part in influencing the return of the papacy from Avignon to Rome.

In the year 1350, Bridget went to live in Rome. Here her visions and prophecies concerned the most urgent political and spiritual questions of her time. She spared no one—rulers, popes, priests, or people—in her criticisms when their transgressions and the punishments they would merit came to her in visions. This did not earn her many friends among those she accused. Before writing or speaking to these offenders however, the saint sought the counsel of her confessors or the pastors of the Church, not trusting, in her humility, her own judgment.

While those she chastised did not care much for her, Bridget was loved by most of the common people. She cared for the poor and regularly fed pilgrims from Sweden who visited Rome. She was, in the words of a companion, "kind and meek to every creature, and had a laughing face."

In response to another vision, Bridget's final journey was to the Holy Land in 1371. Her daughter Catherine, her son Charles, and others joined her on this pilgrimage. On this journey Charles came down with a fever that killed him after a short time. Bridget was devastated, as Charles, along with Catherine, had been a favorite child.

Bridget had been ailing for several months prior to her return to Rome in 1373. She continued to waste away until her death in July of that year. Bridget was initially buried in Rome, but some months later, her remains were carried to Sweden by Catherine and Bridget's confessor, Peter of Alvastra. She was finally laid to rest in her convent at Vadstena.

St. Bridget was canonized in 1391 and is the patron of Sweden.

Bridget's message today: In response to her visions, Bridget criticized some very important people during her lifetime. Not trusting solely her own judgment, however, she first consulted with her confessor or pastor before judging others. When we feel compelled to criticize someone, we may not always be so prudent.

Have you rushed to judge a family member or someone you know? Perhaps your prayers can have a greater effect on their lives.

James the Greater, Apostle: First Century

This James is called "the Greater" because his vocation to serve Jesus preceded that of the other apostle with the same name.

James the Greater was the brother of John and the son of Zebedee. One tradition, derived from information in several of the Gospels, tells us that James and John were first cousins of Jesus. With his brother, James was a fisherman working in his father's business until called by Jesus.

Neither James nor John fully understood at first what they were being called to do. Matthew tells us that their mother asked Jesus to give James and John the places of honor, one at his left hand, the other at his right hand, when his kingdom was established (Mt 20:20–21). We can assume that James was held in high esteem by Jesus. He, John, and Peter were the only apostles present for the raising from the dead of Jairus' daughter, as well as for the transfiguration of Jesus, and these three were in the garden of Gethsemane with Jesus.

James and John were noted for their hot temperament which was probably the basis for the nickname, "sons of thunder" (Mk 3:17), which Jesus gave them. One story illustrates that temperament well. When Jesus was on his way to Jerusalem, he and his disciples passed through a Samaritan town. (The animosity between the Samaritans and the Jews at that time was roughly equivalent to that between the Jews and Palestinians today.) When the Samaritans learned that Jesus' destination was Jerusalem, a city hated by the Samaritans, they refused to house him and the disciples. James and John asked him, "'Lord, do you want us to command fire to come down from heaven and consume them?' But he turned and rebuked them" (Lk 9:54–55).

James was the first of the apostles to be martyred at Jerusalem around the year 42. The story is told of his accuser who, seeing the great and unwavering faith of James before King Herod, became a Christian on the spot and was condemned to be killed together with James. As they were approaching the place where they were to be beheaded, the accuser turned to James and asked his forgiveness for testifying against him. James turned to his accuser, kissed him and said, "Peace be with you, brother."

A doubtful tradition, which sprang up around the eighth century, had this saint preaching in Spain. It is unlikely that James would have traveled to Spain to preach and then return to martyrdom in Jerusalem. Nevertheless, James has become the patron saint of Spain as well as the patron of laborers, pilgrims, and those suffering from rheumatism.

James' message today: "Peace be with you, brother." What a wonderful offering by James to one who has falsely testified against him. The man who testified against James knew that he was giving false testimony, yet, when he realized his error, James forgave him.

If James can forgive one who has falsely accused him, think how much greater is God's forgiveness. Have you asked God's forgiveness for your sins?

Christopher, Martyr: Third Century

Christopher is one of the most popular saints in both the East and in the West. Many stories surround him, some contradictory and confusing.

One of the most popular traditions holds that Christopher was a strong giant who made his living by carrying people across a raging stream. For years, he searched in vain to find someone more powerful than himself. He finally concluded that this could only be Christ, since the devil feared Christ.

One of his passengers was a small child who grew so heavy as they crossed the stream that Christopher thought they would both drown. The child then identified himself as Christ and told Christopher that the heaviness was caused by the weight of the world on his shoulders.

St. Christopher was martyred during the reign of Decius in about 251. His name means Christ-bearer and as a result of this legend, he is the patron of travelers especially, in modern times, of motorists.

Christopher's message today: We are much luckier than Christopher. While we can all carry Jesus within us, he does not burden us with the weight of the world. Rather, he lifts our burdens from us and helps us to carry them if we follow him.

When your burdens seem too heavy for you to carry, do you turn to Jesus for help? Perhaps St. Christopher will intercede on your behalf if you say a prayer to him.

JULY 26—MEMORIAL

Ann and Joachim, Parents of Mary: First Century

Tradition passed on to us in *Protevangelium of James* is our only source of information about the parents of Mary and the grandparents of Jesus. While the trustworthiness of this document is somewhat in question, there are certain things which we can surmise about the parents of the mother of God.

Ann and Joachim were both from the tribe of Judah of the royal house of David. They were childless for many years after their marriage, although both of them prayed that they might be given a child. Finally, an angel appeared to each of them, telling them that their prayers had been heard by God and that they would have a child who would be spoken of throughout the world. In gratitude, Ann promised that her child would be given to the service of God.

Although originally from Galilee, the couple moved to Jerusalem; this is where Mary was born and raised. Mary, we are told, was sent to the temple to be educated and to serve God. As a teenager, Mary chose to accept God's mission for her to be the mother of Jesus. Her life was then devoted to Jesus and to her husband, Joseph. We can easily imagine a role for Ann and Joachim in Jesus' upbringing. Perhaps Joachim, whose name means "preparation for the savior," passed on the tradition of Israel to the young child sitting on his lap. Ann, whose name means "grace," certainly provided the love which only a grandmother can give.

The Church chose to formally honor Ann and Joachim in the middle of the sixth century when the Emperor Justinian I dedicated a shrine to St. Ann in Constantinople. About the same time, Pope Constantine introduced the devotion to these two saints to Rome. Even earlier, a church was dedicated to Sts. Ann and Joachim in the fourth century on the site of their home in Jerusalem.

St. Ann is the patron of Christian mothers, of housewives, and of cabinet makers. She is also the patron of Canada. While not officially proclaimed as such, we might also consider Sts. Ann and Joachim as the patrons of grandparents.

Ann and Joachim's message today: Imagine being the grandparent of Jesus. While they could not know that Jesus was the son of God, Ann and Joachim knew that he was someone special and they loved him very much.

All children are special and need love, not just our own. Do something nice for a child, perhaps a poor child, to make them feel more loved.

Martha: First Century

Martha, her sister Mary, and her brother Lazarus were all close friends of Jesus. He often came to their home simply as a welcome guest.

Luke's Gospel (10:38–42) tells us that, as Martha bustled about with household preparations, Mary sat at the feet of Jesus, listening to him speak. Martha (in frustration, we might imagine), said to Jesus: "Lord, do you not care that my sister has left me to do all the work by myself? Tell her then to help me." To this, Jesus replied, "Martha, Martha, you are worried and distracted by many things; there is need of only one thing. Mary has chosen the better part, which will not be taken away from her." Thus, Martha has become the prototype of the activist Christian, while Mary is the symbol of the contemplative life.

The sisters were such good friends of Jesus that they felt free to call upon him at their brother's death. When Jesus arrived in Bethany, Martha said to him "Lord, if you had been here my brother would not have died" (Jn 11:21). Jesus then asked her if she believed that he was the Messiah, the Son of God. Martha responded in a simple, yet powerful faith statement: "Yes, Lord. I have come to believe that you are the Messiah, the Son of God, the one coming into the world" (Jn 11:27).

St. Martha is the patron saint of cooks and dietitians.

Martha's message today: Jesus gently chided Martha for putting too much emphasis on worldly matters while Mary was more concerned with spiritual things. By this, Jesus did not imply that Martha was wrong, only that Jesus' message of salvation is much more important than the things of this world.

Do you try to achieve some balance between your spiritual life and the everyday tasks of life?

Peter Chrysologus, Bishop and Doctor: 406–c. 450

Like St. John Chrysostom, this saint earned the name Chrysologus, meaning "golden tongue," for his exceptional preaching abilities.

Born and educated in the town of Imola, Peter was ordained a deacon by Cornelius, the bishop of that city. Legend tells how Peter accompanied Cornelius to Rome to participate in the election of a new archbishop of Ravenna. According to this story, the pope had a vision the night before their arrival and refused to accept the results of the election. Instead, he chose Peter to be the archbishop. It is much more likely, however, that Peter was elected archbishop in his own right.

Upon beginning his episcopacy in Ravenna about the year 433, Peter found pockets of paganism and corruption among the Christians as well. He successfully rooted these abuses out, perhaps by the strength and delivery of his sermons. As bishop, Peter was known for his far-reaching charities and his great concern for people. He also built a church dedicated to St. Andrew and a baptistry.

The homilies of Peter which survive are quite short, as he was afraid of losing the attention of his listeners. We have no way of knowing whether the homilies were delivered as written or possibly served as an outline. But because of his given surname, Chrysologus, we do know that his talks must have been impressive.

In about the year 450, St. Peter received a revelation of his approaching death and returned to his home town of Imola. There he presented some of his cherished chalices to the church of St. Cassian. On December 2, he died in his home.

St. Peter Chrysologus was named a Doctor of the Church by Pope Benedict XIII in 1729.

Peter's message today: The gift of eloquence is not given to everyone. Yet all of us are called to conversion, not only our own, but to help others as well. We may spread the good news of Jesus through our words, or through our example and the good works that we do.

Are you setting a good example for your family members and your neighbors? If you have been given the gift of eloquence, do you use it for God's work or merely to advance yourself?

Ignatius Loyola, Priest: 1491–1556

I gnatius was the youngest of thirteen children of a noble family in the Basque region of Spain. He entered the military service and had a promising career ahead of him until he was wounded during the siege of Pamplona in 1521.

During his long recovery, Ignatius spent the time reading religious books, as there was nothing else available to him. These readings included a life of Christ and the lives of the saints, both of which had a profound effect on him. After his recovery, he made a pilgrimage to Monserrat where he hung up his sword at Our Lord's altar. He then spent a year in retreat at Manresa where he experienced visions and began writing his *Spiritual Exercises.*

From 1524 to 1535, Ignatius studied in Paris and received a master of arts degree in 1534. In that same year, along with a group of fellow students who included St. Francis Xavier, he founded the Society of Jesus (the Jesuits). The group vowed to live in poverty and chastity, and to go to the Holy Land. Because of the hostility of the Turks, however, they were unable to achieve this last goal, so they went instead to Rome and placed themselves in the apostolic service of the pope. The Society was formally approved in 1540 by

Pope Paul III. The group took their final vows in 1541, and Ignatius Loyola was named superior general of the order.

Unlike most orders, Jesuits take four vows. In addition to poverty, chastity, and obedience, they also take a vow to go wherever the pope should send them for the salvation of souls. In the case of the early Jesuits, this meant India and Japan where Jesuit missions still exist. (St. Francis Xavier was the earliest Jesuit missionary to go to both countries.)

The Jesuits established many houses, schools, colleges, and seminaries around Europe in the early years of the order. They soon became known for their intellectual prowess and for their work in the field of education. Ignatius Loyola was active against the heresies which spread during the Reformation. (It was in 1517 that Martin Luther had nailed his theses to the church door at Wittenberg.)

By the time of his death in 1556, Ignatius had set in motion three of his goals for the Jesuits: reform of the Church, especially through education and frequent acceptance of the sacraments; widespread activity in the missionary field; and participation in the fight against heresy. Following his advice to treat all people with respect, members of the order have also been at the forefront of the modern ecumenical movement.

St. Ignatius Loyola was canonized a saint in 1622 and proclaimed patron of retreats and spiritual exercises by Pope Pius XI.

Ignatius' message today: The Jesuits today run many high schools and universities which are known for high standards of education. While offering the broadest range of subject matter, these institutions focus much time and energy in teaching about the Church. For all of us, though, most parishes offer adult education courses which allow members to become more knowledgeable about the Church.

Have you made any effort to learn about your Church by attending classes or seminars in your parish?

Alphonsus Liguori, Bishop and Doctor: 1696–1787

Alphonsus was born into a distinguished and aristocratic family in Naples, and given every advantage that his family's wealth and position could obtain. His parents provided tutors for him and sent him to the university at the age of thirteen. Within four years, at the age of sixteen, Alphonsus was awarded doctorate degrees in both canon and civil law.

Alphonsus established a successful civil law practice in Naples and developed a reputation for legal skill. When he was twenty-one, his father arranged a marriage for him, but it never took place. Several years later, after receiving the sacrament of confirmation, he vowed to never marry but continue in his profession until God gave him a sign to abandon it. This sign came just a few months later, when he completely missed an important point in a case before a civil court, causing him to concede the case.

In 1726, Alphonsus was ordained and began several years of missionary work throughout the kingdom of Naples. The preaching style of this period was exemplified by pompousness and excessively ornate verbosity, but Alphonsus kept his preaching simple, which led to a high degree of success for him.

At the age of thirty-three, Alphonsus met and developed a friendship with Father Thomas Falcoia. Many years earlier, Falcoia had tried to establish a new religious order following a vision he had, but was not successful in doing so. He was, however, able to set up a convent in Scala whose nuns observed the Visitandine rule. One of these nuns, Sister Marie Celeste, had also had a vision similar to Falcoia's about setting up a new order of priests.

Falcoia was appointed bishop of Castelamare in whose see Scala was located, and the bishop invited his friend Alphonsus to give a retreat for the nuns. Besides giving the retreat, Alphonsus spent time investigating the visions of his friend and of Sister Marie. Finding the visions to be truly from God, he revised the rule which the convent followed, and expanded on it. He then recommended that the convent be reorganized in accordance with the new rule, to which the nuns readily assented. They became known as Redemptoristines.

Falcoia then proposed that Alphonsus organize a new congregation of missionary priests who would minister to the peasants of rural areas. Thus the Congregation of the Most Holy Redeemer—known as Redemptorists—was born in November of 1732. Alphonsus and his followers became known for the effectiveness of their missions. They focused their work on Naples and the surrounding areas, and preached a message of reconciliation and Christian love.

In the 1750s, Alphonsus began to concentrate on his writing. His work, based on the earlier writings of St. Thomas Aquinas, gave us many of the theological positions which the Church holds today. He clarified, for example, the elements of mortal sin: that the sinner must have full awareness of the matter, that he or she must give full consent, and that it must be a serious matter. Alphonsus was also widely known for his work in moral theology, particularly on the position of probabilism.

Pope Clement XIII appointed Alphonsus as bishop of a small diocese near Naples in 1762. Reluctantly, the saint accepted the appointment and brought the same zeal to this ministry which he had applied to all of his endeavors. He immediately reformed abuses among the clergy, organized general missions for his people and established programs for assisting the poor of the diocese.

The last few years of his life brought Alphonsus into a period of intense interior trial, a "dark night of the soul." He was beset by temptations and every tenet of his faith was shaken. This torment lasted for eighteen months with only brief periods of light and relief. When it finally ended, Alphonsus entered a period of ecstasies, prophetic visions, and the ability to perform miracles.

Alphonsus Liguori died on August 1, 1787. He was canonized in 1839 and declared a doctor of the Church in 1871. He is the patron of vocations, of moral theologians, and of confessors.

Alphonsus' message today: This saint achieved much in his lifetime by applying the talents which God gave him to the tasks at hand. Often, we become overwhelmed by the responsibilities facing us, and a daunting task might bring us to a standstill. Attacking the problem one piece at a time could help us to work wonders.

Do you hesitate to begin a project because of its seeming enormity? Say a prayer to St. Alphonsus, then just dig in!

AUGUST 4–MEMORIAL

John Vianney, Priest: 1786–1859

John Vianney was born in a village near Lyons, France, shortly before the French Revolution. His parents, poor farmers, were devout Catholics and brought up their son to be the same.

John received minimal schooling while working as a shepherd on his family farm, and he longed for more education. From an early age, he developed a desire to become a priest. At about the age of eighteen, he voiced the idea of a priestly vocation to his father, who immediately discouraged him. John was a great help on the farm, and his father could neither afford to lose him, nor finance his education for the priesthood. Yet John did not give up on his dream.

About two years later, John received permission to attend a lower seminary which had been established in a neighboring village by the Abbé Balley, a priest who was to play a major role in John's formation. With John's meager background, learning came very hard to him, and he struggled with his subjects, particularly Latin. During the summer, on a sixty-mile pilgrimage to the shrine of St. John Francis Regis, he sought God's help in becoming a priest. While his studies became no easier, the deep discouragement which John had felt was lifted from him and his goal was reaffirmed.

After years of hard work, John was finally ordained in 1815, and his first assignment was as the assistant pastor for his mentor, Abbé Balley. In this position, his reputation as a confessor began to grow and many sought him as a spiritual advisor. But in 1817, Abbé Balley passed away, and the following year, John was made curé (pastor) of his own small parish in the village of Ars-en-Dombes.

In these years, Abbé John's spiritual gifts began manifesting themselves and his fame as a confessor spread. Drawing people from the region and beyond, the priest would spend twelve to sixteen hours a day in the confessional rather than turn anyone away. The curé had an insight into the souls of his penitents, and on many occasions, would remind them of sins which they had forgotten or how many years it had been since their last confession.

Similarly, he had insight into the future. A widowed noblewoman who had never met the curé traveled to seek his advice when her eighteen-year-old son wished to marry a fifteen-year-old girl. Arriving at his church, she found it packed to the doors with people. Despairing of a chance to speak with him, she was about to leave when John came out of the confessional, walked straight up to her and said, "Let them marry. They will be very happy!"

A small shrine dedicated to St. Philomena was installed by John at his church soon after his arrival, which attracted many pilgrims. There many miraculous cures took place. John also helped to open a shelter and school for homeless girls in Ars. There, too, many unusual occurrences would come about, for example, more than enough food to feed the girls produced from an almost bare larder or the exact amount of money found to pay an important bill.

John Vianney, who was known as the Curé d'Ars, died on August 4, 1859. Even on his deathbed, he called penitents to him to finish hearing their confessions. St. John Vianney was canonized in 1925 by Pope Pius XI. He is the patron of parish priests.

John's message today: John kept the vision of what he wanted firmly in his mind and prayed often that he would achieve his goal. After many disappointments, he experienced success. His formula was simple and one that is available to us today: dedicate yourself completely to your goal and try to minimize distractions.

Do you become distracted from your goal? Have you tried concentrating on your goal in prayer? Anything is possible with God's help.

Dominic, Priest: 1170–1221

The son of the warden of a small town in Spain and Blessed Joan of Aza, Dominic was educated by his mother until about his fourteenth birthday. At that time, Dominic entered the school of Palencia, and studied to become a priest. Upon ordination, he stayed with the community of priests from the school, living under the rule of St. Augustine.

Dominic had been appointed a canon of the cathedral at Osma while still a student and continued in these duties after ordination. When Diego d'Azevedo, the prior of the community, was named bishop of Osma, Dominic was chosen his successor at the age of thirty-one.

In 1204, Bishop Diego was sent to Denmark by the King of Castile, and he asked Dominic to accompany him. En route, they passed through a town in France which was beset by the Albigensian heresy (this heresy held that the body and all material things were evil, therefore they denied the incarnation of Jesus). Dominic, feeling kindness toward their host who professed this heresy, spent the whole night in discussion with him. As a result, the man rejected the heresy. It is commonly thought that this was when Dominic recognized what God's work for him was to be.

Upon return from their mission, Diego and Dominic went to Rome seeking the pope's permission to preach the gospel in Russia. Instead the pope asked them to return to Spain and oppose the heresy there. During this time, Dominic took the first steps toward establishing a preaching order to become known as the Dominicans (officially, the Order of Preachers).

Dominic himself was a very persuasive preacher and ultimately can be credited with stemming the tide of the Albigensian heresy. He later sent his preachers out to other lands, and once more requested permission to preach in Russia. But the pope asked Dominic, now greatly respected throughout the Church, to effect reforms among several orders living in Rome at that time.

One story told about Dominic occurred during this latter stay in Rome. The nephew of a cardinal, a boy named Napoleon, was thrown from his horse and killed. The saint ordered the body to be brought into the house where he offered Mass. Following this, he arranged the bruised limbs of the body, then knelt down to pray. When he arose, he made the sign of the cross over the body and called out, "Napoleon, I say to you in the name of our Lord Jesus Christ, arise." In that instant, in the sight of all, the young man arose with no signs of any injuries.

Dominic was known not only as a great preacher, but as a gentle, charitable, and humble person. In 1220, he visited Bologna and halted construction of a priory for his friars when he judged it too stately and not consistent with his idea of poverty. Indeed, when he died on August 6, 1221, he died in a brother priest's bed because he had none of his own.

When Gregory IX canonized Dominic in 1234, he said that he no more doubted the sanctity of Dominic than he did that of Sts. Peter and Paul. St. Dominic is the patron of astronomers.

Dominic's message today: Dominic had great faith in God. With this gift, he was able to turn back a heresy and perform miracles. God has given the same gift to each of us and if we strengthen that faith, anything is possible. As Jesus told us, "If you have faith, nothing will be impossible for you" (Mt 17:20).

Are you working to make your faith grow strong? Prayer, attendance at Mass, and frequent reception of the sacraments will help you to move mountains, if you so desire.

Lawrence, Deacon and Martyr: died c. 258

Lawrence was appointed a deacon under Pope St. Sixtus II. It was Lawrence's job to handle the treasury, distribute alms to the poor, and take care of the sick, of which more than 1000 were under the care of the Church at this time.

In 257, Emperor Valerian issued an edict against all Christians. A year later, Pope Sixtus was arrested and led off to be executed. It is written that Lawrence followed the Pope, weeping, and asked him, "Father, where are you going without your deacon?" The pope replied, "I do not leave you, my son. You shall soon follow me." Lawrence was overjoyed to think that God would soon call him.

The deacon set out to find the poor, the widows, the orphans, and all others whom the Church had been caring for. He distributed to them all of the money which he had and even sold the chalices and other sacred vessels of the Church in order to increase the amount which he could give to the unfortunates.

The prefect of Rome, hearing of Lawrence's charity, sent for Lawrence and demanded that the treasures of the Church be handed over to him. Lawrence promised that he would hand over these treasures, but needed time to assemble and inventory them. He was granted three days.

On the third day, Lawrence had assembled hundreds of poor, the old, the lame, the blind, lepers, widows, and orphans. Then, going to the prefect, he presented the assembled as the treasures of the Church. The prefect failed to see the humor in this, and sentenced Lawrence to death. He ordered a large grill to be constructed and placed over hot coals so that Lawrence would die a slow and painful death.

When Lawrence had been on the grill for some time, apparently feeling no pain, he is said to have told his persecutors, "You can turn me over now; I'm done on this side." After his death, his great faith led to the immediate conversion of several Roman senators who took up his body and buried it on the Via Tiburtina. There a church was later built in his honor.

St. Lawrence is the patron of Rome, of the poor, and, perhaps with a hint of his own humor, cooks.

Lawrence's message today: We sometimes have a tendency to take ourselves too seriously, and forget that God has the ultimate sense of humor. We too are blessed with this gift, and should manage the sufferings which we experience with the best possible grace.

Are you able to use a bit of humor when navigating through life's trials?

Clare, Virgin: 1193–1253

Clare was born into the house of Offreduccio, a powerful noble family in Assisi. According to the mores of the time, her mother, Ortolana, raised Clare and her sisters in a strict, almost cloistered environment until they were of marriageable age.

When Clare was eighteen, St. Francis came to preach the lenten sermons at her church. These had a profound effect on her. She sought out the saint and asked him how she could live in the manner of the gospels. Francis spoke to Clare about leaving worldly ways behind and growing in love for God.

On Palm Sunday night in the year 1212, Clare ran away from home. She went about a mile out of town to the Portiuncula where St. Francis lived with his community of friars. There the saint and his brothers met Clare at the chapel of Our Lady and led her to the altar, where Francis cut her hair. Clare then exchanged her fine clothes for a penitential habit. In effect, this was the founding moment of the Order of Poor Clares, the second Franciscan order.

At first, her family was vehemently opposed to Clare's choice. But seeing her determination and her absolute devotion to Christ, they accepted her decision. Francis sent Clare to the nunnery of Sant' Angelo di Panzo, where her younger sister, Agnes, soon joined her. Eventually, Francis established a convent next to the church of San Damiano with Clare as superior. They were joined there by many other women, including Clare's mother. This convent was to become (and still is) the motherhouse of the Poor Clares.

The community practiced a life of extreme poverty and austerities, similar to the Franciscans. According to Clare's wishes, they were not to own property, either in common or individually, and were to rely only on daily almsgiving for their sustenance. The Poor Clares prayed constantly, and kept a cloister-like existence. (It had been said by Francis himself that Clare never left the walls of San Damiano.)

Clare was given many gifts by God, and stories of the miraculous cures which she affected abound. The toll for the austerities which Clare imposed on herself was high, and she became an invalid for at least the last third of her life. During this time, however, her miracles never ceased. Once, when San Damiano and the city of Assisi were under attack by the Saracens, Clare had her sisters carry her to the door of the convent. There she prayed that her convent and the city be spared. Shortly after, for no apparent reason, the Saracens lifted the siege and left without doing any damage.

Clare also had St. Francis' way with animals. One story tells of a time when Clare, confined to her bed, wished to have a certain small cloth brought to her. Since all of her sisters were at prayer, there was no one available to carry the cloth to her. At that moment, a little cat which lived in the monastery started to drag the cloth to her. Clare gently chided the cat, "O naughty one, you don't know how to carry it. Why do you drag it along the ground?" At those words, the cat began to roll up the cloth and brought Clare the cloth in its mouth so that it no longer touched the floor.

Clare of Assisi was a great inspiration to many in her lifetime, including popes and bishops, and is still an inspiration to us today.

Clare's message today: Clare's faith was ignited in her teens by a spark from the lenten sermons of St. Francis. We never know when someone or something we see or hear might be a spark which God is sending into our lives.

Are you listening for God's call in your life? Will you be ready when it comes?

Pontian, Pope and Martyr, and Hippolytus, Priest and Martyr: died c. 235

One could not find two saints more opposite than Pontian and Hippolytus, pope and anti-pope. Yet these two suffered martyrdom in the same place and under the same circumstances, and share a feast day.

Hippolytus was a priest in Rome who, with his followers, felt that even orthodox teaching and practice in the Church was not strict enough. In a bold gesture, Hippolytus censured Pope Zephyrinus for not coming down hard enough on heresy. At the same time, Hippolytus accused the pope of being under the influence of his deacon, Callistus. Upon the death of Zephyrinus, Callistus was chosen as his successor. This angered Hippolytus and his followers, who soon accused Callistus of being too lenient with sinners. His disciples then proceeded to elect Hippolytus as their pope, and he served in the role of antipope for eighteen years. His tenure lasted through three popes, the last of whom was Pontian.

Although at times, he came close to crossing over the line into heresy, Hippolytus was certainly one of the most important theologians in the first three centuries of the Church. He was a prolific writer, and it is from his *Church Order* that all of the eucharistic prayers which we use in the Church today are derived.

Pontian was elected pope in 230. Very little is known of his pontificate other than that he called a synod in Rome to denounce a heresy which had spread into the Church in Alexandria.

When the emperor Maximinus came to power in 235, he began a new persecution of Christians. Hippolytus was banished to the mines in Sardinia, as was Pontian; it was here that the two men, pope and antipope, finally met. Before his death, Hippolytus was reconciled to the Church, perhaps through the influence of Pontian.

Pontian and Hippolytus' message today: Hippolytus tended to judge sinners harshly while the popes whom he opposed treated them with compassion. Yet Hippolytus reconciled with God before he suffered martyrdom. Today, it is a compassionate God whom we believe in.

Do you tend to rush to judgment on others? Before you do judge another, ask yourself: what would Jesus say or do in this situation?

Maximilian Kolbe, Priest and Martyr: 1894–1941

M ost often, we think of martyrs as those who suffered for their faith during the the early days of the Church. Yet Maximilian Kolbe was a martyr in our own century.

Maximilian was the prior of the largest friary in the world, which was located at Niepokalanow, a small village near Warsaw in Poland. When World War II began in 1939, Hitler's army quickly overran Czechoslovakia, then Poland. The friary was turned into a deportation camp for refugees, political prisoners, and Jews. Yet Kolbe and the few priests remaining with him saw this as an opportunity to conduct a ministry to the sick and terrorized prisoners.

Under the Nazis, priests were expected to preach what the Nazis told them and to keep the people submissive. But Kolbe could not subscribe to this dictate. Arrested in February, 1941, he was found guilty of writing unapproved materials and sentenced to Auschwitz, the infamous Nazi concentration camp.

Like other prisoners who were not scheduled for immediate execution, Maximilian was assigned to a labor detail. One time, Maximilian collapsed under a heavy load. He was kicked and beaten by the guards, then shoved into a ditch and left for dead. Another prisoner somehow got Maximilian to the camp hospital where he miraculously survived and regained his strength. After his recovery, Maximilian was assigned to another barracks and work detail. He continued his ministry, offering encouragement and the little food which was his ration to his fellow prisoners.

In the camps, prisoners who tried to escape—if caught—were subjected to a slow and agonizing death as a lesson to others. If a prisoner was successful in an escape attempt, the Nazis would usually select several of his or her barracks mates to die. This happened in Maximilian Kolbe's barracks, and ten of his fellow prisoners were chosen to be starved to death in a bunker. One of these cried out, "My poor wife! My poor children! What are they to do?"

Hearing this, Kolbe stepped up to the commandant and offered to die in the man's place. Approaching the commandant was unheard of and could, of itself, bring a death sentence. But the Nazi officer accepted his offer. Maximilian marched off with the other prisoners to the windowless bunker where all food and water were cut off. Normally, those assigned to die in the starvation bunker could be heard throughout the camp wailing and crying in despair and attacking one another. This time, those in the camp heard singing from the bunker.

Maximilian Kolbe was the last of the prisoners to die. On August 14, 1941, when the Nazis needed the bunker for another batch of prisoners, a doctor, several SS troops, and another prisoner went into the bunker. Kolbe, barely alive, was sitting against the wall with a smile on his face, as if seeing some distant vision. The doctor injected him with a poison and, in a moment, Father Maximilian Kolbe was dead, still with a smile on his face.

Maximilian Kolbe was canonized on October 10, 1982. We celebrate his memorial on the date of his death.

Maximilian's message today: Maximilian Kolbe was a twentieth-century martyr who gave up his life for another. In many ways, we all suffer as martyrs in some form. Think of those with AIDS or cancer, or those who have undergone a traumatic change in their lives such as death or divorce. It is how we approach this suffering, this martyrdom, which counts.

The next time some seemingly intolerable event takes place in your life, try to assume an attitude of acceptance and perhaps find some good in what has occurred.

Stephen of Hungary: 975–1038

Stephen, called Vaik at birth, was the son of Geza, the leader of the Magyars, a fierce tribe which had settled into the land that is now Hungary. Geza deemed it politically expedient to become Christian, therefore, he, his family, and his nobles were baptized in 985. While Geza and the nobles were Christian largely in name only, Stephen became a practicing Christian.

In 997, Stephen succeeded his father as leader of the Magyars. One of his first undertakings was to put down rebellions among rival tribal leaders so that he could assume leadership of all Hungary. Having overcome the warring tribes in the region, Stephen then sent St. Astrik, whom he had designated Hungary's first archbishop, to Rome to request an ecclesiastic organization for Hungary. Stephen also asked the pope to grant him the title of king in order to solidify his position among the tribes of Hungary. The pope granted both requests and sent back a crown, which Stephen officially received on Christmas Day, 1001.

Over the next several years, Stephen established episcopal sees throughout his country and was a strong force in promoting the Church in Hungary. He abolished pagan practices and ordered that every person, except priests and religious, should marry.

Stephen built a church in his capital city in which all later kings were to be crowned and buried. He further ordered that every tenth town would build a church and that all people tithe to support the Church and the poor. Stephen himself was strong in his support of the poor. While he made himself accessible to all of his people, he was especially attentive to the needs of the poor.

Stephen instituted a just code of laws, based on Christian principles, to govern his people. Although meant to improve living conditions for all people, it made enemies for Stephen among those who were less fervent Christians. Nevertheless, Stephen was successful in bringing the Magyars together as one people and establishing the independent kingdom of Hungary.

Stephen's only son, Blessed Emeric, was to have succeeded his father as king, but was killed in a hunting accident in 1031. A series of intrigues and squabbles around the succession to the throne followed. Stephen's nephews attempted to kill him, and his sister, Gisela, seeking the throne for her son, plotted to that end. Stephen himself was plagued by illness during the last years of his life.

Stephen died on the feast of the Assumption in 1038, and he was canonized by Pope Gregory VII in 1083.

Stephen's message today: Stephen recognized that he had obligations reaching far beyond governing his people, and used Christian principles to create an environment of change. We, too, can use our Christianity to better the lives of those around us.

What opportunities do you see for Christian service in your neighborhood? Parish? Community?

Jane Frances de Chantal: 1572–1641

D aughter of the president of the Burgundy parliament, Jane
Frances was born in Dijon, France. At the age of twenty, she
married Baron Christopher de Chantal. The couple had seven children, three of whom died in infancy.

Jane reestablished the custom of daily Mass in her castle residence and engaged in numerous charitable works. When her husband died in a hunting accident in 1601, Jane Frances sank into a
depression. She and her children moved into her father-in-law's
house when he threatened to disinherit her children. Despite his
oppressiveness, she managed to regain her cheerfulness and raise
her children in a happy atmosphere.

When she was about thirty-two, Jane heard St. Francis de Sales
preach and recognized him from a vision which she had earlier
seen. Greatly affected by his words, she convinced him to become
her spiritual director. Jane indicated her desire to enter the
Carmelites, but Francis de Sales convinced her that this was not
her calling. A few years later, however, he explained to her his
concept for a new congregation which he wished to found. This
order would be open to women who, because of health, age, or
other circumstances, could not enter the established orders. This
order would undertake spiritual and corporal works of mercy and
exemplify the virtues shown by Mary at the Visitation.

Jane made provisions for her children's care. She then, along
with three other women, formed the first community of Visitation
nuns. It was for Jane and her nuns that St. Francis de Sales wrote
his great spiritual classic *On the Love of God*. In the remaining three
decades of her life, Jane was active in spreading the order over all ·
of France; more than sixty houses were founded in her lifetime.

During the last years of her life, Jane suffered a spiritual dryness. She told St. Vincent de Paul that her mind was so filled with

all sorts of temptations that she had to strive not to look within herself. Despite this, St. Vincent noted that "her face never lost its serenity, nor did she once relax in the fidelity God asked of her. And so I regard her as one of the holiest souls I have ever met on this earth."

Jane Frances overcame these cares and worries by losing herself in God. "To live no more in oneself, but lost in God, is the most sublime perfection which the soul can reach," was Jane Frances' advice to those with misgivings and concerns.

St. Jane Frances de Chantal died on December 13, 1641 and was canonized in 1767.

Jane's message today: All of us experience spiritual dryness at some point in our lives, a time when God seems to have abandoned us. Jane's advice, "to live no more in oneself, but lost in God," offers wise words of counsel. We can persevere, as she did, in our faith life despite not feeling connected to God.

Do you remain faithful to God even when life is routine and you feel a lack of spirituality in your daily existence? Remember that God doesn't turn away from you at any time.

AUGUST 19–OPTIONAL MEMORIAL

John Eudes, Priest: 1601–1680

John's early training came from the Jesuits, but his own interest was in the Congregation of the Oratory, a group of secular priests who took no vows, but had a common goal of reinvigorating the spiritual life of their communities. John was ordained in 1625 and celebrated his first Mass on Christmas Day that year.

Almost immediately, John became seriously ill and was not able to preach the missions which the Oratorians were noted for. He was finally able to fully join the Congregation after a year of recovery and retreat and several more months of study.

Shortly after his recovery, a letter from his father informed him of a plague that had struck his native region in Normandy. John sought and, after some delay, received permission to go to Normandy to minister to the sick, the dying, and their families. His ministry was most welcome because many of the priests in the region had fled the area to avoid the plague.

When the plague had been eradicated, John was directed to the Oratorian house in Caen to continue his preparation for conducting missions. But in 1631, John's relatively quiet life was disturbed when a plague hit Caen. Once again, the priest turned his attention to the sick, and together with some Jesuits and Capuchins, established a hospital for the plague victims. When the superior of the Oratorians, a priest who had been John's mentor some years before, visited Caen and discovered that his protégé had not yet been sent out to do missions, he urged that to happen. Thus John Eudes began a long preaching career which was to include 110 missions.

While working in Caen, one of John's works had been to find temporary homes for prostitutes who were returning to God's graces. As he was passing one of these homes, the woman with whom he had placed some of these women demanded of him, "Where are you off to now? To some church, I suppose, where you'll gaze at the images and think yourself pious. And, all the time, what is really wanted of you is a decent home for these poor creatures who are being lost for want of attention and guidance." Her words deeply troubled John and led him, in 1641, to establish a permanent facility for the women. The Visitandine nuns later took on this ministry as their primary duty and formed the order of Sisters of Charity of the Refuge.

Meanwhile, John was not satisfied that he or the Oratorians were doing quite enough to train priests. Against much opposition, he left the order and formed the Congregation of Jesus and Mary in 1643. This new community was modeled after the

Oratorians, but placed more emphasis on training priests. To that end, John Eudes founded several seminaries for secular priests.

In 1670, the saint published *The Devotion to the Adorable Heart of Jesus,* a book which included a Mass and devotions to the Sacred Heart. The Mass was first celebrated on August 31, 1670 at one of the seminaries which he founded and was soon observed in other dioceses. Together with St. Margaret Mary Alacoque, St. John Eudes is credited with establishing the devotion to the Sacred Heart of Jesus.

St. John Eudes died on August 19, 1680 and his feast day is celebrated on that date.

John's message today: John ministered to the sick and to the fallen, conducted missions, founded religious orders, and established new devotions. When he felt overwhelmed by all the tasks he had taken on, he prayed for help from God and found new strength in that grace.

Do you stick with a mission until you feel satisfied that your share of the task is completed? Whom do you turn to when you feel overburdened by the demands in your life?

AUGUST 20—MEMORIAL

Bernard of Clairvaux, Abbot and Doctor: 1090-1153

Bernard, the third son of seven children of a noble family, was born at the family castle near Dijon. Upon the death of his mother and after a misspent youth, Bernard decided to lead a religious life.

In 1112, he persuaded thirty-one of his friends and relatives (including his brothers) to go with him to the Cistercian monastery at Cîteaux. This community, which followed a very strict

Benedictine rule, had been on the verge of dying out when Bernard arrived. With his help, the group recovered its vitality and, in 1115, Bernard was sent to open a new monastery at what was later to be called Clairvaux. This monastery was to become the motherhouse of sixty-eight Cistercian monasteries.

Bernard was noted for his wisdom and the eloquence of his preaching. He was often consulted by rulers and popes and soon became one of the most powerful influences in Europe. He led the successful struggle to support the legitimacy of Pope Innocent II's election against the claims of an antipope, and was the leader in gaining Lothaire II's acceptance as Emperor.

In 1142, Peter Bernard Paganelli, whom Bernard had brought to Clairvaux as a postulant, was chosen as pope, taking the name Eugene III. Three years later, Pope Eugene asked Bernard to preach against the Albigensian heresy growing in southern France. The next year, he was asked go throughout Europe to encourage a crusade against the Turks who had captured Edessa, one of the four principalities of Jerusalem, in 1144. Bernard succeeded in rallying all of Europe around the Second Crusade, which was headed by Emperor Conrad II and King Louis VII of France.

Bernard was given many other assignments by the pope and rulers and was certainly the dominant influence in religious and political affairs of the twelfth century. His works included, among other things, a treatise written for the guidance of Pope Eugene, more than three hundred sermons, and five hundred letters. Through all of this, Bernard's greatest desire was to return to the strict monastic life of his youth. He had a great devotion to Mary and to the Baby Jesus, fostered by a vision, which he had experienced in his youth, of the divine birth. He said, "In dangers, in doubts, in difficulties, think of Mary, call upon Mary: under her protection, you have nothing to fear; if she walks with you, you shall not grow weary; if she shows you favor, you shall reach the goal."

St. Bernard, called the "mellifluous Doctor" for his way with the spoken word, was canonized in 1174 and declared a Doctor of the

Church in 1830. He is considered the last of the Fathers of the Church. St. Bernard is the patron of chandlers (a person who makes or sells candles).

> **Bernard's message today:** Though Bernard was called upon to use his wisdom and counsel in world affairs, he had a great desire to lead a quiet contemplative life. He took on the missions assigned to him and completed them successfully while deeply grounded in his spiritual roots. In the turmoil of today's world, it is worthwhile taking some time to get back to basics, as Bernard did.

Though our lives are busier than ever these days, we too can keep a connection to the simple path to eternal life, as Bernard did. How can prayer help help you in this practice?

Pius X, Pope: 1835–1914

Born into a poor family and raised in the simple life, Guiseppe (Joseph) Sarto was an unlikely candidate for pope. Yet this pope changed some of the practices in the Church which had been around since the Middle Ages and faced down a government which sought to control Church affairs.

Joseph was the second of ten children of the local postman and cobbler in a small town in Veneto, Italy (near Venice). His parents could not afford a fine education for him, but with the encouragement of his parish priest and a scholarship, Joseph was able to continue his schooling. By a special dispensation, he was ordained a priest at the age of twenty-three. For several years thereafter, he worked at being a simple parish priest for his people.

In 1884, he was named a bishop and appointed to the diocese

of Mantua. At the time, this diocese had been rundown by widespread schism and indifferent clergy. Over the next few years, Bishop Sarto was successful in bringing his episcopacy back to the fold. Recognizing this accomplishment, Pope Leo XIII appointed him a cardinal and patriarch of Venice. Here, Joseph's simple tastes contrasted sharply with the pomp and majesty common to Venice.

After the death of Pope Leo XIII in 1903, the cardinal favored to replace him was vetoed by the Austrian emperor, a practice which was not unusual back then. Cardinal Sarto was then elected pope, and chose the name Pius X. One of his first acts as pope was to end the practice of civil leaders meddling in papal selections.

Pope Pius X began the codification of canon law and instituted changes in both the psalter and the breviary. He also simplified the papal court. Having a strong interest in politics himself, he encouraged Italian Catholics to become more actively involved in the affairs of their country. He encouraged the practice of daily communion when possible, and directed that children should be allowed to receive the Eucharist upon reaching the age of reason (seven).

Pope Pius X was noted for his charity. He sent relief missions to the scenes of many disasters and housed refugees at his own expense. He was so generous in providing assistance throughout the world that people wondered where all the money came from.

Throughout his pontificate, Pius X remained a man of simple tastes and one with a strong sense of concern for his people. After his death, a Church historian wrote that Pius was a man of God who knew the unhappiness of the world and the hardships of life, and in the greatness of his heart wanted to comfort everyone.

Pope Pius X had predicted the outbreak of World War I in the summer of 1914. When it occurred on the eleventh anniversary of his election as pope, it nevertheless dealt him a mortal blow. Pius became ill and died within a few days. In the final days of his life, he is reported to have said, "This is the last affliction that the Lord will visit on me. I would gladly give my life to save my poor children from this ghastly scourge."

Pius' message today: This saint recognized that receiving the body and blood of Christ at Mass is a great gift, and source of divine nourishment. He sought to make communion a part of everyone's life who was above the age of reason. By his life of charity and good works, Pius X further lived out Jesus' example for us.

Do you take advantage of the great gift of Eucharist as often as you possibly can? If you are waiting to be received into full communion in the church, pray for those who have fallen away from the practice of receiving Eucharist.

AUGUST 23–OPTIONAL MEMORIAL

Rose of Lima, Virgin: 1586–1617

Isabel de Santa Maria de Flores was the daughter of wealthy Spanish parents. Because of her beauty, she was called Rose by her parents and took this name at her confirmation.

Rose took St. Catherine of Siena as a model when she became an adult and practiced great austerities, even beyond what most ascetic saints carried out. For example, when her parents wished her to marry and a caller admired her beauty, she rubbed pepper on her face to disfigure it. Another time, when her fair skin was complimented, she applied lime to it, burning herself so severely that she was unable to dress herself for a month.

Though she refused her parents' enjoinders to marry, Rose was not disobedient to them in any other way. When an investment went bad for her parents, Rose worked all day in the garden and sewed late at night in order to help them. In response to their struggle to get her to marry, Rose became a Dominican tertiary and lived almost as a recluse in a small shed in the garden. There she experienced visions and mystical gifts. A group of priests and doctors called in to examine her concluded that these occurrences were of supernatural origin, and stories of her holiness spread throughout the city. When earthquakes struck in the area, her prayers were credited with sparing Lima.

Rose did not give herself up entirely to asceticism. She spent much of her time consoling the poor, the sick, the Indians, and slaves. For this she has come to be regarded as the originator of social service in Peru. Rose was so well known that when she died on August 24, 1617, senior officials of Peru and of Lima took turns carrying her casket to burial.

St. Rose of Lima was canonized in 1671 by Pope Clement X, the first saint of the Americas. She is the patroness of South America.

Rose's message today: All of us are called to help those less fortunate than ourselves, whether they be the poor, the sick, those uneducated in their faith—any person or group to which injustice has been done. While it may not be possible to help all of these people except through prayer, we can and should do what we can.

What are you doing to help those who need your help? Do you ever pray for guidance and opportunities to give of yourself to those in need?

AUGUST 24–FEAST

Bartholomew, Apostle: First Century

Most of our knowledge of Bartholomew comes down to us from early writers and from tradition. This apostle is often thought to be the apostle called "Nathanael" whom John refers to in his gospel, although the other evangelists refer to him as "Bartholomew."

While Bartholomew's home in Cana was several miles from the Sea of Galilee, it is most likely that he was a fisherman like many of his fellow apostles when Jesus chose him. John tells us that after the resurrection, Bartholomew was fishing with Peter and several other apostles when Jesus called to them from the shore and asked if they had caught any fish (Jn 21:2–14).

Tradition has Bartholomew preaching in Asia Minor and Armenia as well as India. He apparently joined his old friend, Philip, in Phyrgia for a short time around the year 58, having earlier preached in Armenia. The strongest evidence available about Bartholomew points to a mission in India where a copy of Matthew's Gospel, written in Hebrew and said to be carried to India by Bartholomew, was found hundreds of years later.

Bartholomew is said to have cured the insane daughter of the governor of a region in India and, by that act, received permission to preach in the region. When a later miracle by Bartholomew converted the governor and many of his people, the king, a brother of the governor, declared war on the new Christian community. The apostle was beaten and skinned alive, and finally beheaded. The dreadful means of his martyrdom explains why, in sacred art, Bartholomew is often depicted holding a knife in one hand with his skin draped over his other arm.

St. Bartholomew is the patron saint of plasterers.

Bartholomew's message today: Bartholomew traveled far to preach the word of God, risking his life in the process. Yet he persevered in his work, answering the call he had heard so long ago from Jesus.

When have you most strongly heard your call from God? If you have answered this call, where are some of the more risky places it has taken you?

Monica: 332–387

This saint's life demonstrated the effectiveness of persevering in prayer. She provides a model for parents whose children have drifted away from their family values and their Church.

Monica was born in Tagaste, North Africa and raised a Christian by her parents. When she was old enough to marry, her parents arranged a marriage with Patricius, a pagan who was also from Tagaste. Patricius was described as a man with good qualities, but having a raging temper and inclined to dissoluteness. Her mother-in-law, a quarrelsome woman, lived with them, as well. Though the early years of her marriage were a trial, Monica persisted in prayer for her husband and mother-in-law; eventually, they were converted to Christianity.

Monica and Patricius had three children, the oldest of whom became St. Augustine. Augustine showed much promise from his earliest days and his parents gave him the best education possible. But while he became a catechumen at an early age, Augustine drifted away from Christianity during his school years. About two years after the death of her husband, Monica was crushed to learn that he had taken up a life of immorality, and was caught up in the Manichaen heresy.

When Augustine returned to Tagaste to teach, she at first refused to let him into her house. But a vision caused her to relent when a voice told her to dry her tears, "Your son is with you." Monica continued to pray and fast for her son's spiritual health. She sought help from her priests and bishop whom she hoped could convince Augustine of his error. They recognized that such argument would have no effect on him in his state of mind. Her bishop sent her away gently with the words, "Go now, I beg of you; it is not possible that a son of so many tears should perish."

Augustine decided to move to Rome to teach when he was

twenty-nine, and Monica decided to follow him there. But by the time Monica reached Rome, her son had already moved on to Milan. In that city, Augustine fell under the influence of the bishop, St. Ambrose. When Monica finally arrived in Milan, Augustine announced that he no longer believed in the Manichaen heresy. Though this delighted Monica, he reminded her that he was not yet a Christian. She responded with patience that he would be before she died.

Monica also fell under the influence of St. Ambrose. When the bishop was in the midst of confronting the Arian Catholics, he was added to her prayers. Monica deferred to Ambrose's judgment on most matters, something that Augustine suspected would never happen with another bishop. When she found the rules on fasting in Milan different and confusing from the rules in Rome, Ambrose gave her the advice which has been shortened to "When in Rome, do as the Romans do."

Monica's prayers for Augustine were finally answered when he was baptized by St. Ambrose at the Easter Vigil in 387. Augustine, who had been living with a mistress and had fathered a son, declared that, henceforth, he would live a celibate life. Together with his mother and son, Augustine made plans to return to North Africa. Monica, though apparently in good health, knew that she would not return to her home. She spoke of her death and told Augustine, "Son, nothing in this world now affords me delight; all my hopes for this world have been fulfilled. All I wished to live for was that I might see you a Catholic and a child of heaven. God has granted me more than this."

A few days later, Monica became ill and died shortly after that. St. Monica is the patron of mothers and for those seeking perseverance in prayer.

Monica's message today: Monica provides an excellent example of the power of prayer. While it took several years before all of her prayers were answered, she died a happy woman, knowing that God had granted her wishes. We too can trust that God hears and answers all of our prayers, even though the response may not come exactly when we would like it to come or in exactly the way we would like.

When you are having difficulty in your prayer, ask St. Monica to intercede on your behalf, that you might receive the grace to persevere in prayer.

Augustine, Bishop and Doctor: 354–430

A ugustine was the eldest son of St. Monica and Patricius, a pagan Roman official. As a young man, he studied at the university at Carthage with the intent of becoming a lawyer, but gave up law to devote himself to literary pursuits. Along the way, he abandoned the Christian faith.

For about fifteen years, Augustine adopted the Manichean heresy. The Manichaens believed that evil was caused by an outside force, thus, people were relieved of guilt for their sins. Augustine lived with a mistress who bore him a son. He studied and taught rhetoric at Tagaste, Carthage, Rome, and Milan.

In Milan, Augustine was impressed by the sermons of St. Ambrose, the bishop of the city. His influence, as well as the prayers of his mother, brought him back to Christianity and he was baptized by Ambrose at the Easter Vigil in 387.

Later that year, Augustine set out to return to Tagaste accompanied by his mother and son. He planned to teach and to live a life of prayer and meditation in community. On the way, his mother died; two years later, his son died. Soon after, Augustine was ordained a priest at Hippo and three years later, became the Bishop of Hippo. Though he preferred the monastic life,

Augustine became the dominant figure in African church affairs, writing profusely, preaching, and defending the faith.

To this day, many of his two hundred treatises, some three hundred letters, and nearly four hundred sermons are of major importance in the study of theology and philosophy. His towering intellect has molded the thought of Western Christianity to such an extent that his ideas dominated the thinking of the western world for a thousand years after his death. He and Thomas Aquinas are considered to be the greatest intellects the Catholic Church has ever produced.

St. Augustine is the patron saint of brewers, printers, and theologians. His memorial is celebrated on the day following the memorial to his mother.

Augustine's message today: It took over thirty years for Augustine to recognize what God was calling him to do. When he accepted that call, he became one of the Church's greatest theologians. We all know people whose talents could be of great service to God if they were to acknowledge and embrace their calling. Are you one of those people?

Do you pray for those who might perform wonders if they turned their lives around? Or do you just dismiss these people?

SEPTEMBER

Vibiana, Virgin and Martyr: c. Third Century

In 1851, Pope Pius IX bought a vineyard located just outside of Rome. When ancient catacombs were discovered underneath the land, the pope directed the Pontifical Commission for Sacred Archeology to explore the vast underground network.

About two years later, an intact tomb was uncovered which was sealed by a marble tablet. When the tomb was opened, the skeleton of a young woman was discovered who had apparently died a violent death. The inscription on the tablet, while not revealing the exact year of her death, bore markings which indicated that the victim had been martyred. The wording, "To the soul of the innocent and pure Vibiana" also suggested that the young woman had died a virgin.

The pope ordered an investigation to authenticate the designation "virgin and martyr" for Vibiana. The favorable decision, just a few weeks later, led the pope to declare an "equivalent canonization" for this third-century servant of God. With canonization, a devotion soon developed in Rome to honor this saint. Pius IX was himself a leader in this veneration and took an active hand in spreading her devotion to the universal Church.

When Thaddeus Amat, the newly consecrated bishop of Monterey in California, was received by the pope on March 18, 1854, Pius IX presented the relics of St. Vibiana to him with instructions to build a cathedral in her honor. The bishop arrived in his diocese and carried the relics to Santa Barbara, where they were placed in a reliquary in Our Lady of Sorrows church. In 1856, Pius IX named Saint Vibiana as the principal patroness of the diocese of Monterey and designated a special feast day in her honor.

In August of 1863, a fire completely destroyed Our Lady of Sorrows church. The relics of Saint Vibiana, encased in a wax figure covered with silk, escaped unharmed. This apparently miraculous occurrence caused the devotion to this saint to spread even further. Since no provisions had been made in the new church for the relics, they were brought to Los Angeles where they were eventually installed in a new cathedral dedicated, in 1876, to Saint Vibiana's honor.

As the Catholic population of southern and central California grew, Los Angeles was established as a separate diocese (and later, as an archdiocese) with Saint Vibiana as its patron. The original cathedral named in her honor was closed in 1995 due to earthquake damage and a new cathedral commemorating the saint is planned.

An interesting story is told of this saint's intercession in recent years. A homeless man had found shelter in the cathedral for some time. Praying to the saint, he asked her intervention with God to improve his state. After a while, it is said, the homeless man won the lottery, moved to the Midwest, and turned his life around. Each year, on the saint's feast day, he returns to thank Saint Vibiana for her help and donates a substantial sum of money to the church to care for other homeless people.

Vibiana's message today: This saint is remarkable in that we know so little about her life and death. But what is striking is that, through her intercession with God, she has interceded on behalf of many people in our times, and helped those who need her assistance.

Perhaps Vibiana can inspire you to help someone who has need of your service. Ask her to seek direction for you.

Gregory the Great, Pope and Doctor: 540–604

Now best known for the chants which take his name, Pope Gregory contributed much to the Church. Born and raised in a patrician family at a time when the Roman Empire was disintegrating, Gregory began his career as a public official. At the age of thirty, the Lombard invasion came alarmingly near Rome. Gregory, who was then prefect of Rome, the highest civil office in the city, showed some of the wisdom and leadership that were to characterize him later and helped to avert the invasion.

Gregory felt a higher calling, however, and eventually left civil service to devote himself to God. Though he was one of the richest men in Rome, Gregory gave up his wealth and turned his house into a monastery under the patronage of St. Andrew. Shortly after, the pope ordained him as a deacon and sent him as ambassador to the emperor's court in Constantinople.

Recalled to Rome around 586, Gregory returned to the monastic life and was soon elected abbot of his community. In 590, a terrible plague hit Rome, and among its victims was the pope. Gregory was immediately and unanimously elected pope, and consecrated on September 3, 590.

Soon after becoming pope, Gregory wrote the *Regula Pastoralis,* a work that addresses the office of a bishop. In it, he declared that a bishop should, first and foremost, be a physician of souls whose chief duties are preaching and the enforcement of discipline. The work was an immediate success, and for hundreds of years provided the guidance for the pastoral mission of a bishop.

In temporal affairs as well, Gregory filled a huge void. The Lombards had continued their aggressive move into Italy and no help was forthcoming from Constantinople. When, in 593, they reached the gates of Rome, it was not the prefect or the military which went out to meet them, but Pope Gregory. The pope persuaded the Lombard king to withdraw his army. Some years later, when his efforts to effect a settlement between the emperor and the Lombards failed, Gregory negotiated his own treaty with the Lombard king which finally left Rome and its surrounding districts in peace.

As pope, Gregory introduced many reforms in the Church, and preached often on the scriptural readings of the day. Many of his homilies still exist. In addition to the many sermons and letters which he wrote, in 593, he published *Dialogues,* a collection of visions, tales, prophecies, and miracles gathered from oral tradition. This was one of the most popular books of the Middle Ages.

Gregory was canonized a saint by acclamation almost immediately after his death. For all of his works, only a few of which have been mentioned here, he has been called St. Gregory the Great. He is the patron of singers. We celebrate his memorial on the anniversary of the date on which he was consecrated as pope.

Gregory's message today: Gregory would have preferred the quietude of the monastic life. But God had other plans for Gregory. Sometimes we are called upon to minister in ways which are not ones which we would choose for ourselves. If this is what God is calling us to do, we must respond with our best efforts just a Gregory did.

Has God given you talents to be used in his service? Are you responding to God's call or are you trying to ignore it?

Adrian, Martyr: died c. 304

Adrian, the first of several saints by that name, was a pagan officer at the imperial court in Nicomedia. Impressed by the courage of a group of Christians who were being tortured during the persecution of Emperor Diocletian, he declared himself to be a Christian and was imprisoned with them.

Adrian's wife Natalia, who was also a Christian, bribed her way into the prison to take care of him and the others. He suffered excruciating tortures before being put to death, and was ordered killed by having all of his limbs broken and his hands and feet cut off. Natalia was present at his death and comforted him in his agony.

Shortly after the executions, the Romans piled up the bodies of the martyrs to be burned. Rain extinguished the fire, however, allowing the Christians of Nicomedia to gather up the relics of the martyrs for burial. Natalia recovered one of Adrian's severed hands and fled with it to Argyropolis near Constantinople, in order to escape an imperial official who wanted to marry her. She died there soon after and was buried with the martyrs.

St. Adrian is a patron of soldiers and of butchers.

Adrian's message today: Here is a saint who won his faith by observing how Christian martyrs conducted themselves in the face of torture and death. Their example was enough to convert Adrian to a belief in God.

Do you set an example by your faith for those who observe you? Do they look to you as a model of Christian living?

Peter Claver, Priest: 1580–1654

Born in Spain, Peter was educated at the University of Barcelona. After graduating about the year 1601, he resolved to join the Society of Jesus and received his early training at the Jesuit college in Palma, Majorca. Peter soon declared his desire to minister to those most in need in the New World, and in 1610, left Spain for Cartagena in what is now Colombia. Completing his studies in the New World, Peter was ordained in Cartagena in 1615.

During this time, Cartagena was a major center for slavery, with ten thousand slaves arriving in the port every year from West Africa. Forced to live on board under the most horrible conditions, the trip generally killed more than one third of the slaves who had originally set out. Upon arrival in Colombia, the survivors were herded into cattle pens where they were put on display until they were shipped out to the mines or to estates.

Peter realized that these slaves were those most in need of his help. The priest would go aboard each arriving slave ship and take care of the sick and the dying in the stinking holds. As the slaves were moved out to the pens, he went among them with medicine, food, brandy, tobacco, and lemons.

To be able to converse with the slaves, Peter had a corps of interpreters who were familiar with many of the African dialects. Through these translators and the use of pictures, he preached God's love to the slaves. He instilled a sense of self-worth in them as God's creatures and taught them that they must not abuse that love by sin. In his forty years of ministering to the slaves, he is said to have baptized more than 300,000 of them. Once, when a comment was made to him on his saintliness for working in the unspeakable conditions among the slaves, he attributed this to his lack of sensibility: "If being a saint consists of having no taste and having a strong stomach, I admit that I may be one."

Peter also went out to the plantations to minister to the slaves there and insure that they were being dealt with in accordance with the law. Whenever possible on these treks, he avoided the hospitality of the plantation owners and lived in the slave quarters. Peter had declared himself "the slave of the slaves forever."

Beyond his ministry to the slaves, each week Peter would visit the two hospitals of Cartagena where he is said to have worked miraculous cures among the sick and dying. Peter also worked with condemned prisoners. During his lifetime in Cartagena, no prisoner was executed there without the priest being present to console him.

Peter became ill during a journey to the plantations in 1650 and returned to Cartagena to recover. A viral epidemic struck that city during his recovery, and Peter was hit hard by the disease. While he recovered from this, he was disabled for the remainder of his life. The remaining few years of his life were spent in his cell, ignored and largely forgotten.

Peter Claver died on September 8th, which is also the day we celebrate the birth of Mary. The civil authorities and other clergy who had looked skeptically on his concern for slaves now showered honors upon him. They ordered that he have a great funeral and be buried at public expense. The slaves themselves also arranged for a Mass to be said in his honor.

St. Peter Claver was canonized in 1888 and was declared the patron of all missionary work among blacks by Pope Leo XIII.

Peter's message today: Peter found that his call was to work among the most unfortunate of people: slaves, the seriously ill, and prisoners. Not all of us have the "strong stomach" which Peter had for this type of work, but we can offer our support to those who work among these groups by our prayers and financial offerings.

What is your gut reaction to the undesirables in our society today? Do you pray for them, turn away in revulsion, or help?

John Chrysostom, Bishop and Doctor: 349–407

Born the son of an imperial military officer, John studied rhetoric and theology under the best Roman scholars before converting to Christianity in 369. John preferred the simple life of a monk, and in 374, he became a hermit under the guidance of St. Basil. The austere life undermined his health, however, and he was forced to return home.

John became a deacon in 381 and was ordained in 386 by the bishop of Antioch, whom he served for the next twelve years. It was during this time that his reputation for preaching began to spread. John became noted for the eloquence of his sermons which earned him the surname Chrysostom, meaning "golden mouth." In his sermons, John often called for justice and charity, enjoining the rich to share their wealth with the poor.

In 397, John became the object of an imperial ruse to make him the Archbishop of Constantinople, then the greatest city in the Roman empire. It was known that if the popular preacher were to leave Antioch there would be a general uproar by the people. So the emperor's agent came to Antioch, and secretly asked John to accompany him out of the city to the tombs of the martyrs. Once outside the city, John was delivered to an imperial officer who took him straight to Constantinople, where he was consecrated bishop in 398.

John immediately instituted reforms in his own household by cutting down on the expenses of the office. The sums which were saved in this manner were applied to hospitals and for the relief of the poor. John's preaching and Christian practice gained him many enemies, both in the imperial court and among less worthy bishops. In 403, Theophilus, Archbishop of Alexandria (who had desired the see in Constantinople when John was named archbishop) came to Constantinople and convened a council of thirty-six bishops. Here a list of false and frivolous charges was drawn up against John and handed over to the emperor, who then ordered John to be exiled.

Soon after John left Constantinople, an earthquake struck. This so unnerved the empress Eudoxia, who had been the object of some of John's sermons and the instigator of his exile, that she implored the emperor to return John to his see.

Some time later, public games were held at the dedication of a statue of Eudoxia in front of a church. John once again spoke out against the evils sponsored by the empress; this time, Eudoxia had enough of John. At her instigation, he was driven into final exile in 404 and died in 407.

St. John Chrysostom is the patron saint of preachers and orators.

John's message today: Taking an unpopular view is certain to gain enemies. Yet John, like many other saints, spoke out against the excesses of his time. Most people in our times would shy away from pointing out the immoral positions of certain groups.

Do you speak out against injustice? Do you write to the editor when your paper publishes stories slanted toward immoral views?

SEPTEMBER 16–MEMORIAL

Cornelius, Pope and Martyr, and Cyprian, Bishop and Martyr: Third Century

Cornelius, Bishop of Rome (another name for the pope), and Cyprian, Bishop of Carthage, were friends who guided the Church through a difficult period. It was during their time that differences concerning penance split the church into factions, and the persecution of Christians reached its most violent peak.

Cornelius was elected pope a year after Pope St. Fabian was martyred by the Emperor Decius in 250. During a brief lull in persecutions, the schism regarding the forgiveness of sin arose. A priest who was a leader among Roman priests, Novatian, set himself up against Cornelius and declared himself Bishop of Rome, in effect becoming the first antipope. Novatian claimed that the Church did not have the power to forgive apostasy—the sin of giving up one's faith, not uncommon during the persecutions—and certain other sins, no matter how repentant the sinner might be.

Cornelius felt that repentant apostates, after appropriate penance, should be readmitted to the Church. In this he had the support of most of the bishops, including his friend, Cyprian. But before the conflict could be resolved, Cornelius was exiled by the Emperor Gallus when persecution of Christians began anew in 253, and died in that year. Cyprian wrote to Cornelius shortly before his death, congratulating him that he was able to suffer for Christ. Cyprian also noted that, in this persecution, not a single Roman Christian had apostatized from the Church.

Cyprian, known as Thascius Cyprianus, was an orator, a teacher, and a lawyer who did not become a Christian until he was middle-aged. Upon his conversion, Cyprian began a comprehensive study of Scripture and the works of religious writers. He became a strong advocate of the faith, and turned his speaking and writing talents to this work. A short time later, Cyprian became a priest and, in 248, was named bishop of Carthage.

The schism that faced Cyprian was quite the opposite of the one which his friend Cornelius faced. Novatus, a priest who had opposed the naming of Cyprian as bishop, openly accepted all apostates with no penance whatsoever. Cyprian was a strong supporter of Pope Cornelius, both as supreme pontiff and as a defender of the Church against Novatian's heresy. He also denounced Novatus and, together with Cornelius, steered a middle line between the opposing heresies of Novatian and Novatus.

In the years between 252 and 254, a plague ravaged Carthage. With kindness and courage, vigor and steadiness, Cyprian urged his people to care for everyone, even their enemies and persecutors. Much was accomplished in this regard under his leadership. The wealthier people gave money for the care of the plague victims, while those who were not as well off gave of their time.

Under the first edict of Valerian, the Christian persecution reached Africa in the year 257. Cyprian was sent into exile. When he refused to sacrifice to the Roman gods, Cyprian was sentenced to death. A great crowd of his supporters followed Cyprian to his place of execution. After his death, they carried his body off for burial in a triumphant parade of candles and torches.

Cornelius and Cyprian's message today: These two saints faced the same type of situations that exist in our Church today. There are those who believe the Church has become too liberal and others who take the opposite stand. We sometimes forget that this is a universal Church and as such, there is room for opposing views.

Jesus never turned away anyone who accepted him as the Savior. Can you accept and love those members of your community with whom you disagree?

SEPTEMBER 17–OPTIONAL MEMORIAL

Robert Bellarmine, Bishop and Doctor: 1542–1621

Robert demonstrated a remarkable precociousness as a young child, writing Latin verses, playing the violin, and knowledgably discussing many subjects. The rector of the Jesuit school which he attended as a teenager described Robert as "the best of our school, and not far from heaven."

Despite opposition from his father, Robert entered the Jesuits where he was ordained in 1570. Before and after ordination he devoted himself to the study and teaching of Church history and the Fathers of the Church. He later became famous for his treatises on these and other subjects.

Bellarmine became theologian to Pope Clement VIII and was named a cardinal by that pope in 1598. Even with these honors, Robert lived an austere life, eating only the food available to the poor and using the hangings of his Vatican apartments to clothe the needy. During this period, he prepared two catechisms for Clement VIII which had a great impact on the church and remained in use into modern times.

In 1602, Robert Bellarmine was named archbishop of Capua, his only pastoral assignment. Setting aside his books, the great scholar went about his duties with the zeal of a much younger man. Alban Butler tells us that, "He preached constantly, he made visitations, he catechized the children, and he won the love of all classes." As he had at the Vatican, he also cared for the poor, supplying their needs to the best of his ability.

Three years later, a new pope, Paul V, recalled the cardinal to Rome to be his advisor. In this position, Bellarmine was in the center of many controversies, ranging from the defense of the Church's rights to formulating a response to two books written by King James I. The first of these books put forth arguments which would have required priests in England to take an oath of allegiance to the king. The second book denied the pope's authority over the Church in England. Although he wrote a brilliant defense, the cardinal could not satisfy the extremists on either side of the controversy.

Robert Bellarmine was friendly with Galileo Galilei, who dedicated one of his books to him. In 1616, the cardinal was directed to admonish the great astronomer. His admonition, which Galileo accepted with good grace, was simply that Galileo not put forward any theories which had not yet been proven (although he could present his ideas as hypotheses).

Controversy followed him even after his death. His beatification was stalled by a school of theologians who disagreed with some of Bellarmine's views. St. Robert Bellermine was canonized in 1930 and declared a Doctor of the Church in 1931.

Robert's message today: Robert Bellermine was a brilliant man who produced many works that are still studied today. At the same time, he was a simple man who took seriously his duties as a Christian and a bishop: to feed the hungry, clothe the needy, and tend to the flock. We all have the same obligation to take seriously our duties as Christians.

What do you see as your Christian responsibilities? How willing are you to carry these out each day?

Januarius, Bishop and Martyr: Fourth Century

A ccording to tradition, Januarius was born in Naples, Italy and was Bishop of Benevento at the time that the persecution under the emperor Diocletian began. After four of his followers were jailed for confessing their faith, the bishop visited them in prison to offer comfort and encouragement. When this was reported to the governor of Campania in whose state the prisoners were held, he was himself arrested together with his deacon and a lector from his church.

All of the prisoners were condemned to be thrown to wild beasts. When this happened, none of the animals would harm them. While the witnesses were amazed, they attributed this occurrence to magic. Januarius and his followers were then condemned to be beheaded. This sentence was carried out at Pozzuoli, a small town near Naples, where the martyrs were then buried.

St. Januarius is especially venerated in Naples where his relics are retained in the cathedral. His blood is kept in a glass vial encased in a silver reliquary, and it liquefies on various feast days during the year. Although this has occurred for 500 years, and no one doubts its occurrence or can explain the phenomenon, there is not universal belief that this is a miracle.

St. Januarius is the patron of blood banks.

Januarius' message today: At great risk to his own safety, Januarius visited those of his people who were being held in prison awaiting death. By this act, he comforted them and strengthened their faith. One of the corporal works of mercy which Christians perform is visiting those in prison who need our comfort and strength.

Have you ever visited a prison? Find out if there is a prison ministry in your parish or in a neighboring one.

Andrew Kim Taegon, Priest and Martyr: 1821–1846

This saint and his companions, over one hundred in number, represent the thousands of martyrs who died for their faith in Korea during the nineteenth century. Most of these martyrs were laypersons.

Korea is unique among missionary countries because Christianity sprang up in this country before any missionaries arrived there. Although Korea was a closed society, some Christian books found their way into the country during the eighteenth century. Educated Koreans studied these books and many became believers. On a diplomatic mission to Peking in 1784, one of these believers sought and received baptism. Ten years later, when a Chinese priest came into Korea, he found over 4,000 Christians there, none of whom had ever had any contact with a priest. A few years later, the number had grown to 10,000.

A French bishop and two French priests entered the country in disguise in 1837. Working in secrecy, they ministered to the Catholic community in Korea for two years before they suffered martyrdom. The bishop, Msgr. Laurence Imbert, wrote of the hardships involved with this ministry. Rising at 2:30 AM, they would call the people to prayer, baptize and confirm any converts, and celebrate Mass, all before sunrise so the people could return to their homes under cover of darkness. During the day, they would hear confessions. After two days in the same house, they would move on to the next house after dark. There they would get what little sleep they could before starting the process all over again. The bishop wrote, "You will understand that, leading a life like this, we scarcely fear the sword stroke that may end it at any time."

The sword stroke came for these three when they surrendered themselves to the Korean authorities, in order to avoid a general massacre of Christians. They were tortured, then beheaded in Seoul on September 21, 1839.

Andrew Kim, whose father, Ignatius Kim, was martyred along with him, was the first native-born Catholic priest in Korea. He was tortured and beheaded at Seoul while trying to smuggle missionaries into Korea.

Today, there are almost two million Catholics in Korea. While there is now freedom of religion in South Korea, the persecution of Christians continues today in North Korea.

Andrew's message today: Although Christians are still persecuted today in other parts of the world, few endure martyrdom now. What strong faith these Christians in Korea had to endure the suffering and death they experienced.

Would your faith be strong enough to stand up to torture and death if that were to be your fate?

Matthew, Apostle and Evangelist: First Century

Matthew was probably born in Galilee and was a publican tax collector at Capernaum at the time that Jesus called him. While a tax collector was a rich man, he was no more admired in ancient times than an IRS agent is admired today. The fact that Jesus chose a tax collector as a disciple shows us that he was bringing the Good News not just to the Gentiles and Jews, but also to the rejected people of society.

Matthew was one of the twelve apostles, and the second gospel is attributed to him. His gospel was written sometime between the years 60 and 90, most likely in Aramaic. (The historian Papias records in 130 that Matthew wrote the *Logia,* presumably our gospel, "in the Hebrew tongue"). The gospel which we now have came to us in Greek and, at the very least, is a thorough and substantial revision of the original Aramaic, of which no traces have ever been found.

Without question, the gospel credited to Matthew was written by a Jewish Christian of Palestinian origins for Jewish Christians. The goal of Matthew's gospel was to convince the Jewish people that Jesus was the Messiah, that the old covenant between God and the Jewish people was being replaced by a new covenant through Jesus, and that everyone, not just the Jewish people, was included in God's plan for salvation.

Of the four evangelists, only Matthew presents Jesus as a second Moses, as a lawgiver. To the Jews of that time, the law was paramount and Matthew strove to represent Jesus as the fulfillment of Scripture. He gives an account of Jesus' lineage and draws several parallels between events in the lives of Moses and of Jesus. In his account of Jesus' birth, for example, Matthew tells how Herod's jealousy and hatred forced Joseph to take his family into exile in Egypt. In this way, Jesus, like Moses, came out of Egypt to save his people.

According to tradition, Matthew preached in Judea, then went to the East and to Ethiopia where he suffered martyrdom, according to the Roman martyrology. Another legend has Matthew martyred in Persia.

St. Matthew is the patron saint of accountants, bankers, and bookkeepers.

Matthew's message today: Matthew builds a logical case for Jesus as the Messiah to the Jewish people. In writing this Gospel, he shows a broad knowledge of what we today call the Old Testament. We all need to develop a familiarity with Scripture if we are to understand the basics of our faith.

Do you read Scripture on a daily basis? Have you considered joining a Bible study group?

Thomas of Villanova, Bishop: 1488–1555

Born in Fuentellana in the kingdom of Castile, Spain, Thomas received his early education in Villanueva de los Infantes, the home of his parents and the place from which his surname is derived. He received a masters degree in art and a licentiate in theology at the University of Alcala while still in his teens, and became a professor of philosophy there at the age of twenty-six.

In 1516, Thomas was offered the chair of philosophy at the University of Salamanca, but chose instead to enter the Augustinian order in that city. Ordained in 1518, Thomas devoted himself to the work of his ministry with such zeal that he later became known as "the apostle of Spain." He was noted for the austerity and poverty of his life and for his generosity to the poor and needy. As a priest, Thomas continued to teach within his order. His classes proved so popular that students in the university sought to attend his lectures.

In later years, Thomas served as prior of several monasteries and as provincial of Andalusia and Castile. He sent the first Augustinian missionaries to the New World (to Mexico) in 1533. Thomas was named Archbishop of Valencia in 1544. While he had previously declined the archbishopric of Granada and appealed this appointment as well, he was ultimately obligated to take it.

Thomas proceeded on foot to Valencia. On his arrival there, he spent several days in prayer in an Augustinian friary, asking for God's grace and guidance in his new duties. In Valencia, the archbishop continued his charities and his austere life. Once, as he was mending his old habit (which he had received as a young Augustinian friar), an aide asked him why he didn't pay a tailor a small trifle to sew it for him. Thomas replied that he was still a friar and that a trifle could be better used to feed the poor.

During the eleven years that Thomas was archbishop, he fed several hundred poor every day and cared for many needy orphans. To encourage his people to bring abandoned children to him, he gave a reward for each foundling. When pirates had plundered a town in his diocese, he sent money to ransom the captives.

In September of 1555, Thomas suffered a heart attack. Sensing that he was near death, he ordered that all of the money in his possession be distributed among the poor. Even the bed on which he lay dying was to be given to the jail for use by a prisoner when

Thomas no longer had need of it.

St. Thomas of Villanova is honored on this date by the Augustinian order and by the students in the many schools which bear his name.

Thomas' message today: Thomas had many great gifts, including a brilliant intellect, wise leadership, and a love for the needy. Yet he was exceedingly humble in his work and in his deeds. We can all practice humility in our daily lives, accompanied by a sense of love for those who need our care and concern.

Do you ever get carried away by your own importance?

SEPTEMBER 26–OPTIONAL MEMORIAL

Cosmas and Damian, Martyrs:
Early Fourth Century

According to legend, Cosmas and Damian were twin brothers born in Arabia. They studied medicine in Syria and later became widely known for their medical skills which they offered, without charge, to all. Because of their charities, they were known in their time as the "moneyless ones." They gained the love and respect of the people to whom they ministered, both for their medical assistance and the zeal of their Christian faith.

During the persecution under the emperor Diocletian, Cosmas and Damian, together with three brothers, Anthimus, Leontius, and Euprepius, were arrested, tried, and beheaded for their faith. Over the years following their deaths, many people reported miracles that occurred in the names of Cosmas and Damian. Among them was the emperor Justinian I, who attributed his cure from a serious illness to these saints. In thankfulness, the emperor enlarged a church which had been built on the site of the saints' burial place.

Cosmas and Damian are patrons of physicians and surgeons, along with St. Luke.

Cosmas and Damian's message today: These two brothers completely accepted and lived the Christian life. This was particularly exemplified by their unselfish behavior in caring for the sick. We are not asked to give nearly so much of ourselves as Cosmas and Damian did, but we are asked to give something.

Think about volunteering some of your time to a local hospital or nursing home.

Vincent de Paul, Priest: 1581–1660

Vincent was born at Pouy, France in 1581, the third of six children. His parents, who were poor farmers, recognized his potential and were determined to give him a good education. He was educated at the college at Dax and at the University of Toulouse, then ordained at the early age of twenty.

While not a lot is known about this period in his life, we do know that in 1605, while on a trip to Marseilles, Vincent was captured by pirates and sold into slavery in North Africa. Following his escape from Tunisia in 1607, he became chaplain to the Queen of France and tutor to the children of the Count de Joigny.

At this point in his life, by his own telling, Vincent's ambition was little more than to have a comfortable life. Certainly, there was no sign of the great things which Vincent was to accomplish in later years. Called upon to hear the deathbed confession of a peasant in 1617, however, he became aware of the spiritual needs of the poor people of France. Vincent began preaching to the poor and soon left the house of his patron to become pastor of a church. There he instructed the people in the necessity of repentance, and converted many from a scandalous life style.

The following years brought wide renown to Vincent de Paul. He became noted for his work among the poor, and was a chaplain to galley slaves waiting to be shipped abroad. In 1625, with the help of his former patron, the Count de Joigny, Vincent founded the Congregation of the Missions (known today as the Vincentians), an order devoted to work among the peasants. In 1633, along with Saint Louise de Marillac, he founded the Sisters of Charity.

In his lifetime, Vincent de Paul established hospitals, orphanages, and seminaries; ransomed slaves in northern Africa; sent his priests abroad to preach missions; and organized far-flung relief among victims of war. It is remarkable that one man, without the advantages of birth and fortune so necessary for success in those times, could achieve so much.

Saint Vincent de Paul suffered from ill health in his later years and died quietly while sitting in his chair at the age of 80 on September 27, 1660. He was canonized by Pope Clement XII in 1737 and declared the patron of all charitable groups by Pope Leo XIII.

Vincent's message today: Even though he was ordained a priest at an early age, it took an awakening event for Vincent to recognize what God was calling him to do. The same may be true for many of us, no matter what age we are. God may be asking us to do something as simple as praying for our neighbor. On the other hand, God may be asking us to do much more.

God calls each one of us to be of service, in ways both great and small. What is it that you are being called to do?

Wenceslaus, Martyr: c. 907–930

Wenceslaus was born into the royal family of Bohemia (Czech Republic in modern times), and was raised a Christian by his grandmother, St. Ludmila. At this time, Christianity was not widespread throughout the land; indeed, most of the nobility were very much against it.

In 925, he assumed the throne shortly after the death of his father. Wenceslaus announced that he would support God's law and endeavor to rule with justice and mercy. The severity with which he punished oppression by the nobility, as well as the friendly relations which he established with Germany, raised bitter opposition against Wenceslaus. He was betrayed by his brother, Boleslaus, and other nobles and was assassinated in 930 while on his way to attend Mass.

While the carol which we sing at Christmas time honors his name, there is no evidence to support the particular deeds with which he is credited in that tune. In fact, the carol was written in England sometime during the seventeenth century.

St. Wenceslaus is the patron of the Czech Republic.

Wenceslaus' message today: Being a just and merciful ruler has never been an easy task—not when surrounded by the sycophants who are attracted to those in positions of leadership. Nevertheless, being just and merciful is exactly what our Christian beliefs call on us to do.

If you are a leader or a manager, how do you treat your employees? With justice? With mercy?

Michael, Gabriel, and Raphael: Archangels

The Revelation of St. John tells us that Michael led the heavenly hosts that cast Satan and his followers out of heaven. He was also regarded in the early Church as the protector of Christians against the devil. Appropriately, he is the patron saint of infantry, paratroopers, mariners, and police.

Gabriel was the archangel who was God's messenger. He was mentioned twice as such in the Old Testament (Book of Daniel), but is more prominently known in two New Testament passages. He foretells the birth of John the Baptist to Zechariah (Lk 1: 11–20), and proclaims the birth of Jesus to Mary (Lk 1:26–38). Gabriel is the patron of messengers, postal workers, and those working in various telecommunications fields.

Raphael is the only other archangel identified by name. One of the seven archangels who stand before the Lord, Raphael was sent by God to minister to Tobias and his family (Book of Tobit). He also is the angel who healed the earth when it was defiled by the sins of the fallen angels (Enoch 10:7). Raphael is the patron of physicians, nurses, travelers, the blind, and lovers.

The three archangels are honored together with a memorial on September 29. This date was formerly St. Michael's feast day and has been known for centuries as Michaelmas Day.

The archangels' message today: In Christian tradition, angels are sent by God to guide, guard, and heal us. They also inform people of a particular mission from God. There has been a renewed interest in angels in the past few years as more and more people seek out ways to better communicate with God.

How do you regard the idea of angels? Where do they fit in with your overall spirituality?

Jerome, Priest and Doctor: 340-420

Jerome was born in Dalmatia and studied in Rome under the famous pagan grammarian, Donatus. There he acquired great skill and knowledge of Latin, Greek, and the important classical authors.

Baptized by Pope Liberius in 360, Jerome then joined a group of scholars working under St. Valerian. He later continued his studies while living as an ascetic in the Syrian desert for several years. Ordained by St. Paulinus in 377, Jerome began an active career of study and writing and immediately jumped into the controversy surrounding the Meletian schism.

In 382, Jerome went to Rome with Paulinus and stayed to become the secretary to Pope Damasus. At Damasus' suggestion, he undertook the revision of the Latin version of the four gospels, as well as Paul's epistles and the psalms. During this period, Jerome made numerous enemies by his fiery attacks on pagan life and on certain influential Romans. Following the death of Damasus, his enemies drove him out of Rome and he settled in Bethlehem. There he headed a monastery and continued his writings, but remained involved in many controversies. In one case, he even attacked St. Augustine who questioned his views.

Jerome's greatest achievements were his translation of the Old Testament from Hebrew and his revision of the Latin version of the New Testament. This version, known as the Vulgate, became the official Latin version, and almost all English translations of the Bible came from it until the middle of the twentieth century.

Jerome was often irascible and sarcastic, and he never hesitated to direct that sarcasm at those who disagreed with his views. He was, however, precisely the instrument whom God needed to combat the many schisms and heresies which arose within this period of Church history. From this, Jerome is venerated as a Doctor of the Church.

Jerome's message today: Jerome's personality was not like the calm, placid saintliness we usually associate with holy people. Yet he surely practiced gospel living in his willingness to speak out against heresy and immorality. Jerome had a powerful understanding of the message contained in Scripture, which gave him a rare measure of authority to defend the Word of God.

Choose one book of the New Testament, and become familiar with it. You may enjoy this so much that you'll undertake another book, and another.

OCTOBER

Thérèse of the Child Jesus, Virgin: 1873–1897

St. Thérèse of the Child Jesus—also known as St. Thérèse of Lisieux and the "Little Flower"—was born Marie-Françoise-Thérèse Martin in Alençon, France on January 2, 1873. She was the youngest of five surviving children, all girls, of Louis and Azélie-Marie Martin.

Thérèse had a happy childhood, surrounded by good influences. She wrote that her earliest memories were "of smiles and tender caresses." When her mother died in 1877, her father sold his watchmaking business and moved the family to Lisieux so that the children could be near an aunt who would help to raise them. Mary, an older sister, ran the household and Pauline, the eldest, took charge of the family's religious training.

When Thérèse was nine, Pauline entered the Carmelite convent at Lisieux, something that Thérèse also longed to do. Mary entered the same convent when Thérèse was nearly fourteen. It was at this time that Thérèse experienced her first vision of the baby Jesus.

During the next few months, Thérèse made known her wish to enter the Carmelite convent. While her father agreed, the Carmelites and the bishop felt that, at fourteen, she was too young. Shortly thereafter, when her father took Thérèse on a pilgrimage to Rome, she boldly spoke up at a general audience with the pope and sought his permission to enter the convent. "You shall enter if it be God's will," Pope Leo XIII told her in kindly dismissal.

Some time later, the bishop gave her permission to enter. Only fifteen, Thérèse joined her two sisters in the Carmelite convent in April, 1888. (A fourth sister, Céline, also entered the convent a few years later after the death of their father.) In the convent, Thérèse was content with the life of hard work and prayer. "I prefer the monotony of obscure sacrifice to all ecstasies. To pick up a pin for love can convert a soul," she said, echoing her way of life.

Thérèse's superiors, one of whom was her sister Pauline, recognized the saintliness of this humble girl and directed her to write her autobiography. This book, *L'histoire d'une Ame (The Story of a Soul),* was instantly successful, and is still read and loved throughout the world.

During Holy Week in the year 1896, Thérèse took ill. Over the next eighteen months, her disease worsened and she died on September 30, 1897 at the age of twenty-four. Shortly before that she wrote, "I want to spend my heaven doing good on earth." She also said that "After my death I will let fall a shower of roses," a prophecy that has become a sign of the saint's intercession even to our own time.

Due to her popularity and the miracles which were attributed to her soon after her death, the Holy See dispensed with the period of fifty years which ordinarily elapses before the beatification process may begin. Pope Pius XI beatified her in 1923 and declared her a saint in 1925.

St. Thérèse of the Child Jesus is the patroness of all foreign missions and of all works for Russia. She is also a patroness of aviators.

Thérèse's message today: "To pick up a pin for love can convert a soul." Thérèse understood that anything we do for another in God's name is done for love. Even in doing the most humble and mundane of chores, Thérèse was serving God in the most magnificent manner. We too can dedicate our daily tasks to God and do them with love.

Do you go about your daily tasks with joy or do you complain about what you are asked to do?

Guardian Angels

According to long-standing tradition, each one of us has a guardian angel appointed by God to guard us and help us in our journey toward heaven. While this belief is not a defining tenet of our faith, and therefore not something that Catholics must believe, it has been the teaching of theologians for centuries.

From Scripture, we know of seven archangels, particularly Gabriel, Michael, and Raphael. Angels are mentioned many other times in both the Old and New Testaments. It was an angel of the Lord who released the apostles from prison when the Pharisees had arrested them (Acts 5:19). It was also an angel who later released Peter from prison; in this incident we find an indication of the belief which the early Christians had in guardian angels. After his release, when Peter came to the place where the disciples were praying, they did not believe at first that it was him. The disciples exclaimed, "It is his angel" (Acts 12:15).

Most often, we think of angels as messengers from God, for example, the angel who came to St. Joseph several times. Guardian angels are a little different. Their role is to guide us and inspire us, but they cannot command us. Instead, they exert influence over us by suggesting what we should (or should not) be doing and generally protecting us from evil. Some believe that this pure spirit is what we often call our conscience.

On this date, we honor all guardian angels who look out for us.

The Guardian Angels' message today: Tradition teaches that our guardian angel is with us all of the time and can help us in our daily lives. Here is a popular prayer to guardian angels which children learn and say each day:

Angel of God, my guardian dear,
To whom God's love commits me here,
Ever this day be at my side,
To light, to guard, to rule, and guide. Amen.

Francis of Assisi: 1182–1226

Born the son of a wealthy merchant, Francis spent his youth in extravagant living and pleasure-seeking. Although he was wont to lavishly spend his money, he was also generous. Francis never refused a beggar who asked for alms in the name of God.

When a war broke out between the cities of Assisi and Perugia about the year 1200, Francis was taken prisoner and held for a year. Upon his release, he was stricken by a long and serious illness which he bore with great patience. Francis recovered and for a while returned to his former way of life, but found that he no longer had the heart for it.

At one point, he heard a voice from heaven which told him "to serve the master rather than the man." While Francis did not immediately recognize what he was being called to, he began to devote himself to a life of poverty, and care of the sick and poor. For this he was angrily denounced by his father and disinherited.

Francis had a vision of Christ who told him to "build up my house, for it is nearly falling down." Seeing this call first in the physical sense, Francis rebuilt several churches in Assisi which had fallen into disrepair. Eventually, Francis saw a deeper meaning in Christ's words.

Many people were attracted to the simple way of life espoused by Francis, and he founded the Order of Friars Minor (Franciscans) in 1209. Within a few years, his order had spread over the Alps to France, Spain, Germany, and Hungary. In 1219, he sent missionaries to Tunis and Morocco, and he himself went to Egypt to evangelize the Mohammedans. Though he met with the Sultan at Damietta, Egypt, which was then under siege by Crusaders, his mission was a failure.

At Christmas, 1223, Francis built a crèche at Grecchia, Italy, and thus popularized a custom observed all over the Christian world to the present day. In September of the following year, Francis received the *stigmata*, where his feet, hands, and left side were marked as were Jesus' during his passion and death.

Though never ordained, Francis had an enormous impact on religious life. Probably no saint has affected so many people in so many different ways. Francis of Assisi, born to wealth, devoted his life to poverty and delighted in God's works as revealed in nature. Alban Butler, in writing of St. Francis two centuries ago, said that "he is the one saint whom, in our day, all non-Catholics have agreed in canonizing."

St. Francis of Assisi is the patron of Italy. He is also the advocate for Catholic Action and the protector of merchants.

Francis' message today: This saint discovered the "selfless secret" which is made clear in his prayer, "It is in giving that we receive; in loving that we are loved." Francis received much and was loved greatly, for he himself gave generously and loved abundantly.

Do you recognize that giving of your time reaps tremendous rewards? That loving the unloved will bring love back to you many times over?

Bruno, Priest: 1035–1101

Bruno was born in Cologne, and sent to Rheims at an early age for his education. When this was completed, he returned to his home in Cologne where he was ordained and made canon of the collegiate church of St. Cunibert.

In 1056, while still a young man, Bruno was offered a professorship at his school in Rheims. For over eighteen years, Bruno taught "the most advanced and the learned, not young clerics." After his term as teacher, Bruno was appointed chancellor of the diocese by the archbishop, Manasses, a man who was less than worthy of high clerical office. Bruno and others testified against him at a council called in 1076 to judge his fitness, but Manasses refused to appear. When he learned of the testimony against him, however, Manasses had the houses of Bruno and the others sacked and their possessions sold.

This incident strengthened a resolve which Bruno had considered earlier, that is, to give up all of his material goods and take up the life of a hermit. Eventually, Bruno and a small group of friends resigned their positions and proceeded to Grenoble. There, with the help of St. Hugh, bishop of Grenoble, they established themselves in the almost inaccessible high desert of Chartreuse. The monks were called Carthusians, which was derived from the place of their settlement. They built a church and cells for themselves and began to live the simple life which Bruno had prescribed.

The life of the Carthusians centered around prayer and work. Twice a day, the monks gathered for prayer in the church. At other hours they prayed in their cells. Except on major feasts, they had no more than one meal per day which they ate in their cells. The monks' principal work was to copy books and the income from this labor provided the meager subsistence on which they lived.

Even in this reclusive life, the fame of Bruno and of the

Carthusians spread. Other monasteries opened as the order grew. St. Hugh, who had helped Bruno to establish the first monastery, was so impressed by him that he took him as his spiritual director. Hugh often made the long, difficult journey to Chartreuse to visit with Bruno and seek his advice and guidance.

One of Bruno's pupils from the school in Rheims, Eudes de Châtillon, became Pope Urban II. Hearing of Bruno's holiness and knowing from personal experience of his wisdom, the pope summoned Bruno to Rome to assist him in governing the Church. As the pope's advisor, Bruno advised Urban in his reform of the clergy. Urban wished to name Bruno archbishop of Reggio in Calabria, but Bruno demurred with such resolution that the pope did not press him. The pope permitted Bruno to retire to the solitary life in Calabria which was close to Rome.

Bruno died on October 6, 1101. He was never formally canonized since, following his example, the Carthusians shunned any occasion for publicity. In 1514, however, the Carthusians sought and received from Pope Leo X permission to observe his feast. Pope Clement X later extended this observance to the whole Western Church.

Bruno's message today: In our times, it is difficult to conceive of anyone with even a trifle of fame to shun publicity. Bruno was an eminent scholar, sought after by popes, yet he retained his humility and his simple life. Much good can be done in the world if we forgo seeking credit.

Go about quietly doing good for someone whom you know can use your help.

Simeon: First Century

As Luke tells us in his gospel, this saint was the first to recognize Jesus as the Messiah. A righteous and devout man, Simeon was "looking forward to the consolation of Israel, and the Holy Spirit was upon him" (Lk 2:25). The Spirit made known to Simeon that he would see the Messiah of the Lord before his death. When Mary and Joseph brought Jesus to be presented at the temple, the Spirit prompted Simeon to be there.

Taking the infant Jesus in his arms and praising God, Simeon uttered the words which have come to be known as the Canticle of Simeon, or the *Nunc Dimittis,* sung in the evening prayers at monasteries worldwide.

Master,
now you are dismissing your servant in peace,
according to your word;
for my eyes have seen your salvation,
which you have prepared in the presence of all peoples,
a light for revelation to the Gentiles
and for glory to your people Israel. (Lk 2:29–32)

Simeon then blessed Mary and Joseph and said to her, "This child is destined for the falling and the rising of many in Israel, and to be a sign that will be opposed so that the inner thoughts of many will be revealed—and a sword will pierce your own soul too" (Lk 2:34–35).

This is all we know of St. Simeon. While his feast is not on the liturgical calendar, he is honored in some communities on this date.

Simeon's message today: Imagine holding the infant Jesus, and knowing that this is the promised Messiah from God. With that experience, we could all likely write poetry as marvelous as the Canticle of Simeon. Yet in truth, we hold Jesus each time we receive the Eucharist.

How do you feel when you receive Jesus in the Eucharist? Does it make you want to write poetry? To sing? To offer praise and thanksgiving?

Denis, Bishop and Martyr: died c. 258

There has been more than a little confusion about this saint. Due to an accident of history, the story of St. Denis (sometimes known as Dionysius of Paris) has been mingled with that of St. Dionysius the Areopagite, and Denis' life has been placed anywhere from the first century to the third century. What follows seems to be the story of St. Denis who was the bishop of Paris.

In the year 250, Bishop Denis and six others were sent to Gaul as missionaries. Together with a priest and a deacon, St. Rusticus and St. Eleutherius, Denis made his way to Paris. The men established themselves on an island in the Seine where they began preaching, but they were so effective in their evangelizing that they were arrested during Decius' persecution of Christians.

After a long imprisonment, the three were beheaded and their bodies thrown into the Seine. Recovered by their converts, the bodies were given a Christian burial. Later, a chapel was built over their tomb which became the site of the abbey of St. Denis.

St. Denis is known as the "apostle of France" and is the patron of that country. This memorial honors St. Denis and his companions in martyrdom.

Denis' message today: While little is known of St. Denis, it is apparent that he and his companions were not afraid to speak out for their Christian faith. Even today, we can be called upon to defend the principles of our faith when it is attacked by others.

Do you know enough about your faith to defend it in the face of attacks?

Teresa of Avila, Virgin and Doctor: 1515–1582

Teresa, sometimes known as Teresa of Jesus, was born in Avila in Castile, Spain. She was one of nine children of Don Alonzo Sanchez de Cepeda and his second wife, Doña Beatrice Davila y Ahumada. Teresa wrote of her large family that "all, through the goodness of God, were like our parents in being virtuous, except myself."

At the age of seven, Teresa was already intrigued by the lives of the saints. She and a younger brother, Rodrigo, decided that the easiest way to become a saint was to be martyred, since martyrs seemed to have bought heaven very cheaply by their sufferings. With that in mind, the two young children set off from home to travel to Morocco where, they were certain, they would be martyred and thus become saints. An uncle found them not too far from home and returned them to their frightened mother.

After attending school in an Augustinian convent, Teresa became a Carmelite nun in 1536. At that time, the convent parlor acted as the social center of the town. Many of the townspeople would come to the convent on Sunday afternoons; they and the nuns would sit in the parlor and discuss the issues of the day. Teresa participated in this and enjoyed it for some time, even to the point of giving up much of her prayer and meditation.

Teresa eventually came to believe that the Carmelite order was too relaxed, and began to fight for reforms. In that regard, she founded the St. Joseph Convent in Avila and several other convents in Spain for nuns who wished to live a cloistered life. These nuns came to be known as the Discalced Carmelites for the sandals they wore (as opposed to the shoes which the other nuns wore). With St. John of the Cross, Teresa also founded a similar monastery for men.

Teresa chose her novices in a way which might seem strange to us. Before considering their piety, Teresa wanted to know about their intelligence and common sense. A person could train herself to piety, she felt, but not to good judgment. "May God preserve us from stupid nuns!" she exclaimed.

In her efforts to effect reform within the Carmelites, Teresa traveled all over Spain and wrote many letters and books which are regarded as classics of spiritual literature. Her book, *Way of Perfection*, was written for the guidance of her nuns, and *Foundations* was written for their encouragement. Her book, *Interior Castle*, explains the contemplative life for the layperson.

Though a contemplative, Teresa managed to successfully blend a highly active life with spiritual meditation. She was a popular person who combined charm and wit with humility and courtesy, so that even her enemies respected her.

St. Teresa was declared a Doctor of the Church in 1970 by Pope Paul VI, the first woman so honored.

Teresa's message today: What a magnificent combination of characteristics this saint possessed: charm, wit, humility, courtesy, all combined with sanctity. Too often, we picture cloistered nuns as rather grim, but Teresa shows us that this does not have to be. We too should maintain a cheerful demeanor even as we practice penance and sacrifice.

How well do you succeed at keeping time for quiet prayer and meditation a part of your daily life?

Margaret Mary Alacoque, Virgin: 1647–1690

The widespread devotion to the Sacred Heart of Jesus celebrated in the Church today can be directly attributed to St. Margaret Mary Alacoque. In a period of time when religious devotion in France was, at best, cool, this unlikely saint was charged by Jesus with strengthening the love of God in the people.

Born the fifth of seven children to the family of an official in Burgundy, Margaret was a good child. When she was about eight, her father died and Margaret was sent to school in a convent run by the Poor Clare nuns. It was at this time that she began to be attracted to a religious vocation. The nuns, impressed with her piety, allowed her to make her first communion at the age of nine (at that point in time, children were generally not allowed to receive communion).

At the age of twenty, Margaret had a vision of Jesus which made her determined to follow Christ, and she entered a convent of the Visitation nuns. At the time this order had two classes of nuns. The choir nuns were the cultivated, educated nuns who did the teaching and sang in the choir, while the lay nuns were the unschooled women who did the menial chores in the convent. Margaret Mary was a part of this second group. Hers was not an easy life, and she suffered the scorn and ridicule of some of the learned nuns because of her piety. Strongly devoted to Christ, Margaret Mary accepted her suffering in the name of Jesus.

On December 27, 1673, Margaret Mary received the first of the revelations which she was to have. At that time, Jesus told her that the love of his heart must grow and that she was to be the person to make this known to humanity. In later revelations, he said that his heart was to be represented in the image of the Sacred Heart which we are familiar with today. Jesus also told her that as far as she was able, she was to atone for mankind's ingratitude for his loving kindness by frequent reception of the Eucharist, especially on the first Friday of the month, and a one-hour prayer vigil on Thursday nights (the Holy Hour which was popular for many years). In one revelation, Jesus asked Margaret Mary to have a feast of reparation established on the Friday following the feast of Corpus Christi to be known as the feast of the Sacred Heart.

While giving these instructions to Margaret Mary, Christ told her that obedience to her superior was foremost. The superior, Mother de Saumaise, was skeptical of Margaret Mary's revelations and initially treated her with contempt. But when Margaret Mary became very ill and was near death, her superior allowed that if she were to recover from this illness, she would take that as a sign that Margaret's revelations were really from Jesus. Margaret Mary prayed to Jesus and immediately regained her health.

Margaret Mary had a powerful ally in her confessor, Blessed Claude La Colombière. He not only believed in her mission, but encouraged her and was, at least in part, responsible for making her crusade known in the world. He, St. Margaret Mary, and St. John Eudes, are called "saints of the Sacred Heart."

Margaret Mary's message today: Many of the saints were scorned because of their lives of devotion and prayer; Margaret Mary was one of these, although her sanctity was eventually recognized by those in her community. Likewise, we may experience the same reaction when we try to live out our Christian beliefs. Jesus encourages us to persevere, however, as he did in his visions to Margaret Mary.

Was there a time when you were rebuffed because of what you believe in? Were you able to persevere? How?

Gerard Majella: 1726–1755

Gerard was born in Muro, a small town about fifty miles southeast of Naples. His father died when Gerard was twelve, and the boy was taken out of school and apprenticed to a tailor. Though badly mistreated by the tailor's journeyman, Gerard learned his lessons well and accepted the ill treatment as God's will.

Upon finishing his apprenticeship, Gerard sought to enter the Capuchins. When they refused him entry due to his youth and his frailness, he became the servant of the bishop of Lacedogna, a town north of Muro. This cleric was not noted for his kindness and patience; in fact, he could not keep servants for any length of time because of his ill temper. Gerard, however, cheerfully served the bishop for three years until the prelate's death in 1745.

Returning home to his mother and his sisters, Gerard became a successful tailor in Muro. After providing for his family's needs, Gerard would give the remainder of his money earned from his work to the poor and as Mass offerings.

In about 1749, Redemptorist priests came to Muro to conduct a mission. Gerard was so taken by them that he volunteered himself as a lay brother. Again, his health caused him to be turned down, but Gerard would not give up easily. The story is told that when the missionaries were leaving Muro, their superior advised Gerard's family to lock him in his room to prevent him from going after the priests. But Gerard took his bed sheets, knotted them together, and used them to escape out the window and follow the priests.

Father Cafaro, the superior, was impressed by Gerard's persistence, but was still not convinced that he could be effective as a lay brother. So the superior sent him ahead to the Redemptorist community with a letter which said, "I am sending you a useless brother." Gerard soon proved the superior wrong and during the remainder of his life worked as gardener, sacristan, infirmarian, cook, tailor, porter, and carpenter, as well as foreman in the construction of new buildings.

God gave many gifts to Gerard, and these brought him fame in the kingdom of Naples. Many miracles were attributed to the saint both before and after his death, and a number of miraculous cures occurred through his intercession. On one occasion, when Gerard had no money for the workmen under his charge, his prayers brought in an unexpected sum of money which was just enough to pay them. He was also able to read souls, and many cases are recorded of people repenting when Gerard told them of their sins.

In the summer of 1755, the sweltering heat of southern Italy proved too much for Gerard and his consumption overcame him. Even while he was himself dying, he effected the cure of a lay brother who, while assigned to care for Gerard, also came down with consumption. Gerard finally succumbed to his illness at the exact hour and day which he had foretold, just before midnight on October 15, 1755.

St. Gerard Majella is the patron of expectant mothers and childbirth.

Gerard's message today: Gerard did not worry about amassing wealth or power, but was content only to serve and help others. He shows us that the work of God can happen in the most lowly and humble of people, in the simplest of circumstance.

Have you stopped to consider your blessings lately...another day to live...a beautiful sunset...the flowers in the park... good health...a loving family?

Luke, Evangelist: First Century

L uke is the author of the third gospel and of the Acts of the Apostles. He was the only Gentile Christian among the four evangelists and his gospel, written in Greek, was unquestionably written for Gentile Christians.

Tradition has him as Greek-born, from Antioch. St. Paul called Luke "our beloved physician," and Luke was known to have traveled with Paul on his second and third missionary expeditions. He also accompanied Paul on the dangerous journey to Rome, where Paul wrote: "only Luke is with me" (2 Tm 4:11).

During Paul's imprisonment in Caesarea, around the years 61 to 63, Luke most likely did his research on the life of Christ and had the opportunity to interview people who had known Jesus. The Acts of the Apostles, the story of the growth of the Church under the inspiration of the Holy Spirit, were probably written during this period as well. Luke's gospel, sometimes called the "Gospel of the Poor" or the "Gospel of Mercy," is thought to have been written sometime between the years 70 and 90 and may have been written in Greece.

One early legend has Luke as the artist of several paintings of Mary. While there is no hard evidence to support it, it is very likely that Luke did visit Mary in Jerusalem while seeking information about Jesus. Much of the infancy narrative and the account of the finding of Jesus in the temple could only have come from someone like Mary.

Luke is the patron saint of artists, brewers, butchers, glass workers, notaries, painters, and physicians.

Luke's message today: Like the other evangelists, Luke's message is with us today as it has been throughout the history of the Church. They have given us the gospels, which enable us to learn about Jesus' life and ministry. Further, the Acts of the Apostles give us grounding in the work of the Holy Spirit in the early Church.

Are you familiar with Luke's infancy narrative (1:5—2:52)? Read this beautiful story again, and reflect on its relation to your life today.

Anthony Claret, Bishop: 1807–1870

Born in the north of Spain, this saint started out in clothweaving, his father's trade. He used his spare time to learn Latin and printing. When he was twenty-two, Anthony entered the seminary and was ordained six years later.

For ten years, he devoted himself to giving missions and retreats in his native Catalonia. These proved so popular that he inspired other priests to join him to help carry on this work. In 1849, with these other priests, he formed the congregation of Missionary Sons of the Immaculate Heart of Mary, who became known as the Claretians.

Father Anthony was sent by the pope to Cuba where he was to be the Archbishop of Santiago, the largest archdiocese in Cuba. For all of Anthony's speaking and management skills, this assignment proved to be a challenge. Most of the priests were no longer living in their rectories, many had taken mistresses, and the churches were run down. With the clergy in such a state, the laity could hardly be expected to be more sanctified. Many of the faithful had not been confirmed, and thousands of marriages had not been blessed in the Church.

Within his first year, Bishop Claret had instituted reforms, given retreats for his priests, confirmed 100,000 people, and blessed

40,000 marriages. All of this was not without opposition, of course. Several attempts were made on the life of the archbishop, and he was seriously wounded by a would-be assassin infuriated by the loss of his mistress, who had returned to the Church.

In 1857, the pope called on Anthony to return to Spain to become confessor to Queen Isabella. When his presence was not required at court, Anthony devoted himself to the missionary work which had been the basis of his career.

The revolution of 1868 drove the royal family out of Spain, and the bishop, also exiled, went to Rome where he participated in the first Vatican council. It was here that he spoke eloquently in favor of the doctrine of papal infallibility which was adopted at this council. An attempt was made to bring the bishop back to Spain, but a fatal illness overcame him before he could return. He died in France on October 24, 1870.

Anthony Claret is credited with writing over 10,000 sermons, as well as 200 books and pamphlets, for the instruction of his priests and people. As rector of the Escorial, the royal pantheon in Spain, he established a science laboratory, a museum of natural history, schools of music and languages, and other foundations.

Anthony's message today: God sometimes throws us into seemingly impossible situations and asks us to straighten things out. Such was the situation Anthony found himself in as the archbishop of Santiago. With God's grace, he dug in and cleaned up the mess that he found. We can also accomplish much if we rely on God's grace to see us through.

What is your approach to the curve balls thrown at you by life? Do you try to avoid solving them? Complain about them? Try asking for God's help.

Jude, Apostle: First Century

Judas Thaddeus, called Jude to distinguish him from Judas Iscariot, is often regarded as the brother of St. James the Less.

Other than a mention in the listing of the apostles in the Gospels, there is only one reference to Jude anywhere in the New Testament. At the Last Supper, Jesus tells the apostles that he will reveal himself to them. Jude then asked him, "Master, what happened that you will reveal yourself to us and not to the world?" Jesus answered and said to him, "Whoever loves me will keep my word, and my Father will love him, and we will come to him and make our dwelling with him."

There are some rich traditions about St. Jude which have come down to us over the centuries. One of the stories concerns a young Middle Eastern prince, Abgar, who had written to Jesus during his ministry. Abgar invited him to come to visit his domain, a small principality in present-day Iraq. Declining the invitation, Jesus promised to send one of his disciples instead. So after the Ascension, Jude made his way to Abgar's capital, Edessa, where he learned that Abgar was dying from an incurable disease.

When Jude arrived in this new, unevangelized territory, he stayed at the house of Tobias, a Jew. As was the custom of the time, Jude first preached the message of Christianity to the Jews of that territory. When Abgar heard about the wonders which Jude was performing, he sent for Jude to call on him. In speaking with Jude, Abgar told him of his own faith in Jesus and the Father. Jude then cured Abgar and went on to convert many in the principality. Jude later went into Armenia where he preached and then, with Simon the Zealot, into Persia (Iran) where they made many converts. It was here that the two apostles met their martyrdom and were stoned to death.

St. Jude is the patron of lost causes and hopeless cases. Many minor as well as major miracles have occurred through his intercession. The entertainer Danny Thomas was out of work for a long period before praying to St. Jude. Soon after, he found work. Several years later, in thanksgiving, he endowed St. Jude's Children's Hospital where modern miracles take place on a routine basis.

Because of their common martyrdom, St. Jude and St. Simon share a feast day on this date.

Jude's message today: In a vision to St. Bridget of Sweden, Jesus noted that Jude would "show himself most willing to help." Many people who have called on St. Jude, like Danny Thomas, have found work after extended unemployment. Others with terminal illnesses have recovered after turning to St. Jude.

When you have reached the end of your rope and all seems lost, say a prayer to St. Jude. He will help you, too.

OCTOBER 28–FEAST

Simon, Apostle and Martyr: First Century

Perhaps the least known of the apostles, Simon is only mentioned in the lists contained in the Gospels. Matthew, Mark, and Luke all refer to this saint as "Simon the Zealot." This has caused some scholars to link him with the Zealot faction, a radical first-century revolutionary organization which sought to eliminate Roman rule by terrorism. It is entirely possible that in his younger days Simon had been a member of this group, but its philosophy would hardly fit with Christian principles. Equally possible, Simon could have earned his nickname by his dedication and zealous support of Jesus Christ.

Simon is said to have been among the first of the apostles to carry the Word to distant lands. He might well have been among the seventy-two who were sent ahead by Jesus to preach in the towns where Jesus would stop on his final journey to Jerusalem (Lk 10). If this were the case, Simon would have been one of the apostles with some experience in teaching when the apostles began their own ministries.

Since he received no mention in the Acts of the Apostles, which largely concentrated on the activities around Jerusalem and the eastern Mediterranean, Simon may have begun his missionary work among the Jews of Egypt. He may have worked his way westward through Libya and into present-day Tunisia. There is some evidence that Simon then took the Word to Britain, where Christianity seems to have been introduced before the Romans established the island as a colony in the year 43.

Tradition tells us that Simon joined Jude Thaddeus in Persia around the year 66. These two saints converted thousands to Christianity over the next several years, but they also made powerful enemies. The pagan leaders in that region finally mustered a mob to stone the two apostles to death. It is told that when the mob approached the two old men, Jude turned to Simon and said, "The Lord is calling us."

Simon's message today: Whatever the origin of Simon's nickname, we can believe that he was ardent in his preaching of the Word of God. This passion carried him from almost one end of the known world to the other. While we are not asked to travel to the ends of the earth preaching the Word of God, we can set an example of Christian living for all of those with whom we come in contact.

Would your coworkers know you were Christian by the way you conduct yourself? By the language you use?

NOVEMBER

All Saints

This feast, originally set to honor martyrs, now honors all of the saints in heaven, the obscure as well as the celebrated.

The Saints' message today: The millions of saints in heaven include many that we have known: a grandparent, a parent, a brother or sister, a neighbor. They are with God, and are praying for us who are still struggling to achieve salvation.

Say a prayer to persons that you know who are in heaven. They are more than willing to ask God's help for you.

NOVEMBER 2

All Souls

On this day we pray for all of those who have died and are awaiting entrance into heaven.

The Souls' message today: Those who have died but have not yet been purged of their sins (the Church suffering) need our prayers so that they might soon be in God's presence.

Remember these souls in your prayers. They need your help. In turn, they will pray for you when they reach heaven.

Martin de Porres, Religious: 1579–1639

Martin was the illegitimate son of a Spanish knight and a freed Panamanian slave. Born and raised in Lima, Peru, he was part of the poorest and lowest level of society. At the age of twelve, Martin was apprenticed by his mother to a barber-surgeon where he learned to cut hair and to provide medical treatment.

After a few years, Martin applied to the Dominicans to be a "lay helper" because he didn't himself feel worthy to be a religious brother. He often spent his nights in prayer, while his days were filled with caring for the sick and the poor. He founded an orphanage and looked after the slaves brought from Africa. Martin became the procurator for both the priory and the city of Lima and supplied whatever was asked of him: blankets, shirts, candles, candy, miracles, or prayers. After nine years, his example of prayer and penance, charity and humility, led his religious community to ask Martin to make a full religious profession.

God chose to give Martin extraordinary gifts: ecstasies which lifted him into the air; light which filled the room where he prayed; miraculous knowledge; instantaneous cures; and remarkable control over animals. Although many of his fellow religious took him as their spiritual director, Martin continued to call himself a "poor slave."

At his canonization, Pope John XXIII said of Martin, "He forgave the bitterest injuries. He tried with all his might to redeem the guilty; lovingly, he comforted the sick; he provided food, clothing, and medicine for the poor; he helped, as best he could, farm laborers and black people; thus he deserved to be called by the name the people gave him: Martin of Charity."

St. Martin de Porres is the patron saint of interracial justice.

Martin's message today: All of us are children of God and all of us deserve justice in our dealings with others. Martin cared not whether those he helped were slaves or free men, rich or poor. If they needed his help, he was available to them. We should do no less.

Can you be as impartial as this saint was in giving your assistance to those in need?

Charles Borromeo, Bishop: 1538–1584

Charles' father was a count and his mother a member of the powerful Medici family. His early dedication to the Church, at age twelve, might have had as much to do with political considerations as with holiness. Nevertheless, Charles became one of the major forces in bringing about the reforms which took place in the Church in the sixteenth century.

Receiving a doctorate in civil and canon law in 1559, Charles was named a cardinal and administrator of the diocese of Milan when he was twenty-one, shortly after his mother's brother became Pope Pius IV. It would be several years before he would take up residence in his see, however. The pope assigned Charles as his Secretary of State and gave him many other duties in Rome.

Charles was responsible for reconvening the Council of Trent in 1562. This assembly, called originally to institute reforms within the Church to counter the Protestant Reformation, had recessed ten years earlier without completing its work. Charles played a major role in this council, keeping it together when dissent threatened to dissolve it and ensuring that the reforms were finally approved by the bishops. When the council was over, Charles was given the task of preparing a catechism and revising the other liturgical books which the council deemed in need of reform.

When his father died during the council, Charles legally became the head of the Borromeo household. Although he had been named a cardinal, Charles had never been ordained. Thus, it was assumed by family members that he would leave his position in the Church to take up his familial duties and to marry. But Charles resigned his position as head of the family in favor of an uncle and sought ordination as a priest. This occurred in 1563, and two months later he was made a bishop.

Charles' uncle, Pope Pius IV, died in 1565. Shortly after, Pope Pius V allowed Charles to leave Rome and go to his diocese in Milan which was in a deplorable state, having been without a resident bishop for eighty years. Among his first acts was to establish rules implementing the decrees of the Council of Trent in the diocese. These reforms brought about discipline and training for the clergy and instituted changes in the administration of the sacraments. A strong believer in education at all levels, Charles opened three seminaries for priests during his episcopacy, and established Sunday school as a teaching implement for children.

Charles was noted for his charity. He gave most of his income to the poor and lived a very austere life. When a famine struck Milan in 1570, Charles obtained food supplies from several sources and fed 3,000 people daily for several months. Later, in 1576, a plague struck the city, and Charles threw himself wholeheartedly into the care of the sick and the dying. Besides organizing volunteer squads and arranging other forms of relief, the bishop personally ministered to the dying and those in need.

On the evening of November 3, 1584 , Charles Borromeo died at the still young age of forty-six. A strong devotion to the saint sprang up almost immediately in Milan and he was canonized by Pope Paul V in 1610. He is the patron saint of seminarians and catechists.

Charles' message today: This saint provides another example of a wealthy and powerful person who gained salvation by the proper use of his talents. Unlike the rich young man noted in Mark's Gospel (Mk 10) who could not give up his worldly possessions to follow Jesus, Charles used his talent and possessions to look after his people.

Have you become too attached to your worldly possessions? to your position of power?

Dedication of St. John Lateran

Contrary to what most people believe, St. Peter's Basilica in Rome is not the pope's church. As the Bishop of Rome, the pope's cathedral is the Basilica of St. John Lateran.

St. John Lateran is the symbol of our unity with the Bishop of Rome and with all the parish churches throughout the world. The feast of St. John Lateran also tells us what we, as Christians, are here for: to find strength, affirmation, and encouragement from gathering as a local faith community, knowing that we are one with the worldwide faith community as we listen to the Word of God and share in the breaking of the bread.

In the early Church, the persecution which took place meant that Christians had to worship in secret, usually in a home. The emperor, Constantine, ended persecution and Christians could then begin to celebrate in a larger, common building. To this end, the Church of the Holy Savior was constructed on the Lateran hill in Rome.

This church was the first one to have a baptistry in a separate building, which was named after St. John the Baptist. As more and more people became Christian and more churches were built, it became common to ask "Where were you baptized?" For many Christians, the answer was "St. John the Baptist on Lateran hill." This soon was shortened to St. John Lateran, and to this day, the church has been known by this name as well.

The Church's message today: We sometimes lose sight of the fact that Catholicism is one of the world's great relgions. It should strengthen our faith life to know that we are in solidarity with so many others not only in our country, but throughout the world.

Remember to include all the other Christians of the world in your daily prayers, especially those who still suffer persecution at the hands of their governments.

NOVEMBER 13–MEMORIAL

Frances Xavier Cabrini, Virgin: 1850–1917

Frances Xavier Cabrini was the first citizen of the United States to be canonized as a saint. Born Maria Francesca Cabrini at San Angelo, Italy, she was naturalized as a citizen of the United States at Seattle in 1909.

Frances was sent to a convent school at an early age, and dreamed of becoming a missionary in China. At the age of twenty-four, she went to a small orphanage in Codogno called the House of Providence, to help in the management of this institution. During this time, she attracted several other women to help in her work, and in 1877 seven of them took first vows. Shortly after, the House of Providence was closed down, and the bishop encouraged Frances to found her own order of missionary sisters.

The nuns were called the Missionary Sisters of the Sacred Heart, and their minstry was the Christian education of girls. The sisters spent the next few years setting up schools and homes for children throughout Italy. Then, in 1889, Pope Leo XIII asked Frances to sail to the United States to work among the Italian immigrants there, and Frances left for New York with six other sisters.

Within three months of their arrival, Mother Cabrini had already founded an orphanage and a school. In the thirty-five years before her death, she was to open sixty-seven hospitals, schools, orphanages, convents, and other foundations in the United States, Europe, Central America, and South America. Despite a great dread of water, Mother Cabrini sailed the oceans more than thirty times in her missionary work.

Although she discounted talk of miracles in her life, there are several recorded instances of special favors. One account tells of a sister who had suffered for many years from varicose veins. Her doctor had advised her to wear elastic stocking at all times, but somehow, she obtained a pair of Mother Cabrini's cotton stockings. Upon putting them on, she felt instantly cured. Seeing her walking briskly the next day, Mother Cabrini asked her what had happened. When the sister confessed to wearing her stockings, Mother Cabrini told her, "I hope you are not so foolish as to say my stockings cured you. I am wearing them all the time and they do me no good. It was your faith that did it."

St. Frances Xavier Cabrini is the patron of immigrants.

Mother Cabrini's message today: The strength of the United Stated has come from those who have immigrated from other countries to our shores. Mother Cabrini was sent to tend to the needs of these people. Today, we sometime seem to have lost sight of the richness which immigrants have brought to our country.

Would you turn immigrants away or do you seek justice for them?

Albert the Great, Bishop and Doctor: 1206–1280

A lbert was the eldest son of the count of Bollstädt and heir to that title. Despite the strong opposition of his family, he became a Dominican priest in 1222.

Teaching and studying at various universities, Albert soon developed a widespread reputation for his learning and intellect. He received a doctorate from the university at Paris in 1245 and became the regent of a new school established in Cologne in 1248. Among his students was Thomas Aquinas, whose genius Albert early recognized and proclaimed. The two became close friends.

Albert was named provincial of his order in 1254, but in 1257, he resigned this position to continue his teaching and studies. Together with Thomas Aquinas and others, Albert drew up a new curriculum for Dominicans. He was very active in the Council of Lyons in 1274, working toward uniting the Greek Church with Rome. In 1277, he fiercely and brilliantly defended Thomas Aquinas against the bishop of Paris and a group of theologians there who were attacking Aquinas' philosophical stand.

One of the great intellects of the medieval church, Albert was among the greatest of the natural scientists. His knowledge of biology, chemistry, physics, astronomy, and geography was so encyclopedic that he was often accused of magic. He wrote on these subjects as well as on logic, metaphysics, mathematics, the Bible, and theology. The writings of Albert the Great fill thirty-eight volumes. His brilliance and intellect brought him the title "Universal Doctor," conferred on him by his contemporaries. It was also his peers who dubbed him Albert the Great.

St. Albert the Great was canonized and named a Doctor of the Church in 1931 by Pope Pius XI. He is the patron of scientists and philosophers.

Albert's message today: Since Albert's time, scientific break-throughs have wiped out many diseases, improved living conditions for most of the world's peoples, and harnessed power unthinkable in his time. Expanding our knowledge in any field contributes to the betterment of the whole human race.

Think of one or two ways that your knowledge can help better the lives of those in your community.

Margaret of Scotland: 1045–1093

Margaret was born in Hungary, the daughter of royal parents. Brought to the court of King Edward the Confessor in England when she was twelve, she and her family were forced to flee after the Battle of Hastings in 1066. Shipwrecked off Scotland, the family was befriended by King Malcolm of Scotland who married Margaret in 1070.

Margaret and Malcolm had six sons and two daughters. Contrary to the general practice of royalty in that time, Margaret took charge of raising and educating her children. The youngest son, St. David of Scotland, succeeded his father and two older brothers as king. One daughter, who became known as Good Queen Maud, married King Henry I, establishing a line which runs through the present royal family of England.

King Malcolm was goodhearted, but rough and uncultured. Because of his love for Margaret, she was able to soften his temper and she became his advisor in state matters. It was said that the main goals of Malcolm and Margaret were to maintain justice, to establish religion, and to keep their subjects happy. Margaret encouraged arts and education in her adopted country and instigated religious reform. With her husband, she founded several churches.

Despite her heavy involvement in the affairs of her household and her country, Margaret led an austere private life. She ate sparingly and slept little in order to have time for her devotions. She and her husband kept two Lents: one before Easter and one before Christmas. At these times, Margaret, often joined by Malcolm, would arise before midnight to attend Mass. She was always surrounded by beggars and never refused them. Especially during Advent and Lent, Margaret and her husband often fed hundreds of poor people, serving them the same food that they had for their own meal.

St. Margaret is the patroness of Scotland.

Margaret's message today: A heavy responsibility falls on those who have been given exalted positions. Margaret and her husband recognized the need to provide for those who were less fortunate than themselves. We too must do the same.

Have you accepted the responsibility of caring for those who need your assistance?

NOVEMBER 17—MEMORIAL

Elizabeth of Hungary, Religious: 1207–1231

Elizabeth, the daughter of royal parents, became betrothed to Ludwig of Thuringia at the age of four. She was sent to the court at Thuringia where the two children were raised together and became dear friends. In 1221, Ludwig turned twenty-one and became the Landgrave (ruler) of Thuringia. The couple then married and had three children.

Elizabeth became known for her great charity. Despite her high station, she led a life of prayer and penance and service to the poor. She built hospitals to care for the common people and daily took food to the poor who came to her gate. Rather than encourage idleness, however, Elizabeth assigned tasks suitable to the strength and abilities of those whom she fed.

One time, when Ludwig had returned from a journey, his counselors complained to him about Elizabeth's charities to the poor and sick. Ludwig asked if she had lost any of his lands. When they said that she had not, he told them not to worry. "Her charities will bring upon us divine blessings."

Ludwig died of the plague in 1227 while en route to the Crusades. Elizabeth was heartbroken. She was forced to leave her castle by her husband's family who thought that she was squandering her wealth. Yet Elizabeth continued her charitable work, caring for the sick, the aged, and the poor.

Upon the return of her husband's allies from the Crusades, she was reinstated, since her son was the legal heir to the throne. Elizabeth then made provision for the care of her children and, in 1228, became a tertiary of the Order of St. Francis. The last years of her short life were spent in caring for the sick and the poor in a hospital which she had built.

St. Elizabeth of Hungary is the patron saint of bakers, tertiaries, and of Catholic Charities.

Elizabeth's message today: Many times, married people who become saints do so in spite of their spouses. Elizabeth's charitable works, however, were fully supported by her husband, who also became a saint, and is known as Blessed Ludwig (or Louis) of Thuringia. They give us an example of how married life should be a state of mutual love, respect, and support.

What does the sanctity of marriage mean to you?

Rose Philippine Duchesne, Virgin: 1769–1852

Philippine, as she was called by her family, was born into an aristocratic family in Grenoble, France. The marriage of her mother, Rose Périer, to her father, Pierre-François Duchesne, had united the two most prosperous textile manufacturing families of the town. The family traits of strong will and determination were passed on to Philippine, along with a passion for reading and study.

When Philippine was not yet ten years old, a Jesuit missionary visited her family. Telling tales of working with Indians in the Louisiana territories of the New World, he enkindled a desire in Philippine to be a missionary to these Indians, a wish that would take over sixty years to fulfill.

Philippine was schooled in her early years in the Visitandine Convent of Ste-Marie-d'en-Haut, and was greatly influenced by the nuns. At the age of seventeen, Philippine entered the convent there, although her parents, who had been urging her to marry, were reluctant to grant consent for this move. Then, in 1791, the French Revolution reached its peak. All churches and religious houses were closed and confiscated by the government, and all priests and religious were secularized. Philippine was sent back home to her family, where she maintained, as much as possible, her religious practices.

In 1801, a pact was signed by the pope and the leader of France which allowed the churches and religious houses to reopen. While her order had been scattered, Philippine was resolute in her efforts to regain and reopen Ste. Marie. She offered the convent to Mother Madeleine Sophie Barat, who had founded the Society of the Sacred Heart four years previously. Philippine resumed her novitiate with Mother Barat's order, and took her vows in 1805, eighteen years after she first entered the convent.

In 1817, the bishop of New Orleans visited the convent at Ste. Marie and requested that several nuns of the order be sent to his diocese as missionaries. Five nuns were selected for this mission, with Mother Duchesne appointed as their superior. After an arduous fifty-six-day voyage which included several storms and an encounter with a pirate ship, Mother Duchesne and her sisters arrived in New Orleans on the feast of the Sacred Heart, May 29, 1818.

The sisters moved up the Mississippi River to Missouri shortly after their arrival. Over the next several years, Mother Duchesne founded several convents and schools, including the first free school for girls west of the Mississippi. By 1830, the society had six convents in the Mississippi valley with sixty-four nuns, and more than 350 children in their schools.

In 1841, Mother Duchesne, now seventy-two and relieved of her duties as superior, finally realized her childhood dream of working among the Indians. She and three other sisters established a school at a Potawatomi Indian mission in what is now Kansas. When the Indians were leaving in the morning to begin their labors, Mother Duchesne would be on her knees in the chapel praying. When the Indians returned in the evening, they found her in the same position. This gained for her the Indian name, *Quah-kah-ka-num-ad*, Woman-who-prays-always.

Philippine's message today: Philippine contributed much energy to regaining her convent in France, and to organizing schools and convents in the diocese of New Orleans. But perhaps her greatest contributions came from her lifelong dedication to prayer. Much has been accomplished through prayer, and God certainly answered the prayers of this saint.

If you are having difficulty in praying, perhaps you may want to look into a different way of prayer. Ask your pastor or a pastoral minister for some suggestions on resources that can help you in your search.

Cecilia, Virgin and Martyr: Third Century

Much of the knowledge about Cecilia is based on tradition. We do know, however, that a strong devotion to St. Cecilia began toward the end of the fifth century.

Cecilia (or Cecily) was born in Rome, the daughter of patrician parents, and was raised as a Christian. When of a suitable age, she was married against her will to Valerian. After their marriage, she converted Valerian and his brother, Tiburtius, to Christianity. Valerian and Tiburtius devoted themselves to good works until they were arrested by the Roman prefect Almachius. They were martyred, together with Maximus, a Roman official who had been so impressed by their witness to Christ that he too became a Christian. These three martyrs are also saints.

Cecilia buried the three and was, in turn, arrested and called upon to renounce her faith. Instead she converted the people who came to convince her to sacrifice to the Roman gods. Pope Urban visited her in her home while she was awaiting trial and baptized more than four hundred converts who were influenced by Cecilia.

When Cecilia was called into court, Almachius tried to convince her to give up her beliefs. Unable to shake her faith, he sentenced her to death by suffocation. When her death in this manner was miraculously prevented, a soldier was sent to behead her. The soldier struck her neck three times, then left her for dead.

Legend tells us that Cecilia lived for three days following her beheading and, in that time, turned her house over to the pope to be used as a church. Gordian, a high ranking Roman official who was one of Cecilia's converts, established the church in her house which Pope Urban later dedicated in her name.

St. Cecilia is the patroness of musicians and singers and is often portrayed with an organ or viola.

Cecilia's message today: Only a very strong faith could withstand the pressures and threats which faced Cecilia and the martyrs of her time. Instead of caving in to those pressures, Cecilia, her husband, and brother-in-law brought more converts into the Church. By word and by example, we too can both strengthen our faith and brings others to Christ.

Are you living your life in such a way as to draw others to Jesus?

Catherine of Alexandria, Virgin and Martyr: Early Fourth Century

This saint is said to have been born into a patrician family of Alexandria and converted after seeing a vision of Our Lady and the Holy Child.

When the Emperor Maxentius began persecuting Christians, Catherine, only eighteen, went to him and scolded him for his tyranny. Unable to answer her arguments against his gods, Maxentius summoned fifty philosophers to oppose her. The fifty were themselves converted by Catherine and the infuriated emperor had them burned to death.

Maxentius tried other bribes to force Catherine to give up Christianity, but when these failed, he had her beaten and imprisoned. Upon returning from a trip, Maxentius found that Catherine had converted his wife, one of his officers, and 200 soldiers of the guard. The emperor had them all put to death and sentenced Catherine to die on a spiked wheel. When she was placed on it, her bonds were miraculously loosened and the wheel broke. Catherine was then beheaded.

Since about the tenth century, a great devotion to St. Catherine has existed in the Eastern Church and numerous churches are named in her honor. St. Catherine is said to have been one of the voices from heaven heard by St. Joan of Arc. Because of her legendary erudition, St. Catherine is the patroness of philosophers and teachers.

Catherine's message today: Just as Catherine stood up to tyranny, we are called upon to do the same, whether it be tyranny of a foreign country, or something more localized, like the tyranny of a school board. There are many effective ways for Christians to respond, such as offering time, writing a letter, or contributing money.

Do you stand up to tyranny, either in your own community or on a broader scale?

Andrew, Apostle: First Century

Andrew, a native of Bethsaida, was a fisherman like his father, John, and his brother, Simon. When John the Baptist began preaching penance, Andrew became his disciple.

One day, Jesus passed by while John was preaching, and John said, "Behold the lamb of God." Andrew immediately grasped John's meaning and went off after Jesus, staying with him for several hours. Based on this encounter, *Butler's Lives of the Saints* credits Andrew with being Jesus' first disciple. Convinced that Jesus was the Messiah, Andrew brought his brother to meet him whereupon Simon also became a disciple, and later received the name of Peter.

At first, Andrew and Peter did not leave their fishing to join Jesus in his ministry, but listened to him whenever their business allowed. Later, Jesus found Andrew and Simon casting their nets into the lake and said to them, "Follow me, and I will make you fish for people" (Mt 4:19). At that point, Andrew and Peter abandoned their nets and answered Jesus' call.

Little more is known about Andrew beyond an occasional mention in the Gospels and Acts of the Apostles. Legend has it, however, that Andrew preached the Good News in what is now modern Greece and Turkey, and was martyred at Patras.

St. Andrew is the patron of Scotland and Russia. His patronage of Scotland is based on an unsubstantiated myth that his relics were carried by St. Rule to Scotland in the fourth century. The origin of his patronage of Russia is derived from a spurious legend that he preached in that country as far as Kiev.

Andrew's message today: Hearing Jesus' words convinced Andrew that the Messiah had come at last. While we can't hear Jesus' words directly, our faith in Jesus as the Messiah grows as we study the Word of God.

Do you spend some time each day studying the Word of God? Check in a local Christian bookstore or your parish library for books and other resources which may help in your pursuit.

DECEMBER

Francis Xavier, Priest: 1506–1552

Francis Xavier was born in the Basque region of Spain and entered the University of Paris when he was seventeen. While there, he met Ignatius Loyola who repeated the words to him, "For what will it profit them if they gain the whole world but forfeit their life?" (Mt 16:26).

Although Francis didn't immediately fall under the influence of Ignatius, he became one of the first Jesuits who vowed themselves to God's service in 1534. Francis was ordained three years later and, in 1540, was appointed by Ignatius to the first missionary expedition of the young order. He sailed to Goa, on the west coast of India and, for the next ten years, labored to bring the faith to such widely scattered peoples as the Hindus, the Malayans, and the Japanese.

Wherever he went, Francis lived with the poorest people, sharing their food and their living conditions and ministering to the poor and the sick, especially to lepers. He traveled thousands of miles to the most inaccessible of places under the most harrowing conditions, and converted hundreds of thousands. His missionary impact in the East has endured for centuries.

When missionaries returned to Japan in the nineteenth century after a gap of several hundred years, they found many Christians who were descendants of St. Francis' converts. Indeed, with the possible exception of St. Paul, St. Francis Xavier was the greatest of all Christian missionaries. Appropriately, he is the patron of foreign missions.

Francis' message today: Although we are most likely not called to become missionaries in a foreign land, we can try to bring one person to Christ through our prayers and our example. We can also help the missions by financially contributing to the work of the priests, religious, and laypeople who are evangelizing throughout the world.

Have you contributed in some way to the support of missions? Also, pray that you might be a strong and good influence on someone's life.

DECEMBER 4

Barbara, Virgin and Martyr: Fourth Century

There is some doubt that the virgin, Barbara, ever existed. Nevertheless, she was one of the most popular saints during the Middle Ages.

The story of Barbara is that she was the daughter of a pagan official in the time of the Emperor Maximian. The girl was so beautiful that her father built a tower for her to live in to isolate her from the world. Many princes came to woo her, but she resisted her father's efforts to have her marry one of them, choosing instead to dedicate her life to Christ.

While her father was away on a long sojourn, Barbara came down from her tower to inspect a bath house which he was having built. When she saw that they were only putting two windows into the building, she ordered the laborers to install a third window. In this bath house, Barbara was baptized, and she lived there for a time before returning back to the tower.

When her father returned from his journey, he questioned why there were now three windows in his bath house. The workmen told him that Barbara had ordered it. The father angrily confronted Barbara, who explained that the three windows were like the Holy Trinity, bringing light into the world.

Furious, her father took her before a judge who had her tortured. Still not satisfied with her punishment, her father then took Barbara to the top of a mountain where he killed her. On coming down from the mountain, Barbara's father was consumed by a fire so intense that only some ashes from his body could be found. The site of Barbara's martyrdom is variously described as being in parts of modern-day Greece and in Rome.

St. Barbara is the patron saint of architects. She is also invoked for protection from fire, presumably referring to the fire which killed her father.

Barbara's message today: While most parents would not treat their children as harshly as did Barbara's father, many of us do not consider the strong and lasting effects of our words on our children. Gentle guidance, understanding, and prayers can often accomplish much more than harsh words.

When you have a disagreement with one of your children, do you try to resolve it with arguments and anger? Or do you try to talk out the problem, with kindness and understanding as your guide?

DECEMBER 6–OPTIONAL MEMORIAL

Nicholas, Bishop: Fourth Century

A few things are known for certain about Nicholas: he was born of wealthy parents; named bishop of Myra, a city on the Mediterranean coast of present-day Turkey; became known for his holiness, zeal, charity, and miracles; and was imprisoned for his faith during the persecution of the Emperor Diocletian.

To those few facts are added the colorful legends which have made him a favorite of young and old for centuries. Among the stories most often told about Nicholas is the account of the three sisters whose family had lost its wealth. To keep the girls from having to turn to prostitution, Nicholas, on three separate occasions, tossed a bag of gold through a window. This money became a dowry for each of the girls, and saved the family from ruin.

Miracles have also been attributed to Nicholas. He is said to have saved three innocent men from death by bravely defending them. Three imperial officials who witnessed this courageous act were later falsely accused of another crime and sentenced to death. In answer to their prayers, Nicholas appeared in a dream to the Emperor Constantine and to the officials' accuser, whereupon the three were freed.

After his death, St. Nicholas' popularity spread across Europe and the eastern Mediterranean in the Middle Ages, but his greatest popularity was in Russia. Before the Russian revolution at the turn of the twentieth century, that country supported a church, hospital, and hospice in Bari, Italy where St. Nicholas' relics are maintained. Together with St. Andrew the Apostle, he is the patron of Russia.

The custom of giving gifts to children in St. Nicholas' name originated in Germany, Switzerland, and the Netherlands. Dutch Protestants who settled in New Amsterdam brought the tradition of St. Nicholas to America, though by this time he had been converted from a popular saint into a Nordic magician (Saint Nicholas became Sint Klaes, then Santa Claus).

As a result of his wide popularity around the world, St. Nicholas has been named patron of many countries and classes of people, including sailors in the East ("May St. Nicholas hold the tiller" was the way sailors wished each other a good voyage). In the United States (and many other countries), St. Nicholas is the patron of children, brides, bakers, brewers, coopers, and prisoners.

Nicholas' message today: This saint was known for his charity, which is the key characteristic in the many legends which exist about him. These stories tell us not only to be charitable, but to seek justice for those who would otherwise become victims.

What can you do to help someone who is a victim of injustice?

Ambrose, Bishop and Doctor: 340–397

A brilliant young lawyer, Ambrose was appointed in about 372 by the emperor Valentinian to be governor of Liguria and Aemilia. Sending him to his new post, which was located in the city of Milan, Valentinian told Ambrose, somewhat prophetically, "Go; and govern more like a bishop than a judge."

The bishop of Milan at the time, Auxentius, strongly advocated the Arian heresy. In 374, Auxentius died and there was considerable turmoil in the city over who should succeed him. The Arians demanded an Arian bishop while Catholics called for one of their own. To prevent this conflict from breaking out into open warfare, Ambrose went to the church where an assembly to elect a new bishop was being held. He spoke to this group, and urged the people to conduct their selection in a spirit of peace, without malice. While he was talking, a voice shouted, "Ambrose, bishop!" and the whole assembly took up the cry. The bishops of the province, recognizing the will of the people, ratified this selection.

Though a professed Christian, Ambrose was still unbaptized and had no desire to be the bishop. He sought to be excused from this office by the emperor, but Valentinian ratified the selection. Reluctantly, Ambrose accepted the will of the people and of the emperor. He was baptized and, one week later on December 7,

374, consecrated bishop of Milan. Now a man of Christ, Ambrose forsook all of the worldly things which he had acquired in his position as governor. His gave his money to the poor and his lands to the Church. He adopted a simple life-style, fasting on most days, and devoting himself to the service of his people.

Ambrose threw himself fervently into the study of sacred Scripture and the writings of the great religious scholars. He was a gifted speaker, and he used this ability well in his ecclesiastical duties. His sermons and his writings on theological subjects had an influence far beyond his diocese. After gaining an understanding of the Arian heresy, he spoke eloquently against it and largely eliminated it in his diocese after a few years. (A notable exception was the Empress Justina, wife of Valentinian, who would cause considerable problems for Ambrose and the Church in later years.)

During Ambrose' episcopate, St. Augustine, who was teaching rhetoric in Milan at the time, was so impressed by the sermons of the bishop that he began to study with him. Augustine was baptized by Ambrose at the Easter Vigil in 387. He continued to work with Ambrose and be one of his strongest supporters.

Ambrose spent the remaining years of his life writing works of exegesis, theology, and ascetics, as well as poetry. He actively ministered to the needs of the people in his diocese, and was a prominent political figure in both the Eastern and Western empires. St. Ambrose is honored on the date of his consecration as bishop.

Ambrose's message today: As bishop of Milan, Ambrose held much power, both in his diocese as well as in the empire itself. Yet he was very careful to use that power to fair and just ends. Above all, he followed Scripture and church teaching as his true guide.

Do you, as a supervisor, a manager, or a parent, use your authority in a wise and just manner?

Blessed Juan Diego: 1474–1548

Juan Diego was a poor Aztec Indian and devout Christian who lived in the Mexican village of Tolpetlac. Juan and his wife were childless, and after she died, his only companion was an old uncle who had raised him.

Juan had little want for anything but the few vegetables which grew on his small farm. On Saturdays and Sundays, he would start out before dawn for a larger village a few miles away where the Franciscan priest would say Mass for him and the other peasants who came from nearby villages.

En route to Mass on the Sunday following the Feast of the Immaculate Conception (December 8th), Juan followed his usual route which took him over Tepeyac Hill. As he approached the top of this hill, Juan heard beautiful music and the sounds of birds, although on this wintry day there were no birds around. Juan then heard a voice calling him by name. When he looked up, Juan saw a beautiful lady wearing a sky blue veil and a dress the color of roses. Juan recognized at once that this was Mary, the Mother of God.

Mary told Juan that she had a special errand for him. He was to go to the bishop of Mexico City and tell him that she wanted a chapel built on this hill for all who seek her aid. Juan immediately set off for Mexico City and, after waiting many hours, was allowed to see the bishop. He relayed Mary's request to the skeptical bishop, then returned to his village, downcast because he had failed to convince the bishop that Mary had indeed spoken to Juan.

As he came by Tepeyac Hill on his way home, once again Our Lady appeared to Juan. He protested that he was not worthy to carry out her mission, but Mary told him to return to the bishop the next day and repeat the request. So Juan again went to Mexico City, and told his story to the bishop. This time, the bishop found it difficult to believe that this simple man could be making up such a tale. But to be sure, he asked Juan for a sign that this was really a request from the Mother of God.

Juan returned to the hill and told Mary of the bishop's request. Mary instructed Juan to return the next morning for a sign. But when Juan returned to his village, he learned that his uncle was suffering from a high fever. Juan spent all night and the next day with his uncle, but his uncle's condition did not improve. Indeed, Juan thought that his uncle would soon die.

Leaving his uncle in the care of a neighbor, Juan set out for the Franciscan mission to have one of the priests bring the last sacraments to the dying man. When he reached the foot of Tepeyac Hill, Juan decided to avoid another meeting and so took a path around the hill. But as he rounded the hill, Juan saw the Blessed Mother coming toward him. Standing in front of him, she asked why he was taking this route. In tears, Juan told her of his uncle's illness and how he had to bring a priest.

Mary smiled in understanding, but told Juan not to worry, that his uncle was already cured and strong. She told Juan to go to the top of the hill and gather an armful of roses; Juan set off on this heavenly task knowing that he would find the flowers. (Roses did not bloom in Mexico in December and certainly not on that hill, which was covered in cactus.) He gathered as many of the roses as he could carry and took them to the Lady. She, in turn, told him to bring the roses to the bishop, assuring him that, this time, he would be believed.

Juan put the roses in his serape (a woolen cloak) and set off to see the bishop. When he unwrapped the roses from the serape, they fell to the floor, as fresh with the morning dew as when they were picked. But this was not what caught the bishop's attention. On Juan's serape was the image of Our Lady just as Juan had seen her on the hill.

When Juan, anxious to see his uncle, finally returned to his village, the old man and the other villagers came out to greet him. His uncle told him that his fever had mysteriously gone away and that the Blessed Mother had appeared to him and told him of Juan's errand. She also told Juan's uncle that, henceforth, she was to be known as Holy Mary of Guadalupe, Ever-Virgin.

When the chapel was built, Juan Diego was assigned by the bishop to guard it. His serape was displayed there in a place of honor, where it remains to this day. A magnificent basilica now stands on the spot where the chapel was first built. After more than 400 years, the serape, with its vision of Our Lady of Guadalupe, is as fresh and unmarred as it was on the day the bishop first saw it.

Blessed Juan Diego is honored by the Church on the date of his first vision.

Juan's message today: Although Juan was a man of very simple means, he was not afraid to speak to the bishop when emboldened by Mary's request. Our faith can help us to speak boldly as well, whether it be in the name of justice or simply to help someone in need.

Who or what needs your boldly spoken words right now?

DECEMBER 13–MEMORIAL

Lucy, Virgin and Martyr: Fourth Century

Lucy is an early saint who has proved to be very popular over the centuries. Her name is mentioned in the canon of the Mass and many places throughout the world have been named after her.

What is known about Lucy is that she lived in Sicily in the early fourth century, the daughter of noble and wealthy parents. Lucy chose to remain a virgin and wished to give the fortune which she inherited to the poor. She was denounced as a Christian by a disappointed suitor during the Emperor Diocletian's persecution of

Christians. According to tradition, Lucy survived several attempts to execute her, but finally died after being stabbed through the throat.

Lucy's name means light. There is a saying associated with her name and feast day, which goes: "Lucy-light, Lucy-light/ The shortest day and the longest night." She has developed a strong following in Scandanavia where her day is a cause for special celebration. St. Lucy is often portrayed with a wreath of candles on her head.

Perhaps because her name means light, St. Lucy has been invoked by those with eye troubles since the Middle Ages. She is also the patron of writers.

Lucy's message moday: Each of us, no matter what our talents may be, can bring light to others through the way we live our lives. As Christians, we have a directive from Jesus, who said: "You are the light of the world. No one after lighting a lamp puts it under the bushel basket, but on the lampstand, and it gives light to all in the house" (Mt 5:14–15)

Think of a few ways that you can bring some light into the lives of those around you.

Stephen, First Martyr: died c. 34

We learn about Stephen, the first Christian martyr, in the Acts of the Apostles. Stephen was a Jew, but also, apparently, a Greek. His Greek name is Stephanos, which signifies "crown."

As the work of the apostles spread, they attracted a great number of followers. Soon, the care and feeding of these crowds became a problem. The apostles, distracted by this situation, called the faithful together and told them that their own ministry was to attend to the spiritual needs of the people, to preach the good news of Jesus. The assemblage, therefore, should select seven men of good character who could take care of the people's physical needs.

Stephen was one of the seven who were made deacons, and given the care of the Christian faithful. According to the Acts of the Apostles, Stephen "full of grace and power, did great wonders and signs among the people" (Acts 6:8). Certain elders of the synagogues attempted to debate with Stephen, but they proved to be no match for his wisdom and spirit.

Since the elders could not defeat Stephen honestly, they had others charge him with blasphemy against God and Moses. Stephen was led before the Sanhedrin where the false witnesses testified against him. When questioned by the Sanhedrin, Stephen gave a long and stinging condemnation of the group who, like their fathers before them, put to death prophets who foretold the coming of the Messiah. This angered the assembly, who took Stephen out of the city and stoned him to death. As he was dying, Stephen cried out, "Lord, do not hold this sin against them."

Among the spectators at the stoning of Stephen was Saul, later to become St. Paul.

Stephen's message today: Stephen was willing to go up against the Sanhedrin, who had the weight of thousands of years of Jewish teaching behind them. It takes great courage to speak out in defense of your beliefs, especially when they are not popular.

Do you have the knowledge and the courage to be a defender of the faith? What can you do, even in small ways, to demonstrate what you believe in?

John, Apostle and Evangelist: First Century

John and his brother, James, were the sons of Zebedee. Like his father and brother, John was a fisherman on Lake Gennesaret until, with James, he was called by Jesus to follow him. John was the youngest of the apostles. He and James were called "sons of thunder" by Jesus because of their volatile temperaments.

Many events in all of the gospels attest to the fact that John was among those apostles closest to Jesus. Perhaps the best known incident is at the Crucifixion, where Jesus placed his mother, Mary, in the care of John. And he, representing all of us, was commended to Mary as her son.

St. Paul refers to John, along with Peter and James, as "these leaders, these pillars" of the Church in Jerusalem (Gal 2:9). According to tradition, John went to Rome during one of the early persecutions under Emperor Domitian and miraculously escaped martyrdom by emerging from a cauldron of boiling oil unscathed. He was exiled to the island of Patmos where he began his writing with the Book of Revelation. Later, after the death of Domitian, John returned to Ephesus where he wrote the fourth gospel and three epistles. He died there in about 100, the last surviving apostle and the only apostle who did not suffer martyrdom.

John's writings are unique among the evangelists. In many of the events recorded by him, he writes as a playwright would, setting the stage, describing the characters, and presenting the dialogue which took place. Three examples of this quality found in his gospel are Jn 4:5–42 (the woman at the well); Jn 9:1–41 (the man born blind); and Jn 11:1–45 (Lazarus raised from the dead).

St. John the Evangelist is often called St. John the Divine in England and in the Eastern Church.

John's message today: Imagine being one of Jesus' closest friends! Imagine living, working, and sharing your life with the Messiah, traveling where he traveled, witnessing his miracles, listening to his stories. Toward the end of his life, John recorded his experiences as a disciple of Jesus, so that we can have an idea of what it was like to know Jesus.

Reading Scripture will help you develop a stronger relationship with Jesus. Start with John's first letter to get an idea of how much God loves you.

DECEMBER 29–OPTIONAL MEMORIAL

Thomas Becket, Bishop and Martyr: 1118–1170

Thomas Becket (sometimes called Thomas à Becket), the son of the sheriff of London, was educated in Surrey, London, and Paris. His parents died when he was twenty-one, and he went to work for a relative in London.

About three years later, Thomas joined the household of Archbishop Theobold of Canterbury. Thomas had earlier been trained in law, and Theobold sent him to Rome, Bologna, and Auxerre to study canon law. Thomas was ordained a deacon in 1154 and nominated by Theobold as the archdeacon of Canterbury. There he quickly became a close friend and confidant of Henry of Anjou, soon to become King Henry II of England.

The king made Thomas chancellor of England in 1155. Next to the king, Thomas was the most powerful man in England and became famed for the luxury and magnificence of his life-style. Yet he was also known for his generosity to the poor and greatly assisted Henry in formulating the reforms in the justice system which were instituted during his tenure.

Upon the death of Theobold in 1161, the king nominated Thomas to be archbishop of Canterbury. He strenuously objected, and refused the position until told by the Holy See that he should accept the nomination. Thomas warned Henry that naming him chancellor would vastly undermine their good relationship; indeed, this proved to be true. Upon election, Thomas resigned his position as chancellor and was ordained a priest on the day before his consecration as archbishop in May 1162.

As archbishop of Canterbury, Thomas undertook an austere style of living, monastic in practice. He wore a hairshirt underneath his cassock, and devoted much of his time to prayer and the study of Scripture. He became a strong church leader, often taking positions which brought him into conflict with the king. One of these conflicts occurred when Thomas rejected the Constitution of Clarendon which effectively gave the king power over the church. Thomas was forced to flee to France for safety. After several years of acrimony between Thomas and the king, a reconciliation of sorts took place.

Knowing that it would almost certainly mean his death, Thomas returned to England in 1170 from his exile in France. Shortly after arriving in England, Thomas sent letters of excommunication to the bishops of London and Salisbury, and a letter of suspension to the archbishop of York. The three bishops immediately set out for France to seek an audience with Henry II, who was in that country at the time.

When informed of Thomas's deeds, Henry, who was given to fits of uncontrolled rage, cried out, "Won't somebody rid me of this troublesome priest!" While it is doubtful that Henry intended the death of Thomas, four of Henry's knights took him at his word and, on December 29, 1170, murdered Thomas in his cathedral at Canterbury.

Thomas Becket was at once proclaimed a martyr and, in 1173, Pope Alexander III declared him a saint. The following year, Henry II was forced to undergo a public penance for the death of

Thomas in response to the demands of the general populace. Until it was destroyed by Henry VIII in 1538, the shrine of St. Thomas Becket became one of the most visited pilgrimage sites in Europe.

The story of Thomas Becket was popularized in our times by a T. S. Eliot play, *Murder in the Cathedral.*

Thomas' message today: Thomas Becket is an excellent example of someone who made drastic life changes in order to follow his call. Although his personality and methods could be offensive to others, he lived by what he believed was right.

What are the causes and issues in our times that you feel are worth fighting for?

No Date

Matthew Talbot, Laborer: 1856–1925

Through the first twenty-eight years of his life, Matthew Talbot was one of the least likely saints imaginable. He dropped out of school at the age of twelve, not having yet learned to read or write. He went to work as a laborer and, much like his father, soon picked up the habit of daily drinking in the local Dublin pubs. Though short of stature, Matthew became a fighter and learned to swear like the proverbial sailor.

In 1884, Matthew took a week off from work, and with his brother, Joe, visited all the pubs of Dublin until their credit was dead. Not being inclined to give up so easily, Matthew and Joe stood outside of one of the pubs where their fellow workers often met in hopes that someone might offer a drink or two. Strangely, nobody did.

Taking this as a message, Matthew went home, put on a clean shirt, and told his mother that he was going to church. While there, he told her, he was going to pledge to stop drinking. "Go, in God's name," she told him, unimpressed by his apparent determination, "but don't take a pledge unless you mean to keep it."

Matthew vowed not to drink for three months, then confessed to the priest that he had been away from the sacraments for several years. The next morning, a Sunday, Matthew received the Eucharist at Mass. The following day, he surprised his mother by getting up early to attend the 5:00 A.M. Mass before going to work.

The three months were tough for Matthew, but at the end of that time, he renewed his pledge to stop drinking for six more months, and then for life. To maintain his resolve, Matthew developed the habit of attending 5:00 A.M. Mass each morning and, to avoid his old drinking buddies, going to church to pray each evening until the pubs closed.

In the years that followed, Matthew became interested in learning more about his faith. From his confessor, he borrowed books and, praying to the Holy Spirit for enlightenment, taught himself to read and write. He developed a great interest in the lives of saints and Church teachings, but eventually branched out into social issues and world issues during World War I. Over time, he built up a library from which he loaned books to others.

Continuing to work as a laborer, Matthew joined the builders-laborers union when it organized in 1911. When a general strike for a living wage hit Ireland in 1913, Matthew joined the strike with his fellow workers. He was too old to march on the picket line, but, as he told a friend, no one had the right to starve the poor into submission. Out of his strike pay, Matthew gave money to other strikers who were having trouble feeding their families while not working.

Matthew continued his habit of daily Mass throughout the remainder of his life. Essentially a shy man, he sought out of the way places to kneel and pray while his fellow workers stopped for lunch or work breaks. He was also sought out for counsel on many subjects by his peers, and never hesitated to provide what help he could, even to the extent of writing to the United States for a book on one occasion.

Matthew Talbot died of heart failure on Sunday morning, June 7, 1925, while walking to his second Mass of the day. Pope Paul VI declared Matthew Talbot "venerable" in 1975 and his cause for canonization continues. When that occurs, Matthew Talbot is very likely to be named the patron saint of alcoholics. Already, his intercession has been cited in numerous cases in which "incurable" alcoholics have been restored to normal lives.

Matthew's message today: We all know people who did not have a good start in life. Matthew Talbot is an example of determination for anyone who wants to make a fresh start, to turn over a new leaf. It is easy to see how his devotion to God helped Matthew in his resolve to live an exemplary Christian life.

Can you think of a time when you were aware of God's presence in your life, guiding you through a difficult situation? Ask God for help with all the troubles and changes in your life.

Appendix A

Liturgical Calendar of Fixed Feast Days and Solemnities

January

1   Octave of Christmas
    Solemnity of Mary, Mother of God
2   Basil the Great, bishop and doctor
    Gregory Nazianzen, bishop and doctor
7   Raymond of Peñafort, priest
13 Hilary, bishop and doctor
17 Anthony, abbot
20 Fabian, pope and martyr
    Sebastian, martyr
21 Agnes, virgin and martyr
22 Vincent, deacon and martyr
24 Francis de Sales, bishop and doctor
25 Conversion of Paul, apostle
26 Timothy and Titus, bishops
27 Angela Merici, virgin
28 Thomas Aquinas, priest and doctor
31 John Bosco, priest

February

2   Presentation of the Lord
3   Blaise, bishop and martyr
    Ansgar, bishop
5   Agatha, virgin and martyr
6   Paul Miki and companions, martyrs
8   Jerome Emiliani
10 Scholastica, virgin
11 Our Lady of Lourdes
14 Cyril, monk, and Methodius, bishop

17   Seven Founders of the Order of Servites
21   Peter Damian, bishop and doctor
22   Chair of St. Peter, apostle
23   Polycarp, bishop and martyr

March

4   Casimir
7   Perpetua and Felicity, martyrs
8   John of God, religious
9   Frances of Rome, religious
17   Patrick, bishop
18   Cyril of Jerusalem, bishop and doctor
19   Joseph, husband of Mary
23   Turibius de Mongrovejo, bishop
25   Annunciation

April

2   Francis of Paola, hermit
4   Isidore, bishop and doctor
5   Vincent Ferrer, priest
7   John Baptist de la Salle, priest
11   Stanislaus, bishop and martyr
13   Martin I, pope and martyr
21   Anselm, bishop and doctor
23   George, martyr
24   Fidelis of Sigmaringen, priest and martyr
25   Mark, Evangelist
28   Peter Chanel, priest and martyr
29   Catherine of Siena, virgin and doctor
30   Pius V, pope

May

1   Joseph the Worker
2   Athanasius, bishop and doctor
3   Philip and James, apostles
12   Nereus and Achilleus, martyrs
      Pancras, Martyr

14 Matthias, apostle
18 John I, pope and martyr
20 Bernardine of Siena, priest
25 Venerable Bede, priest and doctor
Gregory VII, pope
Mary Magdalene de Pazzi, virgin
26 Philip Neri, priest
27 Augustine of Canterbury, bishop
31 Visitation

JUNE
1 Justin, martyr
2 Marcellinus and Peter, martyrs
3 Charles Lwanga and companions, martyrs
5 Boniface, bishop and martyr
6 Norbert, bishop
9 Ephrem, deacon and doctor
11 Barnabas, apostle
13 Anthony of Padua, priest and doctor
19 Romuald, abbot
21 Aloysius Gonzaga, religious
22 Paulinus of Nola, bishop
John Fisher, bishop and martyr
Thomas More, martyr
24 Birth of St. John the Baptist
27 Cyril of Alexandria, bishop and doctor
28 Irenaeus, bishop and martyr
29 Peter and Paul, apostles
30 First Martyrs of the Church of Rome

JULY
3 Thomas, apostle
4 Elizabeth of Portugal
5 Anthony Zaccaria, priest
6 Maria Goretti, virgin and martyr
11 Benedict, abbot
13 Henry

14 Camillus de Lellis, priest
15 Bonaventure, bishop and doctor
16 Our Lady of Mount Carmel
21 Lawrence of Brindisi, priest and doctor
22 Mary Magdalene
23 Bridget, religious
25 James, apostle
26 Joachim and Ann, parents of Mary
29 Martha
30 Peter Chrysologus, bishop and doctor
31 Ignatius of Loyola, priest

August
1 Alphonsus Liguori, bishop and doctor
2 Eusebius of Vercelli, bishop
4 John Vianney, priest
5 Dedication of St. Mary Major
6 Transfiguration
7 Sixtus II, pope and martyr, and companions, martyrs
  Cajetan, priest
8 Dominic, priest
10 Lawrence, deacon and martyr
11 Clare, virgin
13 Pontian, pope and martyr
   Hippolytus, priest and martyr
14 Maximilian Mary Kolbe, priest and martyr
15 Assumption
16 Stephen of Hungary
19 John Eudes, priest
20 Bernard, abbot and doctor
21 St. Pius X, pope
22 Queenship of Mary
23 Rose of Lima, virgin
24 Bartholomew, apostle
25 Louis
   Joseph Calasanz, priest
27 Monica

28   Augustine, bishop and doctor
29   Beheading of John the Baptist, martyr

SEPTEMBER

3   Gregory the Great, pope and doctor
8   Birth of Mary
13   John Chrysostom, bishop and doctor
14   Triumph of the Cross
15   Our Lady of Sorrows
16   Cornelius, pope and martyr
     Cyprian, bishop and martyr
17   Robert Bellarmine, bishop and doctor
19   Januarius, bishop and martyr
20   Andrew Kim Taegon, priest and martyr
     Paul Chong Hasang and companions, martyrs
21   Matthew, apostle and evangelist
26   Cosmas and Damian, martyrs
27   Vincent de Paul, priest
28   Wenceslaus, martyr
     Lawrence Ruiz and companions, martyrs
29   Michael, Gabriel, and Raphael, archangels
30   Jerome, priest and doctor

OCTOBER

1   Thérèse of the Child Jesus, virgin
2   Guardian Angels
4   Francis of Assisi
6   Bruno, priest
7   Our Lady of the Rosary
9   Denis, bishop and martyr, and companions, martyrs
     John Leonardi, priest
14   Callistus I, pope and martyr
15   Teresa of Jesus, virgin and doctor
16   Hedwig, religious
     Margaret Mary Alacoque, virgin
17   Ignatius of Antioch, bishop and martyr
18   Luke, evangelist

13   Lucy, virgin and martyr
14   John of the Cross, priest and doctor
21   Peter Canisius, priest and doctor
23   John of Kanty, priest
25   Christmas
26   Stephen, first martyr
27   John, apostle and evangelist
28   Holy Innocents, martyrs
29   Thomas Becket, bishop and martyr
31   Sylvester I, pope

Appendix B
Patron Saints

Patron of...	Saint	Feast Day
Abandoned children	Jerome Emiliani	February 8
Accountants	Matthew	September 21
Actors	Genesius the Comedian	August 25
Alpinists	Bernard of Montjoux	May 28
Alcoholics	Matthew Talbot	
Altarboys	John Berchmans	November 26
Amputees	Anthony of Padua	June 13
Anesthetists	Rene Goupil	September 26
Animals	Francis of Assisi	October 4
Apprehension of thieves	Gervase and Protase	June 19
Archers	Hubert	November 3
	Sebastian	January 20
Architects	Barbara	December 4
	Thomas	December 21
Armorers	Dunstan	May 19
Art	Catherine of Bologna	March 9
Art dealers	John the Evangelist	December 27
Arthritis	James the Greater	July 25
Artillerymen	Barbara	December 4
Artists	Luke	October 18
Astronomers	Dominic	August 4
Athletes	Sebastian	January 20
Authors	Francis de Sales	January 29
Aviators	Joseph of Cupertino	September 18
	Thérèse of Lisieux	October 3
Bachelors	Christopher	July 25
Bakers	Elizabeth of Hungary	November 17
	Nicholas of Myra	December 6

Bankers	Matthew	September 21
Barbers	Cosmas and Damian	September 26
	Louis of France	August 25
Barren women	Anthony of Padua	June 13
Basket makers	Anthony the Abbot	January 17
Battle	Michael the Archangel	September 29
Beggars	Alexis	July 17
Birds	Francis of Assisi	October 4
Blacksmiths	Dunstan	May 19
	James the Less	May 1
Blind	Odilia	December 13
	Raphael the Archangel	September 29
Blindness	Lucy	December 13
Blood banks	Januarius	September 19
Bodily ills	Our Lady of Lourdes	February 11
Bookkeepers	Matthew	September 21
Booksellers	John the Evangelist	December 27
	John of God	March 8
Boy Scouts	George	April 23
Brass workers	Barbara	December 4
Brewers	Augustine	August 28
	Luke	October 18
	Nicholas of Myra	December 6
Bricklayers	Stephen	December 26
Brides	Nicholas of Myra	December 6
Brush makers	Anthony the Abbot	January 17
Builders	Barbara	December 4
	Vincent Ferrer	April 5
Butchers	Adrian	September 8
	Anthony the Abbot	January 17
	Luke	October 18
	Peter	June 29
Cab drivers	Fiacre	September 1
Cabinetmakers	Ann	July 26

Canada	Ann	July 26
	Joseph	March 19
Cancer patients	Peregrine Laziosi	May 1
Canonists	Raymond of Peñafort	January 23
Carpenters	Joseph	May 1
Catechists	Charles Borromeo	November 4
	Robert Bellarmine	September 17
Catholic Action	Francis of Assisi	October 4
Catholic Charities	Elizabeth of Hungary	November 17
Cavalry	George	April 23
Cemeteries	Anthony the Abbot	January 17
Chandlers	Ambrose	December 7
	Bernard of Clairvaux	August 20
Charitable societies	Vincent de Paul	September 27
Chemical industry	Cosmas and Damian	September 26
Children	Nicholas of Myra	December 6
Children of Mary	Agnes	January 21
Choir Boys	Dominic Savio	March 9
	Holy Innocents	December 28
Civil servants	Thomas More	July 9
Clergy	Charles Borromeo	November 4
Clerics	Gabriel Possenti	February 27
Clock makers	Peter	June 29
Colleges	Thomas Aquinas	March 7
Comedians	Genesius	August 25
	Vitus	June 15
Composers	John the Evangelist	December 27
Confessors	Alphonsus	August 2
	John Nepomucen	May 16
	John Vianney	August 8
Convulsions in children	Scholastica	February 10
Cooks	Lawrence	August 10
	Martha	July 29
Coopers	Nicholas of Myra	December 6
Coppersmiths	Maurus	January 15

Counsel	Holy Spirit	
Court workers	Thomas More	July 9
Dairy workers	Brigid	February 1
Dancers	Genesius	August 25
Deaf	Francis de Sales	January 29
Dentists	Apollonia	February 9
Desperate situations	Gregory the Wonderworker	November 17
	Jude	October 28
Dietitians	Martha	July 29
Difficult children	Sebastian	January 20
Doctors	Luke	October 18
Dog bite	Hubert	November 3
Dog breeders	Roque	November 17
Domestic animals	Anthony the Abbot	January 17
Doubt	Joseph	March 19
Druggists	Cosmas and Damian	September 26
	James the Less	May 1
	Raphael the Archangel	September 29
Dying	Barbara	December 4
	Joseph	March 19
Editors	John Bosco	January 31
Emigrants	Frances Xavier Cabrini	November 13
Engineers	Ferdinand III of Castile	May 30
	Joseph	May 1
England	George	April 23
Engravers	John the Evangelist	December 27
Enlightenment	Our Lady of Good Counsel	
Epilepsy	Genesius	August 25
Eucharistic Congresses	Pascal Baylon	May 17
Expectant mothers	Gerard Majella	October 16
	Margaret	July 20
	Raymund Nonnatus	August 31
Eye troubles	Lucy	December 13

Eye troubles	Raphael the Archangel	September 29
Falsely accused	Gerard Majella	October 16
Families	Joseph	March 19
Family harmony	Dymphna	May 15
Farmers	George	April 23
	Isidore the Farmer	May 15
Farriers	John the Baptist	June 24
Fever	George	April 23
	Peter	June 29
Fire	Lawrence	August 10
Fire prevention	Catherine of Siena	April 30
Fire, protection from	Agatha	February 5
Firemen	Florian	May 4
Fireworks	Barbara	December 4
First Communicants	Tarsicius	August 15
	Blessed Imelda	May 13
Fishermen	Andrew	November 30
Florists	Dorothy	February 6
	Thérèse of Lisieux	October 3
Foot trouble	Peter	June 29
Foreign missions	Francis Xavier	December 3
Forest workers	John Gualbert	July 12
Founders	Barbara	December 4
Foundlings	Holy Innocents	December 28
France	Joan of Arc	May 30
Fullers	Anastasius	September 7
	James the Less	May 1
Funeral directors	Joseph of Arimathea	March 17
Gardeners	Adelard	January 2
	Dorothy	February 6
	Fiacre	September 1
	Phocas	September 22
	Sebastian	January 20
	Trypho	November 10

Germany	Boniface	June 5
Glass workers	Luke	October 18
	Mark	April 25
Goldsmiths	Dunstan	May 19
	Luke	October 18
Gout	Andrew	November 30
Grandmothers	Ann	July 26
Greetings	Valentine	February 14
Grocers	Michael the Archangel	September 29
Gunners	Barbara	December 4
Happy death	Joseph	March 19
Hardware	Sebastian	January 20
Hatters	James the Less	May 1
Haymakers	Gervase and Protase	June 19
Headaches	Teresa of Avila	October 15
Healing of wounds	Rita	May 22
Heart Ailments	John of God	March 8
Hesitation	Joseph	March 19
Home builders	Our Lady of Loretto	
Horsemen	Ann	July 26
Hospital administrators	Basil the Great	June 14
Hospital workers	Vincent de Paul	September 27
Hospitals	John of God	March 8
	Jude	October 28
	Vincent de Paul	September 27
Housewives	Ann	July 26
Hunters	Eustace	September 10
	Hubert	November 3
Infantrymen	Rock	August 16
Innkeepers	Amand	February 6
Interracial justice	Martin de Porres	November 3
Intestinal disorders	Erasmus	June 2
Invalids	Roque	November 17

Ireland	Patrick	March 17
Iron mongers	Sebastian	January 20
Italy	Catherine of Siena	April 30
	Francis of Assisi	October 4
Jewelers	Eligius	December 1
	Luke	October 18
Journalists	Francis de Sales	January 29
Judges	Ives	
Jurists	Catherine of Alexandria	November 25
	John of Capistrano	March 28
Knowledge	Holy Spirit	
Laborers	James the Greater	July 25
	John Bosco	January 31
	Isidore the Farmer	May 15
Lace makers	Francis of Assisi	October 4
Lamp makers	Our Lady of Loretto	
Lawyers	Ivo of Kermartin	May 19
	Thomas More	July 9
Lead workers	Sebastian	January 20
Learning	Ambrose	December 7
Leather workers	Catherine of Alexandria	November 25
Lepers	Vincent de Paul	September 27
Librarians	Jerome	September 30
Lightning	Barbara	December 4
Lithographers	John the Evangelist	December 27
Locksmiths	Dunstan	May 19
Loneliness	Rita	May 22
Long life	Peter	June 29
Lost articles	Anthony of Padua	June 13
Lost causes	Vibiana	September 1
Lovers	Raphael the Archangel	September 29
Lumbago	Lawrence	August 10

Machinists	Hubert	November 3
Maids	Zita	April 27
Marble workers	Clement I	November 23
Mariners	Michael the Archangel	September 29
	Nicholas of Tolentino	September 10
Married couples	Joseph	March 19
Mass servers	John Berchmans	November 26
Mathematicians	Hubert	November 3
Medical social workers	John Francis Regis	June 16
Mentally ill	Dymphna	May 15
Merchants	Francis of Assisi	October 4
Messengers	Gabriel the Archangel	September 29
Metalworkers	Eligius	December 1
Millers	Arnulf	August 15
	Victor	July 21
Miners	Barbara	December 4
Missionaries	Francis Xavier	December 3
Missions	Thérèse of Lisieux	October 1
Monastics	Benedict	March 21
Moravia	Cyril and Methodius	February 14
Mothers	Monica	May 4
Motorists	Christopher	July 25
	Frances of Rome	March 9
Mountaineers	Bernard of Montjoux	May 28
Musicians	Cecilia	November 22
	Dunstan	May 19
Navigators	Mary, Star of the Sea	
Needle workers	Francis of Assisi	October 4
Negro Missions	Peter Claver	September 9
Negroes	Martin de Porres	November 3
Nerves	Dymphna	May 15
Notaries	Ives	
	Luke	October 18
	Mark	April 25

Nurses	Agatha	February 5
	Alexis	July 17
	Camillus de Lellis	July 18
	John of God	March 8
	Raphael the Archangel	September 29
Nursing	Catherine of Siena	April 30
Orators	John Chrysostom	September 13
Organ makers	Genesius	August 25
Orphans	Jerome Emiliani	February 8
Painters	Luke	October 18
Paper makers	John the Evangelist	December 27
Paratroopers	Michael the Archangel	September 29
Peasants	Lucy	December 13
Peddlers	Lucy	December 13
Pen and pencil makers	Thomas Aquinas	March 7
Peril at sea	Michael the Archangel	September 29
Perseverance in prayer	Monica	May 4
Pharmacists (hospitals)	Gemma Galgani	April 11
Philosophers	Albert the Great	November 15
	Catherine of Alexandria	November 25
	Justin Martyr	April 14
Physicians	Cosmas and Damian	September 26
	Luke	October 18
	Pantaleon	July 27
	Raphael the Archangel	September 29
Piety	Holy Spirit	
Pilgrims	Alexis	July 17
	James the Greater	July 25
Pioneers	Joseph	March 19
Plague	Roque	November 17
Plasterers	Bartholomew	August 24
Policemen/women	Michael the Archangel	September 29
Poor	Anthony of Padua	June 13
	Lawrence	August 10

Poor souls	Nicholas of Tolentino	September 10
Porters	Christopher	July 25
Postal employees	Gabriel the Archangel	September 29
Potters	Sebastian	January 20
Pregnant women	Gerard Majella	October 16
	Margaret	July 20
Priests	John Vianney	August 8
Printers	Augustine	August 28
	John of God	March 8
	John the Evangelist	December 27
Prisoners	Barbara	December 4
	Nicholas of Myra	December 6
Prisoners	The Good Thief	March 25
Prisons	Joseph Cafasso	June 23
	Vincent de Paul	September 27
Protector of crops	Ansovinus	March 13
Public relations	Paul	June 29
Publicity agents	Bernardine of Siena	May 20
Racquet makers	Sebastian	January 20
Radio workers	Gabriel the Archangel	September 29
Radiologists	Michael the Archangel	September 29
Retreats	Ignatius of Loyola	July 31
Rheumatism	James the Greater	July 25
Saddlers	Crispin and Crispinian	October 25
	Lucy	December 13
Safe journey	Raphael the Archangel	September 29
Sailors	Blessed Peter Gonzalez	April 14
	Brendan	May 16
	Cuthbert	March 20
	Erasmus (Elmo)	June 2
	Michael the Archangel	September 29
Salesmen	Lucy	December 13
Scholars	Brigid	February 1
	Thomas Aquinas	March 7

Schools	Thomas Aquinas	March 7
Scientists	Albert the Great	November 15
Scotland	Andrew	November 30
	Columba	June 9
	Margaret of Scotland	November 16
Scribes	Catherine of Alexandria	November 25
Sculptors	Luke	October 18
Seamen	Francis of Paola	April 2
Secretaries	Catherine of Alexandria	November 25
	Genesius of Arles	August 25
Seminarians	Charles Borromeo	November 4
Service women	Joan of Arc	May 30
Servants	Zita	April 27
Sheep raisers	Raphael the Archangel	September 29
Ship builders	Peter	June 29
Shoemakers	Crispin and Crispinian	October 25
Sick	Camillus de Lellis	July 18
	John of God	March 8
Sick poor	Martin de Porres	November 3
Silversmiths	Andronicus	October 11
Singers	Cecilia	November 22
	Gregory the Great	March 12
Skaters	Blessed Lydwina of Schiedam	April 14
Skiers	Bernard of Montjoux	May 28
Skin diseases	Peregrine Laziosi	May 1
Snake bite	Patrick	March 17
Soldiers	Adrian	September 8
	George	April 23
	Ignatius of Loyola	July 31
	Joan of Arc	May 30
Soldiers	Martin of Tours	November 11
	Sebastian	January 20
Solitary death	Francis of Assisi	October 4
South America	Rose of Lima	August 30
Speleologists	Benedict	March 21

Spiritual directors	Charles Borromeo	November 4
Spiritual help	Vincent de Paul	September 27
Stained glass workers	Mark	April 25
Stationers	Peter	June 29
Stenographers	Cassian	December 3
	Catherine of Alexandria	November 25
Stock brokers	Matthew	September 21
Stomach troubles	Charles Borromeo	November 4
Stone masons	Sebastian	January 20
	Stephen	December 26
Storms	Barbara	December 4
Students	Thomas Aquinas	March 7
Surgeons	Cosmas and Damian	September 26
	Luke	October 18
Tailors	Homobonus	November 13
Tax workers	Matthew	September 21
Teachers	Catherine of Alexandria	November 25
	Francis de Sales	January 29
	Gregory the Great	March 12
Telegraph/	John Baptist de la Salle	May 15
telephone workers	Gabriel the Archangel	September 29
Television workers	Gabriel the Archangel	September 29
Temptation	Michael the Archangel	September 29
Tertiaries	Elizabeth of Hungary	November 17
	Louis of France	August 25
Theologians	Augustine	August 28
	Thomas Aquinas	March 7
Throats	Blaise	February 3
	Cecilia	November 22
Tongue	Catherine of Alexandria	November 25
Toothache	Patrick	March 17
Travelers	Anthony of Padua	June 13
	Christopher	July 25
	Raphael the Archangel	September 29
Tuberculosis	Teresa of Avila	October 15

Tumor	Rita	May 22
United States	Immaculate Conception	December 8
Universal Church	Joseph	March 19
Universities	Thomas Aquinas	March 7
Ulcers	Charles Borromeo	November 4
Undertakers	Sebastian	January 20
Vanity	Rose of Lima	August 30
Veterinarians	James the Greater	July 25
Vinedressers	Vincent of Saragossa	January 22
Vocalists	Cecilia	November 22
Vocations	Alphonsus	August 2
WAFs	Joan of Arc	May 30
Wales	David	March 1
Watchmen	Peter of Alcantara	October 19
WAVEs	Joan of Arc	May 30
Weavers	Paul the Hermit	January 15
Wine makers	Francis Xavier	December 3
Wine merchants	Amand	February 6
Wolves	Peter	June 29
Woman's Army Corps	Genevieve	January 3
	Joan of Arc	May 30
Workers	Joseph	May 1
Writers	Francis de Sales	January 29
	John the Evangelist	December 27
	Lucy	December 13
Yachtsmen	Mary, Star of the Sea	
Young Girls	Agnes	January 21
Youth	Gabriel Possenti	February 27
	John Berchmans	November 26
	Aloysius Gonzaga	June 21

Resource List

Atwater, Donald and Herbert J. Thurston, S.J., editors. *Butler's Lives of the Saints,* Volumes I-IV. Collegeville, MN: Christian Classics, 1990.

Ball, Ann. *Modern Saints, Their Lives and Faces,* Books One and Two. Rockford, IL: Tan Books and Publishers, 1983 (Book One), 1990 (Book Two).

Bokenkotter, Thomas. *A Concise History of the Catholic Church.* New York, NY: Image Books, Doubleday, 1990.

Chervin, Ronda De Sola. *Treasury of Women Saints.* Ann Arbor, MI: Servant Publications, 1991.

Delaney, John J. *Pocket Dictionary of Saints,* abridged edition. New York, NY: Image Books, Doubleday, 1983.

Farmer, David Hugh. *The Oxford Dictionary of Saints,* third edition. Oxford, NY: Oxford University Press, 1992.

Foley, Leonard, O.F.M. *Saints of the Day,* Volumes I-II. Cincinnati, OH: St. Anthony Messenger Press Vol. I, 1974; Vol. II, 1975.

Freze, Michael. *The Making of Saints.* Huntington, IN: Our Sunday Visitor Publishing, 1991.

Hoever, Hugo, S.O. Cist., Ph.D. *Lives of the Saints,* New York, NY: Catholic Book Publishing Co., 1977.

Lodi, Enzo, translated by Jordan Aumann, O.P. *Saints of the Roman Calendar.* Staten Island, NY: Alba House, 1992.

Nevins, Albert J., M.M. *A Saint For Your Name,* two volumes (for boys' and for girls' names), Huntington, IN: Our Sunday Visitor, 1980.

O'Malley, Vincent J., C.M. *Saintly Companions.* Staten Island, NY: Alba House, 1995.

Severin, Tim. *The Brendan Voyage.* New York, NY: McGraw-Hill, 1978.

Stevens, Clifford. *The One-Year Book of Saints.* Huntington, IN: Our Sunday Visitor, 1989.

Woodward, Kenneth. *Making Saints: How the Catholic Church Determines Who Becomes a Saint, Who Doesn't and Why.* New York, NY: Simon and Schuster, 1990.

Walsh, Michael. *Book of Saints.* Mystic, CT: Twenty-Third Publications, 1994.